OECD Economic Surveys: Indonesia 2010

OECD

Please cite this publication as:
OECD (2010), *OECD Economic Surveys: Indonesia*, OECD Publishing.
http://dx.doi.org/10.1787/9789264000000-en

ISBN 978-92-64-08340-0 (print)
ISBN 978-92-64-09341-7 (PDF)

Series: OECD Economic Surveys
ISSN 0376-6438 (print)
ISSN 1609-7513 (online)

OECD Economic Surveys Indonesia
ISSN 2072-5116 (print)
ISSN 2072-5108 (online)

Photo credits: Cover © Comstock/Comstock Images/Getty Images.

Corrigenda to OECD publications may be found on line at: *www.oecd.org/publishing/corrigenda*.

Table of contents

Boxes

Tables

Figures

This Survey was prepared in the Economics Department by Annabelle Mourougane, Mauro Pisu and Luiz de Mello under the supervision of Peter Jarrett.

Research assistance was provided by Anne Legendre and secretarial assistance by Mee-Lan Frank.

The Survey was discussed at a meeting of the Economic and Development Review Committee on 16 September 2010.

The Survey is published on the responsibility of the Secretary-General of the OECD.

BASIC STATISTICS OF INDONESIA

(2009 unless noted)

THE LAND

Area (thousands sq. km)	1 911

POPULATION

Total (millions, 2010)	237.6
Inhabitants per sq. km	124.3
Net average annual increase during 2000-10 (in per cent)	1.49
Urbanisation rate (2008, in per cent)	51.5
Age distribution (2010, in % of total population)	
0-14	26.7
15-64	68.2
65+	5.2

EMPLOYMENT

Working-age population (2010, in millions)	171.0
Total employment (2010, in millions)	107.4
Labour force participation rate (2010, in per cent)	67.8
Open unemployment rate (2010, BPS definition, in per cent)	7.4
Informality rate (BPS, in per cent, 2010)	68.6
Headline CPI inflation (average over previous 5 years)	8.9

GROSS DOMESTIC PRODUCT

GDP at current prices and current exchange rate (USD billion)	540.3
Per capita GDP at current prices and market exchange rate (USD)	2 349.4
Average annual real growth over previous 5 years (in %)	5.6

PUBLIC FINANCES (% of GDP)

Revenue	15.4
Nominal balance	–1.6
Gross public debt	28.3
Public infrastructure spending	1.7

INDICATORS OF LIVING STANDARDS

Upper-secondary educational attainment (2007, in per cent of 10+ population)	23.4
Literacy rate (2008, in per cent of 10+ population)	93.1
Doctors per 1 000 inhabitants (2003)	0.13
Infant mortality per 1 000 live births (2008)	26.8
Life expectancy at birth (2008)	70.8
Human Development Index (2008)	71.2
Income inequality (2008, Gini coefficient)	0.35
Poverty incidence (March 2010, national poverty line, per cent)	13.3
Internet users per 1 000 inhabitants (2008)	79.1
Improved sanitation facilities (% of population with access)	52.0

FOREIGN TRADE

Current account (USD billion)	10.7
In % of GDP	2.0
Exports of goods (USD billion)	118.0
In % of GDP	26.9
Average annual growth over previous 5 years (%)	14.9
Imports of goods (USD billion)	85.3
In % of GDP	19.5
Average annual growth over previous 5 years (%)	19.6
Outstanding external debt (USD billion)	172.3
In % of GDP	32.0

Executive summary

Indonesia's economy withstood the recent global crisis very well, thanks to appropriate stabilisation policies and increased economic and financial resilience. Major social and economic progress has been achieved over the last decade, leading to several upgrades of its sovereign rating toward investment grade. Nevertheless, a number of institutional reforms and policy changes will be needed to deal with several cross-cutting challenges of decentralisation, capacity building at the local level and improved economic governance. Only with such reforms can Indonesia hope to meet its ambitious medium-term targets for growth and poverty reduction and to move to an environmentally sustainable development path.

The macroeconomic framework has improved

Real GDP growth was the third highest in the G20 in 2009 and is projected to accelerate to around 6% this year and next. However, inflation pressures may re-emerge, and the monetary authorities should thus start to raise the policy rate before the end of 2010. The policy framework – which combines inflation targeting, a flexible yet not completely freely floating exchange rate and rules-based fiscal management – is sound. Bank Indonesia has also sought to strengthen monetary transmission mechanisms. Finding the fiscal room to finance the expansion of growth-enhancing programmes, such as investment in infrastructure and education at the secondary level, and the increase in coverage of formal social protection and health insurance will require enhancing tax enforcement and eliminating energy subsidies. Greater ambition with respect to price stability by bringing down the inflation target range in the medium term closer to those in regional peers would signal a move to a low-inflation environment, reduce uncertainty and allow markets to function better.

Phasing out energy subsidies will free up fiscal resources

Energy subsidies fail to achieve their social objectives and entail significant economic, fiscal and environmental costs. The government should stick to its commitment to eliminate those on fossil fuels by 2014 but needs to go further and cut back on electricity subsidies as well, since these share most of the weaknesses of those on fossil fuels. Widespread communication of the benefits of subsidy removal and recourse to existing well-targeted cash-transfer schemes will help to overcome resistance to reform. Fiscal support for biofuels should be reviewed, given the limited knowledge on their net life-cycle benefits.

Boosting investment in infrastructure would overcome obstacles to faster potential growth

At Indonesia's current stage of economic development, returns to financing investment in infrastructure are likely to be large. Public outlays on infrastructure could be moderately increased without endangering fiscal sustainability. Attracting sufficient private investment will be challenging and will require establishing independent sectoral regulators, strengthening the powers of existing regulators, better co-ordination between national and local authorities, removing legal obstacles to land acquisition and relying on well designed public-private partnerships. The authorities should also consider further relaxing barriers to foreign direct investment.

Extensive safety nets and high-quality education and health services would favour inclusive growth

Indonesia is working toward expanding the coverage of its formal safety net as one means of tackling poverty. Workers would be better protected against employment-loss risks by introducing some form of unemployment insurance. In turn, generous severance payments could be scaled back and minimum-wage increases linked to trend gains in productivity. A comprehensive costing of all existing and new social protection programmes, including public health insurance, is imperative to ensure their long-term fiscal sustainability. Participation in the health insurance scheme for private-sector employees could be fostered by revoking the employer opt-out clause and extending enrolment to the self-employed and employees of small firms. Budget conditions permitting, additional public spending could be allocated to smooth the transition from primary to secondary education and enhance the quality of teaching.

Assessment and recommendations

Economic performance in recent years has been impressive

Indonesia weathered the global crisis very well. At 4.6%, real GDP growth in 2009 was the third highest in the G20, after China and India, and the economy is on track to achieve growth of around 6% this year and next. Lower international commodity prices, a sharp currency appreciation and a slowdown in domestic demand growth caused inflation to decelerate to a nine-year low of an average 4.4% in 2009 (2.8% year-on-year in December). Strong aggregate performance can be attributed to successful macroeconomic management, combining accommodative monetary policy and a moderate but timely fiscal impulse. But it also underlines the increased resilience of the economy in the face of external shocks, which stems from substantial macroeconomic and structural reforms undertaken since the Asian crisis. Indeed, the tremendous improvement in economic fundamentals over the last decade has led rating agencies to upgrade Indonesia's sovereign rating, with an investment grade in prospect. The country has also benefited from its increasing integration with other ASEAN economies, and more recently with China. At the same time, low reliance on international trade with OECD countries and under-developed capital markets, together with low exposure to toxic assets, made the economy less vulnerable to advanced economies' financial and economic developments. In addition, losses in formal-sector employment were absorbed by an expanding informal labour market. While the overall impact of the crisis was muted, the poorest appear to have been more affected, notwithstanding government assistance programmes.

Growth prospects are favourable

The OECD's short-term projections point to strong growth driven by domestic demand. Despite significant currency appreciation, exports are also expected to be robust, boosted by demand from China for Indonesia's commodity exports. The budget balance is likely to be only modestly negative. Vigorous activity and diminished effects of currency appreciation are likely to put upward pressures on inflation. Primary reserve requirements have been raised to remove excess liquidity, but *further monetary tightening, in the form of increased interest rates, will need to get underway before the end of the year to achieve the 2011 inflation target*. Risks to these projections are somewhat to the downside. Even if the Indonesian economy is relatively immune to weaker growth in OECD economies, large capital inflows over the past year have increased the vulnerability of its financial markets to abrupt reversals.

The government has set ambitious growth objectives

A sound and stable macroeconomic and political environment, favourable growth prospects and healthy public finances offer Indonesia a unique opportunity to pursue its reform agenda and achieve lasting, strong and inclusive growth. The country is endowed with the fourth largest population in the world and abundant and diversified natural resources. But a number of policy and institutional weaknesses have long been holding back economic development, and, in the absence of reform, their effects are likely to persist. Real GDP has been growing at a rate of a little over 5% on average per year over the past decade, although with an underlying uptrend resulting from ongoing structural reforms. However, this is still lower than the objective of 7.0-7.7% for 2014 set by the government in its Medium Term Development Plan. Further institutional changes, including a rapid implementation of bureaucratic reforms, to improve both efficiency and governance are a pre-requisite to meet these ambitious economic development goals. Growing greenhouse gas emissions and the depletion of environmentally important forest resources also cast some doubt on the sustainability of the current development path. Finally, although poverty has declined since 2000, other emerging-market economies have experienced a more rapid fall in their poverty rates.

A lower inflation target could help to shift the economy to a low-inflation environment

The monetary policy framework combines inflation targeting and a flexible exchange rate but with interventions to smooth its volatility in a context of free capital movements. This framework has helped to bring down inflation from the high levels experienced in the past. In the Medium-Term Development Plan, the authorities have opted for a gradual decline in the inflation target range to 3.5-5.5% in 2014. This is still above the average inflation of around 3% observed in regional peers. Greater ambition on inflation is called for to reduce its deleterious effects. *Once set, inflation targets for a given year should not be re-adjusted the following year. Committing and sticking to this declining target range will help move the economy toward a low-inflation environment, which will enhance macroeconomic stability and safeguard households' purchasing power.*

Monetary transmission channels could be strengthened

The monetary authorities adopted an Inflation Target Framework (ITF) in July 2005, with the target set by the government. Monetary policy is implemented in a forward-looking and transparent way. Bank Indonesia is responsible for setting the policy rate (BI rate) and accountable for achieving the target. In practice, it seeks to influence money market rates and in turn deposit and lending rates in the banking system. Operationally, Bank Indonesia Certificates (SBIs) are the main tool for the conduct of monetary policy. With a low risk-return ratio and no collateral requirement, SBIs have been an extremely attractive investment vehicle for banks and other institutional investors. This has hampered the development of the interbank market and has contributed to diverting portfolio allocations from longer-term instruments, so crucial for financing investment spending. Bank

Indonesia is seeking to improve the efficiency of the monetary policy transmission mechanism by gradually extending the maturity profile of SBIs, lifting the requirement of a minimum one-month holding of SBIs, creating a term-deposit facility and widening the policy-interest-rate corridor. However, over the medium term, *a more promising option would be to use repurchase agreements as Bank Indonesia's main tool for open-market operations*. This is common practise in OECD countries and many Asian economies and could enhance the effectiveness of monetary policy by focusing on a pure short-term liquidity-management instrument. It would also have the advantage of cutting SBIs' issuance, thereby lowering the attractiveness of these financial products as a carry-trade instrument.

Reforms to the financial regulatory framework are underway

The country is currently in a transition phase, having decided to move toward a unified supervisor model whereby a new Financial Services Authority (OJK) is scheduled to oversee all financial activities from the end of 2010 onward. However, important facets of the OJK, including its specific functions and degree of autonomy, still need to be clarified. A draft bill, currently under discussion in Parliament, sheds light on some of these aspects. Remaining *uncertainties bear a cost and should be removed as soon as possible*. It will also be important to *ensure that the new body is independent from government and industry and works in close collaboration with Bank Indonesia*, which has already built up expertise in bank supervision.

Public spending should be shifted toward growth-enhancing outlays

Thanks to prudent management and robust economic growth, fiscal achievements have been significant. The public debt-to-GDP ratio declined from its peak of 90% in 2000 to less than 30% in 2009, while the budget deficit had been maintained below 2% of GDP since 2002. The 2011 State Budget points to a continuation of these trends. While clear progress has been made in shifting spending from inefficient subsidies towards pro-poor programmes, Indonesia is still spending too little on infrastructure and education at the secondary level, which are major drivers of potential output growth, especially at its early stage of economic development. Increasing the coverage of formal social protection and health insurance would help to reduce the effects of widespread poverty. There are efficient ways to finance these programmes without hampering long-term fiscal sustainability. On the revenue side, the tax-to-GDP ratio appears to be consistent with the country's stage of economic development, but *tax collection could be made still more effective and higher revenues collected through sustained improvement in governance and enforcement*. This goal would be well served by current plans to separate tax collection and policy-making functions within the Ministry of Finance. *A phasing out of inefficient tax expenditure – in particular in the energy sector – will help to expand the tax base*. Moreover, the *introduction of a carbon tax* would help the country to efficiently reach its emissions-reduction targets. On the spending side, important savings could be achieved by the *elimination of both fuel and electricity subsidies*. This is consistent with the G20 call to phase out such subsidies at the international level. In addition, the efficiency of all *existing programmes should be thoroughly reviewed and resources redirected to measures that are the most beneficial to long-term growth and social inclusion*. Making a more extensive use of long-term analysis in budget and planning documents, including the implications of ageing, would be helpful in this context.

Eliminating energy subsidies would spare fiscal resources

Consumer energy subsidies, in the form of underpricing of retail energy, were initially introduced to make a basic need available to the poor. Despite some laudable moves to reduce them, the overall amount of consumer energy subsidies, especially for petroleum products, remains high by international standards. These subsidies entail significant budgetary and non-budgetary costs. They blur price signals, distort consumption and investment decisions and increase the vulnerability of public finances to oil-price volatility. By keeping prices artificially low, they also encourage energy consumption and reduce incentives to improve energy efficiency. In addition, they are a poor means of redistributing income because they mostly benefit richer households. Against this background, the Indonesian authorities plan to reduce overall energy subsidies by 10-15% per year until 2014, including the full elimination of the fossil fuel component by that point. However, that may well leave subsidies on electricity untouched, an unsatisfactory outcome, given that they suffer from most of the same disadvantages as their fossil-fuel counterparts. It will therefore be important to *extend the medium-term elimination commitment to electricity subsidies and stick to the planned removal timetable* for fossil fuels in order to bolster the government's credibility, remove energy pricing from the political process and reduce uncertainty associated with *ad hoc* rises in energy prices.

The main challenge is to deal with the negative side-effects of subsidy reductions. *Communicating broadly the benefits of this reform*, along with its distributional impact will be crucial. A new independent productivity commission could be tasked with such an assessment and the communication thereof. The success of reform will also rely on the *introduction of effective compensation policies* to support the real incomes of the poorest households and prevent an increase in poverty. Past experience, including in Indonesia, suggests that cash transfers, whose cost is known with certainty, are less distortive than other social tools and easier to target. Subsidising new connections of poor households to the electricity grid would promote wider and more equitable access. In addition to direct price subsidies, Indonesia also grants implicit subsidies through a range of tax expenditures, such as support to biofuels. However, full-cycle energy savings associated with these energy sources, especially if they are produced with palm oil or jatropha, as in Indonesia, is still open to in-depth assessment. Hence, *current support to biofuels needs to be carefully reviewed*.

Investment in infrastructure is needed to overcome a major barrier to long-term growth and social development

Since the Asian crisis, the infrastructure sector has suffered from recurring under-investment, leading to poorer infrastructure quality in Indonesia than in regional peers. Despite a recent increase, the current rate of investment is insufficient to meet official long-term growth objectives. In its Medium Term Development Plan, the government has thus announced significant investment plans – amounting to 5% of GDP on average over five years –, of which around 64% is to be financed through private funds in the form of public-private partnerships (PPPs). The private-sector share appears very ambitious in a context where the business environment and significant regulatory uncertainties are likely to hold back private participation, until further reforms are undertaken. Removing obstacles to bank lending and developing long-term debt instruments would facilitate private-sector participation. At the same time, *there is scope for an increase in public spending of around 0.2% of GDP beyond what is already planned*. To be successful the strategy set out in the Medium Term Development Plan should ensure that *the private sector bears the appropriate share of risk and the choice of PPPs focus on relative and absolute affordability* whereby a project should not only offer the best value for money (as demonstrated by thorough cost-benefit analysis) but should also be consistent with long-term fiscal sustainability. In addition to launching new infrastructure projects, national and sub-national authorities need to focus more on maintenance. It will thus be useful to *commission sectoral studies to gauge required yearly maintenance expenditure in different sectors and allocate budget resources accordingly*. To make the most of this additional spending, the investment choice and the spending allocation processes could be improved. *A better co-ordination between ministries and levels of government* would ensure the consistency of the overall infrastructure strategy and exploit synergies between projects. In addition, *making more extensive use of the multi-year budgeting framework*, as envisaged for 2011, will help to prevent capital outlays from being concentrated at the end of the fiscal year as currently the case, and more generally would improve budget resource allocation.

Strengthening the regulatory framework will attract private investment

A well designed regulatory framework and a healthy business environment are key to efficient infrastructure development. In this respect, *creating independent authorities in sectors where they are currently lacking – for instance, in the water supply and rail transport sectors – would help to reduce uncertainty and encourage investment. Similarly, assuming they have built sufficient technical expertise, granting more independence to existing regulators – in the road transport and telecommunications sectors – would go some way towards reducing regulatory uncertainty and eliminating the conflicting roles the government still plays in many sectors as both regulator and service provider*. More generally, *the powers of the regulatory authorities across all sectors should be further enhanced*, by increasing their responsibilities for implementing regulations, verifying compliance and applying fines and sanctions. Strengthening the authorities' powers also requires making them more accountable. This could be done by *formally evaluating their operations at regular intervals*. Indonesia would benefit from *softening foreign direct investment (FDI) barriers*, which, despite some progress through the publication of a negative investment list, have remained quite stringent in Indonesia, in the telecommunication, transport and, to a lesser extent, electricity sectors. There is particularly ample room to relax restrictions on equity acquisition and on the hiring of foreigners in key positions. These reforms would have the double advantage of enlarging the pool of resources to finance investment and favouring technology transfer. These issues are examined in more detail in the OECD's 2010 *Investment Policy Review: Indonesia*.

Restrictions should also be freed up at the sectoral level

In different network industries, the country has undertaken several pro-market reforms over the past two decades. *Efforts should be pursued to remove the remaining obstacles to investment and to realign prices to cost-recovery levels*, especially in electricity, and water and sanitation.

- Rapid economic growth and a rising number of household connections to the electricity grid will result in a growing demand for electricity, which is crucial for sustaining the development process. In addition to the fast-track programmes already planned, capacity could be expanded by *developing a clear strategy to integrate captive power plants (which are solely used for the production of their owners and account for about a sixth of total production) into the grid. Electrification in rural areas could be fostered by auctioning subsidies*, as has been done in telecommunications.
- Investment in the water supply sector has been hindered by the limited access of local-government utilities (PDAMs) to long-term financing. *Accelerating the programme of PDAM debt restructuring and creating revolving funds managed by provinces* to pool project risks would alleviate these financing constraints in addition to improving co-ordination of water infrastructure projects among neighbouring districts. In addition, *raising water tariffs to cost-recovery levels*, while compensating poor households through existing conditional cash-transfer programmes, would spur investment in the sector, which is vital for the health and welfare of the population.
- Land acquisition appears to be the main obstacle to toll-road development due to legal impediments to agree on fair compensation to owners and, as a result, endless legal disputes over valuation. This issue could be solved *by assigning the responsibility to determine fair compensation for land expropriation to a dedicated independent agency*, for instance the National Land Agency, which already has the expertise to undertake this task. Some of these issues will be addressed by the new land acquisition law, currently under discussion.
- The telecommunication sector has so far managed to attract substantial private investment, but there is still a significant digital divide between urban and rural areas. The government is rightly addressing this issue by auctioning subsidies to extend telecommunications services in underserved areas. The *introduction of a unified access service licence* could make the industry more competitive and would speed the move toward the provision of offers combining internet, television and telephone services.
- Finally, the authorities have recently adopted a new shipping law which injects competition in the sector but falls short of liberalising passenger and freight tariffs. In addition, a ban on cabotage by foreign vessels has been gradually re-introduced since 2005, leading to a decrease in the share of ships operated by foreign firms. The productivity and service quality of the shipping industry could increase with the *alleviation of restrictions on foreign cabotage and by letting shipping companies freely determine their tariffs. If necessary, the authorities could auction subsidies on unprofitable routes to meet the social objective of a national coverage of services.*

Participation in formal labour markets needs to be promoted

Indonesia is characterised by a dual labour market, with a small formal market and a much larger informal sector, where workers lack social insurance. The current labour code was originally introduced to protect formal-sector workers, in the absence of unemployment insurance, through generous severance payments and high minimum wages. However, such protection is a deterrent to hiring workers on formal contracts and encourages informality. Extensive informality is detrimental to long-term growth by limiting training opportunities, capital accumulation and, in turn, productivity gains. A large informal sector also undermines the collection of tax revenues.

An effective way to fight informality would be to rely on a *two-pronged strategy of introducing some form of unemployment benefits, which are currently non-existent, and reforming the labour code, in particular by reducing onerous severance payments*. The urgency of labour-market reforms is acute, given the foreseeable demographic trends, which point to population ageing starting in mid-decade. Several options are available for the design of a future unemployment insurance system. OECD experience suggests that unemployment benefits should be time-limited, decline as the spell of unemployment lengthens and be conditional on a minimum duration of employment. A "mutual obligations approach", whereby the unemployment benefit is conditional on fulfilling job-search requirements, would also enhance the efficiency of the system but would require the development of employment services to deliver support facilities and monitor job-search behaviour. This may not be feasible for some time to come. Unemployment benefits would thus need to be modest at the start to ensure that work incentives are maintained. Severance payments could be reduced, for instance by *introducing a cap on their level at a lower number of workweeks. Increases in the minimum wage should not be allowed to exceed trend productivity gains*, to avoid the adverse impact of the high minimum wage on informality and employment, especially for low-skill workers.

The social safety net needs to be developed further

The government is committed to alleviating poverty and has set the ambitious target of lowering the poverty rate from 13.3% in March 2010 to 8-10% by 2014. Indonesia is shifting attention in the design of its social-protection programmes from crisis mitigation to strengthening support for vulnerable households in a manner that: helps them to pull themselves out of poverty; links social protection to sustained improvements in social outcomes; and equips the poor with the means to prevent a long-lasting fall into poverty following adverse income shocks. Poverty-alleviation programmes need to be multi-faceted to address the roots of material deprivation across several areas. A simple and efficient way to exploit synergies across policy domains would be to *make further use of conditionality in income-transfer programmes*, for instance by requiring beneficiaries to keep their children at school or to pay regular visits to health clinics.

Indonesia's flagship conditional income-support measures – community-based PNPM and household-based PKH – are well thought out and are working satisfactorily, although there is room for improvement. *The different social-protection mechanisms need to be better integrated, so that entry into these empowerment schemes is a natural step following exit from conditional income support*. Efforts to boost co-ordination among the authorities overseeing the various social-protection programmes include the creation of a Poverty Commission under the Vice-President's purview in 2009. This is a step in the right direction. At the same time, Indonesia needs to strengthen contributory social insurance while increasing the coverage of formal social safety nets. Because such policies can involve considerable expenditure, *a comprehensive costing of all existing and new social-protection programmes, including the public health insurance* (see below), *is imperative* to ensure their long-term fiscal sustainability and to identify appropriate financing instruments.

Access to high-quality health-care services should be expanded

Government spending on health care and utilisation rates are lower in Indonesia than in regional peers. Outcomes are also comparatively poor. To tackle these deficiencies, the authorities are working to expand health insurance, building on a publicly funded programme (*Jamkesmas*) that aims to cover the entire population of very poor, poor and near poor individuals against the risk of falling into poverty as a result of illness. This, together with a rising demand for sophisticated care, is likely to put pressure on the budget in the years to come, even though part of health insurance is privately funded. *Adequate resources should be maintained to finance programmes that can make substantial improvements to health outcomes, such as access to water and sanitation, female education and literacy and early childhood nutrition.*

Moving away from intergovernmental transfer arrangements based on historical budgeting to a system based on expected expenditure needs would encourage local governments to seek efficiency gains and ensure a better match between health-service provision and actual requirements. At the same time, to remove obstacles to utilisation, budget conditions permitting, consideration should be given to including *indirect costs in Jamkesmas coverage, such as for transport in remote areas, which often deter low-income individuals from using health-care facilities*. Moreover, there are options for raising participation in the privately financed health-insurance scheme for private-sector employees (*Jamsostek*), which is currently low in part because of an opt-out clause for employers who prefer to offer alternative arrangements for their employees and due to the exclusion of self-employed and employees in small firms. This is problematic because it prevents risk-pooling and can lead to cream-skimming, whereby firms would prefer to hire younger, less risky individuals to minimise insurance costs. *The opt-out clause should therefore be revoked, enrolment could be extended to the self-employed on an optional basis, and eligibility for membership should be opened to those working in firms with fewer than ten employees. A pre-requisite to these changes would be to enhance Jamsostek's technical capacity and to improve regulation to protect the interests of enrolees.*

There is room to improve the quality of compulsory education and increase enrolment in secondary schools

Government expenditure on education has risen sharply over the years, in part as a result of a legislated spending floor at 20% of government outlays. But student performance, which is somewhat weaker than in comparator countries, has yet to improve in line with the increase in expenditure. Enrolment is particularly low in secondary education, suggesting the need to make the transition from primary to higher levels of education smoother. This policy objective could be met *by allocating additional government spending to extend conditionality in income-support programmes to include attendance in secondary education.* This would contribute to avoiding early dropping out and raise awareness of the benefits of continued education. Incremental spending could be financed by reallocating outlays within the general government budget and within the education sectors, toward cost-effective programmes. Efforts are also needed to enhance the quality of teaching. The 2005 Teacher Law created incentives for teachers to engage in training, but it needs to be complemented by *regular assessments of teachers' pedagogical skills. The cost-effectiveness of service delivery could also be boosted by increasing the autonomy of local governments (assuming local administrative capacity shortfalls can be overcome)*, especially regarding human-resource management. Finally, financial support to students from disadvantaged backgrounds could be improved by introducing *a higher per-student transfer under the School Operations Fund (BOS) programme – which includes direct block transfers to schools to finance non-payroll recurrent expenditures – for schools located in remote areas and catering for poor students.*

Chapter 1

Achieving sustainable and inclusive growth

Indonesia's economic performance in 2009-10 has been impressive. The country has come out of the global crisis relatively unscathed when compared both with previous episodes of economic distress and with other emerging markets. Appropriate macroeconomic management, a low exposure of financial markets to toxic assets and a high reliance on domestic demand, rather than on international trade, explain this strong performance. Macroeconomic and structural reforms have also improved the country's capacity to withstand adverse economic shocks. But progress have been more rapid in some areas than in others, and potential output growth is expected to slow in the coming decade, when the effects of population ageing will begin to kick in. Over the long term, reforms will be needed to realise the government's economic growth targets, as set out in its Medium Term Development Plan (Rencana Pembanginan Jangka Menengah Nasional, RPJMN), and to speed up economic progress.

Over the last two decades, Indonesia has undergone major economic and social changes and has managed to achieve substantial macroeconomic and political stability. The country was profoundly affected by the Asian crisis, which triggered a vast programme of reforms, opening up the economy to international trade and capital inflows and putting in place a well-functioning framework for macro-stabilisation policies. The benefits of these changes have taken time to materialise, and the speed of convergence toward developed economies' living standards was slow until recently, when the global crisis revealed the economy's increased resilience and sound fundamentals. Although output is expected to grow at a strong pace over the next couple of years, a number of weaknesses are still holding back progress. Changes to the policy and institutional framework will be necessary if Indonesia is to achieve its economic growth objective of 7.0 to 7.7% in 2014 and reach the intended poverty rate of 8-10% (13.3% in March 2010). Reforms will need to cover a range of areas, some of which are covered in detail in this chapter. Other crucial areas where reforms are required are examined at length in the following chapters. They include overhauling energy subsidy policy, boosting the quality and quantity of infrastructure stock, and improving the effectiveness of social policies.

After analysing the impact of the global crisis on Indonesia's economy, this chapter presents short, and medium- to long-term economic growth projections. It then discusses areas where policy changes will be required so as to accelerate the country's development process. Fiscal and monetary policy settings, financial markets, labour markets, environment and governance are reviewed in turn.

Recent economic developments

The country has weathered the global crisis very well

Indonesia experienced substantial positive growth in 2009, contrary to most other countries (Table 1.1). Indeed, the impact of the global financial crisis on GDP was comparable to the 2002 episode of financial duress and much more muted than during the Asian crisis. The economy was also less affected than regional peers (Figure 1.1). This stems from some of the specificities of the Indonesian economy, such as a lower dependence on international trade than other Asian economies and the importance of micro enterprises and SMEs, which rely on internal and informal financing (Box 1.1). The exploitation of natural resources, which enjoyed strong growth in global demand and simultaneously high prices, also supported the economic development. Impressive macroeconomic performance also demonstrates the economy's much improved capacity to withstand large shocks, as well as good macroeconomic management and the efficiency of the policy response to sustain demand at end-2008 (Box 1.2).

Like other Asian emerging markets, demand for Indonesian exports and imports contracted considerably at the beginning of the crisis, but started to recover vigorously after just a few quarters. As the crisis unfolded Indonesian financial and monetary markets were hard hit by a sudden rise in risk aversion and ensuing capital outflows. This was

Table 1.1. **Selected macroeconomic indicators**

	2001	2002	2003	2004	2005	2006	2007	2008	2009
Supply and demand									
GDP (in current million *rupiah*)	1 646.3	1 821.8	2 013.7	2 295.8	2 774.3	3 339.5	3 949.3	4 951.4	5 613.4
GDP (in current USD billion)	160.4	195.7	234.8	256.8	285.9	364.6	432.0	510.5	540.3
GDP per capita (in USD PPP)	2 515.1	2 638.8	2 786.3	2 970.2	3 197.2	3 440.6	3 710.7	3 974.9	. .
GDP growth rate (real, in per cent)	3.7	4.5	4.8	5.0	5.7	5.5	6.3	6.1	4.6
GDP growth rate (real, in per capita terms)	2.3	3.1	3.4	3.7	4.4	4.2	4.9	4.8	3.3
Demand (in per cent)									
Private consumption	3.5	3.8	3.9	5.0	4.0	3.1	5.0	5.3	4.9
Public consumption	7.5	13.1	10.1	3.9	6.6	9.5	3.8	10.4	15.8
Gross fixed investment	6.4	4.8	0.7	14.6	10.9	2.4	9.5	11.8	3.3
Exports	0.6	–1.3	5.9	13.5	16.6	9.4	8.5	9.6	–9.7
Imports	4.3	–4.3	1.5	26.7	17.7	8.6	8.9	10.1	–15.0
Supply (in per cent)									
Agriculture	3.3	3.4	3.8	2.8	2.7	3.3	3.4	4.9	4.1
Mining	0.3	1.0	–1.4	–4.5	3.2	1.7	2.0	0.6	4.4
Manufacturing	3.3	5.3	5.3	6.4	4.6	4.6	4.7	3.7	2.1
Services[1]	4.9	5.3	6.3	7.1	7.8	7.4	8.8	8.7	6.0
Supply (in per cent of nominal GDP)									
Agriculture	15.3	15.5	15.2	14.3	13.1	13.0	13.7	14.5	15.3
Mining	11.0	8.8	8.3	8.9	11.1	11.0	11.2	10.9	10.5
Manufacturing	29.1	28.7	28.3	28.1	27.4	27.5	27.1	27.9	26.4
Services[1]	44.6	47.0	48.2	48.7	48.3	48.5	48.1	46.7	47.8
Public finances (central government, in per cent of GDP)									
Revenue	18.3	16.4	17.0	17.6	17.9	19.1	17.9	19.8	15.1
Expenditure	20.7	17.7	18.7	18.6	18.4	19.9	19.2	19.9	16.7
Nominal balance	–2.5	–1.3	–1.7	–1.0	–0.6	–0.8	–1.3	–0.1	–1.6
Gross debt	77.3	67.2	61.2	56.6	47.3	39.0	35.2	33.1	28.3
Balance of payments (in USD billion)									
Current account balance	6.9	7.8	8.1	1.6	0.3	10.9	10.5	0.1	10.7
In per cent of GDP	4.3	4.0	3.5	0.6	0.1	3.0	2.4	0.0	2.0
Trade balance	22.7	23.5	24.6	20.2	17.5	29.7	32.8	22.9	35.1
Exports	57.4	59.2	64.1	70.8	87.0	103.5	118.0	139.6	119.5
Imports	34.7	35.7	39.5	50.6	69.5	73.9	85.3	116.7	84.3
International reserves (gross)	28.1	32.0	36.3	36.3	34.7	42.6	56.9	51.6	66.1
Outstanding external debt	133.1	131.1	135.4	141.3	134.5	132.6	141.2	155.1	172.9
In per cent of GDP	82.9	67.0	57.7	55.0	47.1	36.4	32.7	30.4	32.0

1. Includes electricity, gas, water and construction.
Source: World Bank, Ministry of Finance, BPS and OECD calculations.

totally attributable to large portfolio capital outflows as global risk aversion increased, starting a deleveraging process where flows to credit and capital markets were shifted to low-risk assets, particularly US government securities.

The monetary authorities responded promptly to the crisis by cutting interest rates and intervening in the foreign-exchange market to ease excessive pressure while sterilising interventions through open-market operations.[1] Foreign-exchange reserves have risen to USD 86.5 billion in September 2010, corresponding to around six months of imports and servicing of official external debt. Bank Indonesia (BI) also strengthened bilateral and multilateral co-operation with regional central banks in the form of currency swap agreements. Overall, these measures were appropriate and well targeted. They restored ample liquidity to the interbank market and financial conditions improved. Net inflows of portfolio investments were also bolstered by renewed investors' risk appetites in

Figure 1.1. **The global economic crisis in Indonesia, OECD and Asia**

t_0 = 100 for July 2008 (2008Q3 for GDP, export, import and terms of trade)

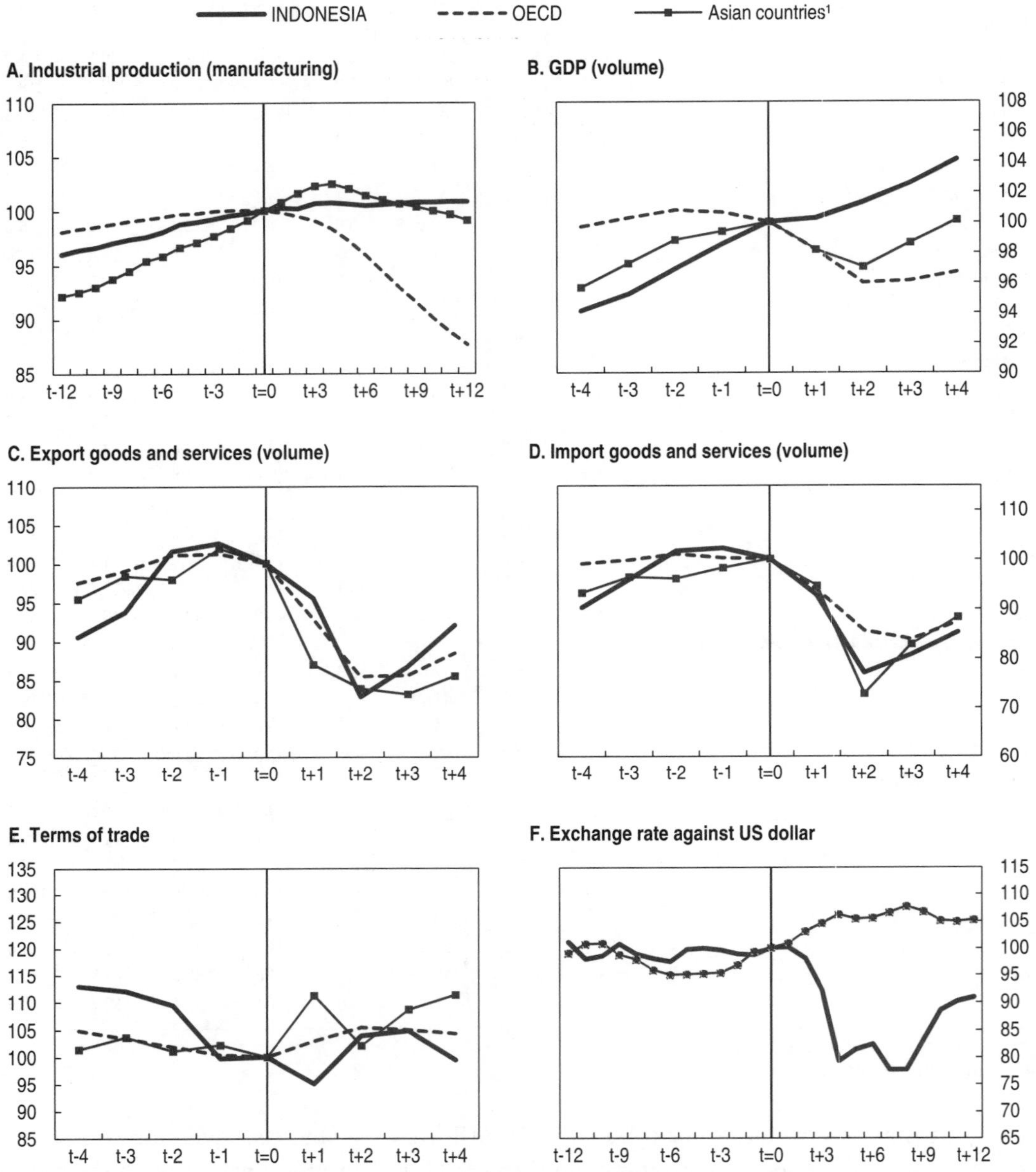

1. "Asian countries" is the simple average of Malaysia, Philippines, Thailand and Vietnam.

Source: World Bank (*World Development Indicators*), *MEI* and OECD calculations.

StatLink http://dx.doi.org/10.1787/888932341138

the second half of 2009, low returns on developed countries' safe assets, propitious domestic economic conditions and an upgraded sovereign credit rating for Indonesia awarded in 2009 by two agencies, which reinforced investors' confidence.

The strong upsurge in foreign capital flows to Indonesia resulted in soaring asset prices. Indonesia's stock market rallied 88% in 2009. This increase in stock prices exceeded what was justified by fundamentals and signalled a potential asset price bubble. Since then, signs of a bubble have faded (Bank Indonesia, 2010).

Box 1.1. **A snapshot of the Indonesian economy**

Indonesia is the world's largest archipelago with approximately 18 000 islands spanning the equator and three time zones. Islands are grouped into 33 provinces gathered into five major groupings: Java-Bali, Sumatra, Kalimantan (Borneo), Sulawesi and the Eastern provinces. Economic activity clusters around some key regional economies, including Java, Bali, Sumatra and Kalimantan. There are large inter-provincial differences in income and welfare. Since 2001, the government has been highly decentralised.

Indonesia is a lower middle-income country and ranked 108th out of 210 countries in terms of GDP per capita in 2008. It is the fourth most populous nation in the world after China, India and the United States. It is ethnically diverse, with around 360 languages spoken. Over two-thirds of the population resides in Java. 36% of the population is currently 20 years old or less. Given this age structure, population ageing will start to affect labour-force developments around 2015. Educational attainment has increased markedly for primary school but remains low for secondary and higher levels of education.

The country is well endowed in natural resources. It is the world's largest producer of palm oil, which is used in biofuels, food and cosmetics. Indonesia has approximately 40% of the world geothermal potential, but only 4% is currently used. It has the world's third largest forest cover (120 million hectares), a topic of considerable controversy, as logging, much of it illegal, shrinks this area. The country is also rich in natural gas, coal and a variety of metals and benefits from very diversified fauna and flora.

Indonesia experienced substantial changes over the last two decades moving at the same time to democracy and market-oriented policies. Although the country is still in a transition, growth and stability have been bolstered by substantial political, economic and institutional reforms. In the early 1990s, the rapid growth of the industrial sector contributed to high economic returns. However, the country was severely affected by the 1997-98 Asian financial crisis and has only recently regained its previous income level relative to the OECD average. While the recovery in GDP has been continuous since 2000, it has not spread equally across sectors. In general, growth has been strongest in capital-intensive services sectors, with the labour-intensive primary and manufacturing sectors experiencing sluggish expansion. Almost 45% of the workforce is employed in agriculture, with the remainder is working in the manufacturing industry, mining and services.

State Owned Enterprises (SOEs) still play an important role in the economy. The successive governments attempted to rationalise their operations and corporatise many of them while keeping state control. According to data of the Ministry of State Owned Enterprises, the number of SOEs decreased from 158 in 2002 to 141 in 2009. Their share of loss-making diminished steadily from 28% in 2006 to 17% in 2009 with total profits of SOEs rising from around IDR 46 trillion in 2006 to IDR 86 trillion (USD 9.6 billion) in 2009. The government plans to make SOEs more efficient and carry on with a selected privatisation programme in the coming years.

Indonesia has a relatively open economy. Import tariffs have been reduced steadily since the 1980s. In addition, the country is committed to the ASEAN Free Trade Agreement, implying that the average effective import tariff is lower than average MFN tariffs. However, Indonesia imposes some non-tariff barriers, especially for agricultural products. Restrictions on foreign investment were simplified and in some cases eased in the 2007 and 2009 Investment Laws. Energy dominates trade patterns, both on the export and import side, while the share of high-technology exports is low. The country stopped being a net oil exporter in 2004. Indonesia trades increasingly with ASEAN countries. The share of non-oil imports from ASEAN countries has steadily increased since 2005 and now

Box 1.1. **A snapshot of the Indonesian economy** *(cont.)*

represents about 20% of total imports. Non-oil exports toward China and India have been on an upward trend. Still, Indonesia remains less reliant on external trade than other countries in the region. The degree of trade openness (exports plus imports divided by GDP) in Indonesia was around 53% in 2008, much lower than the 133% estimated for the ASEAN 10 (Kaid and Swindi, 2009). The major impediments to external competitiveness in Indonesia are of a structural nature and include infrastructure bottlenecks, domestic trade barriers, restrictive product market regulation and stringent employment protection legislation.

Poverty has declined since 1998 but remains high, with a poverty rate of 13.3% of the population in 2010, concentrated in rural areas. In addition to the rural-urban divide, important economic disparities also exist between women and men.

The economy is characterised by a very large informal sector. According to some estimates, the informal sector represents around 70% of total employment. The analysis undertaken in the *2008 Economic Assessment* reveals that women have a higher probability than men to be employed in the informal sector. Informality is also less widespread among workers living in rural than urban areas, and among prime-age individuals. In addition, informality is found to decline with educational attainment.

Box 1.2. **Policy response to the crisis**

In response to the global crisis, the Indonesian government took a range of actions to restore confidence in financial markets and cushion the economic downturn.

Monetary and financial reaction

Bank Indonesia (BI) implemented several measures to prevent a credit crunch from late 2008 through 2009. These included: cutting the policy interest rate by a cumulative 300 basis points to 6.5% from December 2008 to August 2009; interventions in foreign-exchange markets to mitigate the effect of the global liquidity crisis on domestic forex liquidity, keeping, at the same time, an adequate level of international reserves; the creation of new temporary and emergency liquidity facilities in addition to new credit lines for micro and small enterprises located in rural areas; the removal of the daily limit on net short-term foreign borrowings; lowering the minimum bank reserve requirement to 7.5% of depositor funds; the opening of local-currency money-market repo windows of one- and three-month tenors to enhance banking liquidity; the lengthening of the FX swap tenor from 7 days to 1 month; the reduction in foreign exchange reserve requirements for banks from 3% to 1%; and currency swap arrangements with regional central banks under the Chiang Mai Initiative as part of ASEAN+3 financial co-operation.

BI and the government also took specific measures aimed at enhancing banking industry resilience. These included: providing BI with the legal basis to supply credit to finance banks experiencing difficulties in raising short-term funds and to extend the emergency financing facility (FPD) to systemically important banks; a reduction in the risk weighting for credit to micro, small and medium-sized enterprises to make finance more easily available to such firms; the implementation of risk management and prudential principles in activities related to structured (derivative) products; and the improvement of the banking payment system infrastructure through the continuing development of the Bank Indonesia Real Time Gross Settlement Generation II.

Box 1.2. **Policy response to the crisis** *(cont.)*

Fiscal measures

In the aftermath of the global crisis the fiscal authority implemented a range of fiscal measures to support domestic demand, complementing the monetary policy easing by BI. The parliament approved a fiscal stimulus package in February 2009 of IDR 73.3 trillion (around 1.5% of GDP). It introduced an import duty and VAT exemption on inputs and raw materials in selected labour-intensive sectors as well as income tax subsidies on geothermal (IDR 13.3 trillion). It also included an increase in fuel and electricity subsidies (IDR 4.2 trillion) and a hike in infrastructure spending (IDR 12.2 trillion). However, the bulk of the package consisted of income-tax cuts (IDR 43 trillion) already approved in 2008. This stimulus package was subsequently increased in the revised 2009 Budget. Basic salaries were raised by an average 15%, and a 13th month of salary was paid to civil servants. Subsidies for fuel, electricity and food were increased (see Chapter 2).

The fiscal package is officially estimated to have boosted economic growth by 1.3 percentage points in 2009 and by almost 0.8 percentage point in 2010 (Figure 1.2). At 1.6% of GDP, the 2009 general government budget deficit turned out to be smaller than initially planned (2.4% of GDP), as a result of lower outlays on subsidies and on debt interest, and lower spending by line ministries.

Figure 1.2. **Impact of the fiscal package on real GDP**

Annual percentage growth

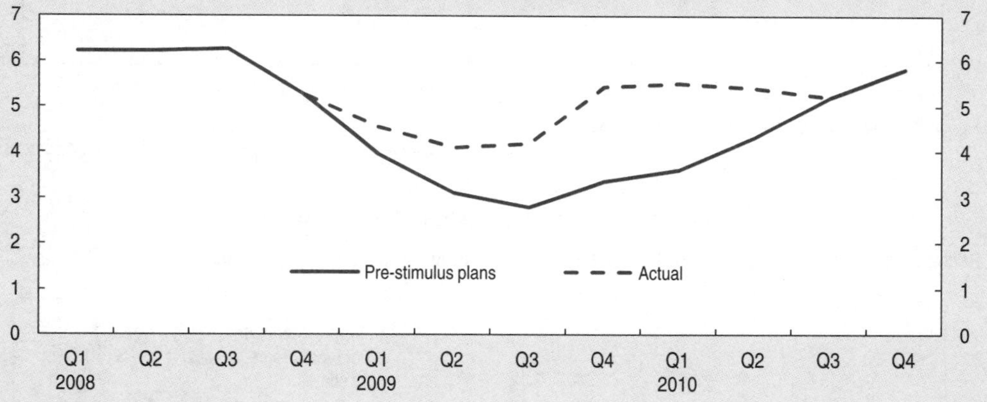

Source: Fiscal Policy Office.

StatLink http://dx.doi.org/10.1787/888932341157

Source: Bank Indonesia (2010), Fiscal Policy Office.

The marked appreciation of the *rupiah* up until May 2010 helped to tame inflation (Figure 1.3). This is consistent with the empirical evidence, which points to the foreign exchange rate and activity as the most important factors predicting future inflation over short and medium horizons (see Annex 1.A1). As activity recovered inflation remained well below target, allowing the central bank to keep interest rates low for longer than elsewhere.

Labour markets appear to have been relatively shielded from the crisis. Employment has continued to grow albeit at a slower pace (Figure 1.4). At the same time, unemployment has kept trending down, as the informal sector acted as a buffer in absorbing additional manpower in a context of slowing economic growth and reduced job opportunities in the

Figure 1.3. **Monetary policy, inflation and exchange rate**

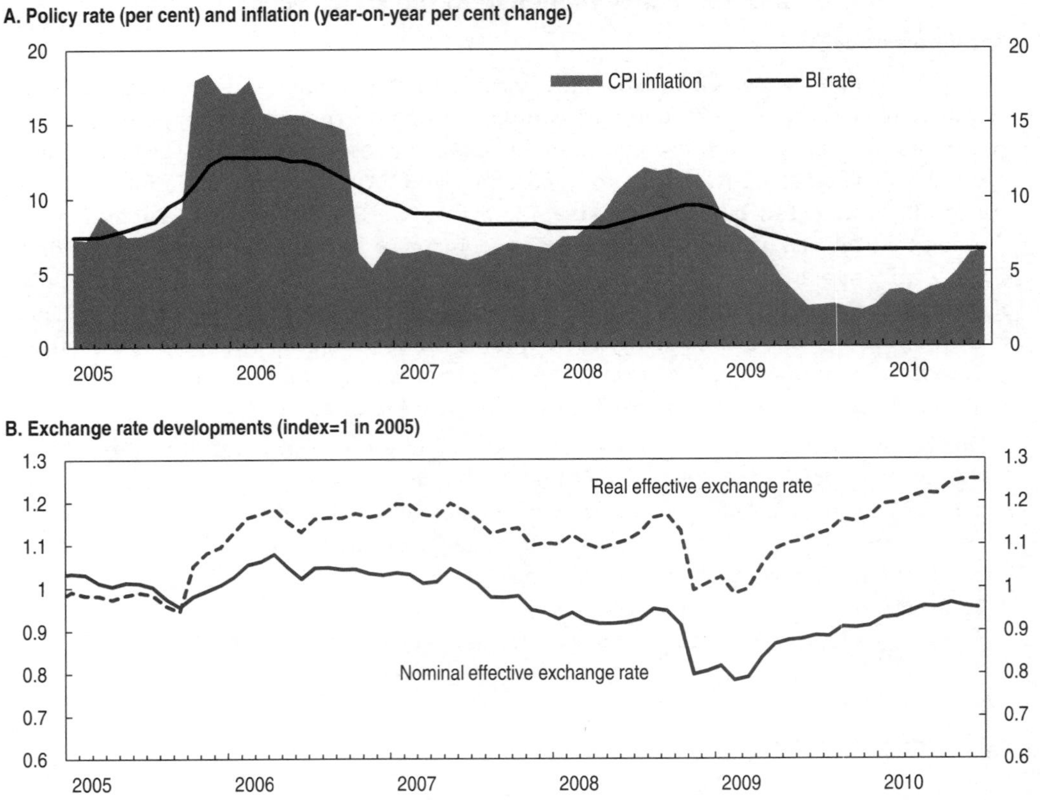

Source: OECD calculation, BPS and Bank Indonesia.

StatLink http://dx.doi.org/10.1787/888932341176

Figure 1.4. **Labour-market indicators**

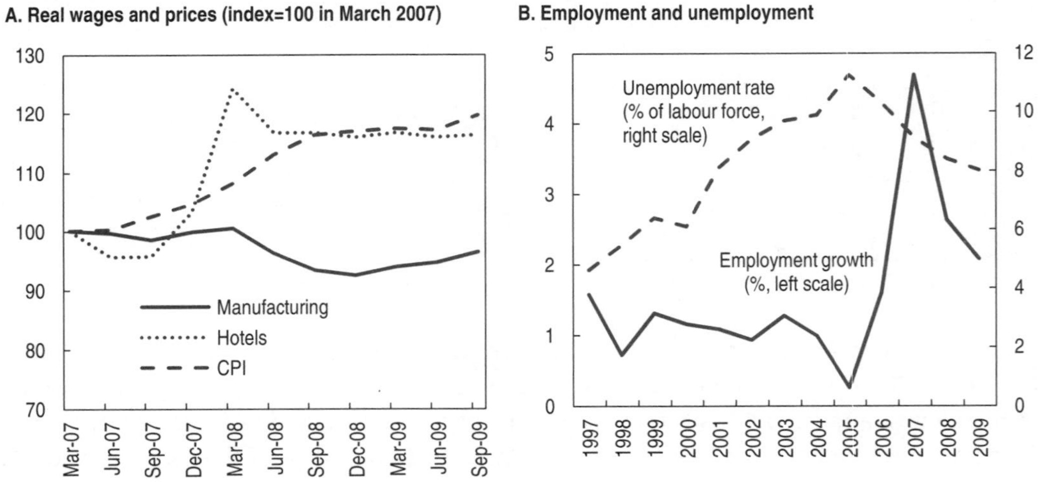

Source: BPS.

StatLink http://dx.doi.org/10.1787/888932341195

formal sector. Estimates from BPS-Statistics Indonesia suggest that employment in the informal sector rose to 72.7 million in August 2009 from 71.4 in August 2008. Informal self-employment explains most of this increase.

Various groups in society have been affected to a different degree (SMERU, 2009). Although the more affluent households have experienced income losses, they could rely on other resources or savings to cope with the downturn. Poorer groups, such as farm labourers and motorcycle taxi drivers, have been hit harder. Government assistance programmes mitigated the impact of the crisis on poverty, by supporting food consumption and school attendance (see Chapter 4). By contrast, the crisis has threatened enrolment at the senior high school level (SMERU, 2009).

Financial markets have proven more resilient than in the past

Indonesia's capital markets have been little affected by the global financial crisis, mostly because of their relative underdevelopment (see below). The turmoil erupted in the most sophisticated end of financial markets, to which Indonesian financial institutions are hardly exposed. The soundness of the banking sector was preserved even at the height of the crisis. Bank liquidity and solvency problems were limited and swiftly dealt with.[2] This good overall performance reflects the effectiveness of the policy reaction as well as the progress accomplished since the Asian crisis in restructuring the banking sector. In addition, the impact of share-price movements on the banking sector was mitigated by BI regulations that prohibit banks from purchasing shares.

The counterpart of prudent bank lending has been a marked slowdown in credit growth (Figure 1.5). The sharp deceleration in loan growth was largely attributable to working-capital loans, whose contribution to the growth in total loans fell from more than 50% at its peak to less than zero in early 2010. From early 2010, loan growth has

Figure 1.5. **Credit outstanding by type of bank and loan**

Year-on-year growth rate

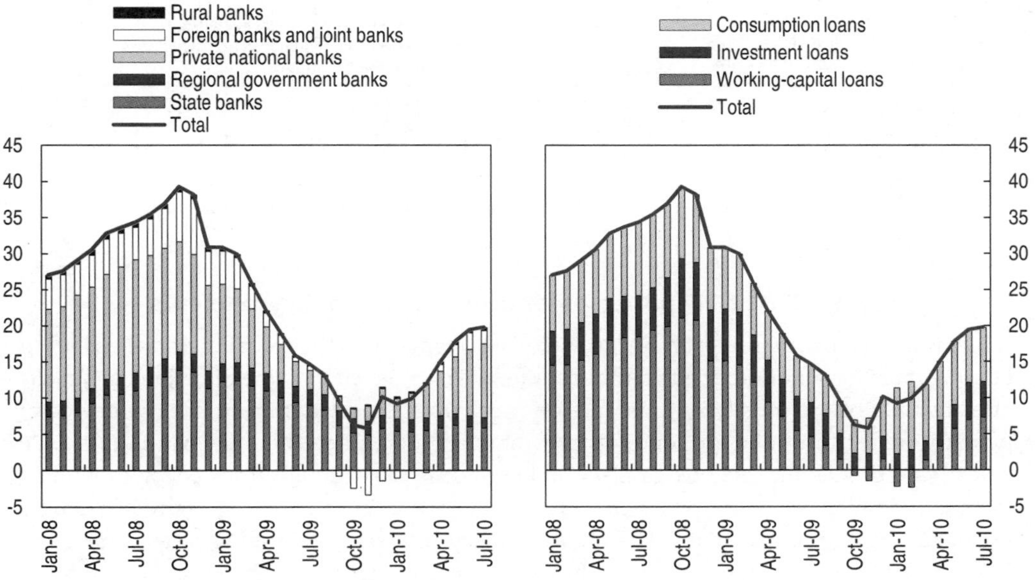

Source: Bank Indonesia.

StatLink http://dx.doi.org/10.1787/888932341214

gradually started to accelerate as the recovery has become entrenched. Whereas lending by private banks has rebounded strongly, state and regional development banks have been more cautious. Among the different types of loans, consumption loans have led the way to renewed credit growth.

An explanation often put forward to explain subdued credit growth at the beginning of the year is the level of lending rates, which have been persistently higher in Indonesia than in regional peers. Lending rates did not come down as rapidly as the policy rate during the crisis (Figure 1.6). However, the muted reaction of lending rates appears to be consistent with the traditional low pass-through from policy to lending rates in Indonesia (Box 1.3). Higher lending rates could then stem from structural characteristics such as low interbank competition. Moreover, modest credit growth could also reflect mistrust between banks and non-financial corporations, which restricted both demand for and supply of loans. Indeed, firms in the financial sector, but also in infrastructure and transportation, have sought alternative financing sources and issued corporate bonds to finance their investments. At the same time, there is some evidence that banks have been reluctant to lend to so-called sunset industries, which are expected to suffer from the ASEAN-China Free Trade Agreement (Box 1.4). In addition, the apprehension concerning a potential rise

Figure 1.6. **Lending rates**

Per cent

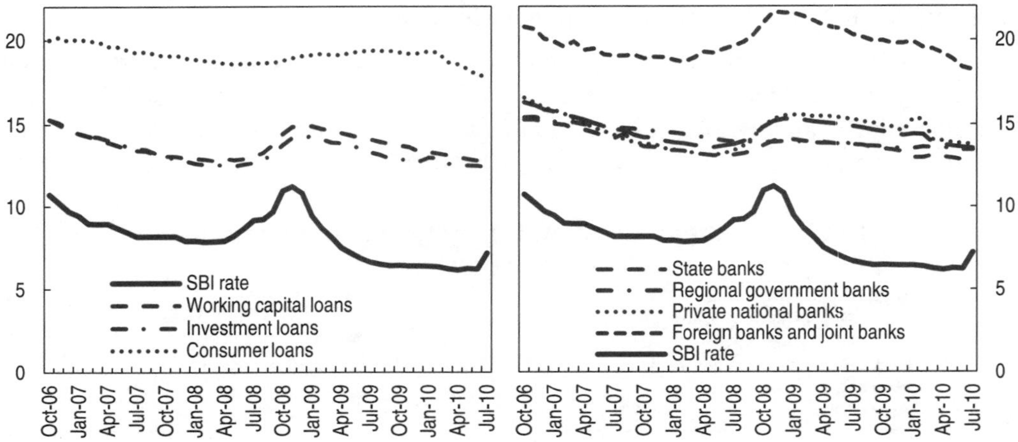

Source: Bank Indonesia.

StatLink http://dx.doi.org/10.1787/888932341233

Box 1.3. **The response of lending rates to policy rate cuts**

BI has cut the policy interest rate aggressively in response to the global financial crisis, but lending rates have not dropped commensurately. This has led to some questions about the effectiveness of the monetary transmission mechanism and whether or not the degree of pass-through from policy to lending rates has declined since the start of the crisis. To investigate this point, this box gauges the long-term pass-through from policy to lending rates in Indonesia and selected Asian countries by estimating an autoregressive distributed lag model using monthly data. The data on policy interest and lending rates come from Datastream and start from mid-1999, at the earliest, to early 2010, but availability varies across countries. Findings appear to be robust to changes in model specification.

Box 1.3. The response of lending rates to policy rate cuts *(cont.)*

The evidence shows that the pass-through in Indonesia is far from complete but of the same order of magnitude than in other Asian countries (Table 1.2), with the exception of Korea where it is much stronger. Given the actual change in the policy interest rate, the model explains all the decrease in lending rates in Indonesia. The model is also relatively successful in explaining the movement in lending rates of the comparator countries, especially Korea and Malaysia. Finally, despite some claims to the contrary, monetary transmission mechanisms in Indonesia have not become less effective during the latest financial crisis. If anything, there is some evidence that the pass-through has slightly increased.

Table 1.2. Long-term pass-through from policy to lending rates and mean lag[1]

	End-period long-term pass through	Mean lag (in months)	Change in the policy rate (basis points)			Change in the lending rate (basis points)	
			From	To	Observed	Observed	In-sample prediction
Indonesia	**0.4****	**1.7**	**Nov. 08**	**Aug. 09**	**–300**	**–117.0**	**–126.0**
Malaysia	0.4**	1.3	Oct. 08	Feb. 09	–150	–95.0	–55.5
Thailand	0.2**	1.4	Oct. 08	Apr. 09	–250	–133.8	–52.5
India	0.2**	1.1	Sep. 08	Apr. 09	–425	–200.0	–93.5
Korea	1.1**	4.2	Aug. 08	Feb. 09	–349	–444.0	–383.9
Japan	0.2*	1.2	Nov. 08	Dec. 08	–20	–15.1	–4.4

1. Mean lag is the number of months necessary to get the full long-term pass-through. ** and * denote 5 and 1% statistical significance.

Source: Datastream, Central Banks and OECD calculations.

Box 1.4. The impact of the ASEAN-China Free Trade Agreement on Indonesia

The ASEAN-China Free Trade Agreement (FTA) came into effect on 1 January 2010. It involves the complete elimination of tariff barriers for around 6 600 products in different industries – twelve in manufacturing and five in agriculture, mining and maritime sectors (see Table 1.3). The implementation of this agreement has been accompanied by growing fears in Indonesia relating to its possible negative impact on output and employment and the risk of turning the country into a supplier of solely primary products.

Kiyota *et al.* (2008) conclude that the long-term effects of the ASEAN-China FTA on Indonesia are positive. According to their results, based on the general equilibrium multi-country and -sector Michigan Model of World Production and Trade, the welfare effects, generated by the reallocation of resources towards sectors with comparative advantage, are equivalent to around 1.2% of GDP in the long term. More specifically, reflecting the comparative advantage of labour-intensive industries, exports of wearing apparel, textiles and leather industries would rise substantially. Also, the rice sector would expand, whereas mineral, capital-intensive manufacturing and service sectors would contract. A study using sectoral equilibrium models also concludes the ASEAN-China FTA would provide welfare gains to Indonesia, by lowering prices and expanding its exports to China (Asian Development Bank, 2008).

Box 1.4. **The impact of the ASEAN-China Free Trade Agreement on Indonesia** *(cont.)*

Related to the FTA, the appreciation of the Chinese renminbi following the change in China's exchange rate policy, announced in June 2010, could affect Indonesia through a number of channels, including an increase in price competitiveness for Indonesian firms in the domestic, Chinese and third markets. China's share in Indonesia's exports was around 9% in 2009, with energy and other commodities accounting for the bulk of sales. A limited appreciation of the Chinese currency is estimated to have only a small impact on Indonesia's exports to China (World Bank, 2010a). Indonesia's exports to third markets could decline to the extent that they are vertically integrated with Chinese exports. A higher renminbi is also likely to make Indonesia more attractive for Chinese investors, increasing FDI flows and eventually shifting production facilities to Indonesia. This would require nonetheless that Indonesia be perceived as a more attractive destination than other countries in the region.

Table 1.3. **Indonesia's tariff rates on imported goods by trade agreement, simple average, per cent**

	1995	2002	2003	2004	2005	2006	2007	2008	2009	2010
MFN	15.5	7.4	7.2	9.9	9.9	9.5	7.8	7.6	7.6	7.5
ASEAN FTA		4.3	2.8	3.4	2.8	2.8	2.0	1.9	1.9	0.9
China-ASEAN FTA					9.6	9.5	6.4	6.4	3.8	2.9

Source: Ministry of Finance.

in non-performing loans encouraged banks to place their funds in *Sertifikats Bank Indonesia* (SBIs) and other safe assets rather than to expand credit.

In order to improve liquidity management and quell mounting inflationary pressures, BI has raised the primary reserve requirement from 5 to 8%, effective from November 2010. This move is expected to help to withdraw the exceptional liquidity support provided in response to the financial crisis and remove chronic excess liquidity in the banking system. Moreover, BI has set a loan-to-deposit ratio target for lending institutions of between 78 and 100%, from March 2011, to promote bank intermediation and achieve the 22 to 24% objective for annual credit growth, while upholding prudential banking principles. Banks not meeting the target will have to deposit additional reserves with BI. These measures appear to be consistent with the double objective of stimulating bank lending while trying to remove excess liquidity. However, by imposing constraints on banks they entail the risk of distorting credit allocation decisions. It will thus be important to closely monitor the impact of these measures on financial and banking sector developments.

Short-term economic forecasts point to strong growth

Activity is projected to maintain strong momentum until year end and accelerate slightly in 2011 (Table 1.4). Resilient private consumption and resurgent investment have been the main drivers of growth. Foreign demand for resource-based commodities is underpinning robust export growth, offsetting the effect of currency appreciation. On the supply side, the economic activity is being driven by the construction and service sectors, especially trade, hotel and restaurants, but it has yet to broaden to manufacturing

Table 1.4. **Short-term economic forecasts**

	2007	2008	2009	2010	2011	2012
Real GDP growth (per cent)	6.3	6.1	4.6	6.1	6.3	6.0
CPI Inflation (per cent, end-year)	6.6	11.1	2.8	6.5	6.0	4.9
Fiscal balance (per cent of GDP)	–1.2	–0.1	–1.6	–1.4	–1.3	–1.3
Current account balance (USD billion)	10.5	0.1	10.6	2.4	–0.4	–4.0
Current account balance (per cent of GDP)	2.4	0.0	1.9	0.3	–0.1	–0.4

Source: Preliminary *OECD Economic Outlook 88 Database.*

industries. Unemployment has been trending down. Bank Indonesia's expectations surveys point to a continued robust economic activity, supported by rising households' disposable income and retail sales.

Domestic demand should remain the main driver of growth over the next two years, supported by resilient consumers' loans growth and rising purchasing power. Investment is expected to pick up strongly on the back of rising credit extensions and receding risk aversion. Import demand is poised to recover as economic activity accelerates, shrinking and even reversing the current account surplus.

The risks associated with these projections are somewhat on the downside. Public capital implementation bottlenecks may hinder the recovery in investment growth. Social and political opposition to the attendant rise in energy prices could postpone or soften the energy subsidies reform, resulting in a higher budget deficit than projected. On the upside, a faster-than-anticipated recovery in global demand would provide an additional boost to exports. Growth could also be higher than projected, provided that the government implements its pro-growth reform agenda, especially with regard to infrastructure projects.

Tail risks emanate from the external sector. The direct effect of a weaker recovery in OECD countries is likely to be muted, as Indonesia trades little with them. Although Indonesia's external debt to GDP ratio declined steadily from over 150% of GDP in 1998 to 31.5% in 2009, the surge in capital inflows over the last year has accentuated the vulnerability of the country to a sudden change in risk aversion and outflows of volatile capital. Thus far, contagion fears from sovereign-debt problems in the euro area have weighed rather modestly on foreign investors' financial decisions (Figure 1.7). However, rapid changes cannot be excluded as evidenced in late 2008. The country is also vulnerable to asset price deflation in China, which could precipitate a reversal of capital flows from emerging-market economies. The danger of massive capital inflows should not be underestimated as they could complicate the task of monetary policy and would need to be properly addressed (see below).

Subdued inflationary pressures have allowed BI to keep rates on hold at 6.5% since August 2009. The July 2010 hike in electricity tariff is expected to have a small and short-lived effect on inflation and survey-based expectations point to softening inflationary pressures in the near future. Still, favourable economic prospects and fading currency appreciation effects are likely to exert further pressure on inflation in 2011. Given the past history of high inflation, anchoring inflation expectations is of paramount importance, if Indonesia is to lower its consumer price inflation to less burdensome levels on a sustainable basis. Monetary policy normalisation in the region has already started. The central banks of Taiwan, India, Malaysia and South Korea have hiked their policy rates by a

Figure 1.7. **Share of local currency government bonds held by foreign investors**

Per cent

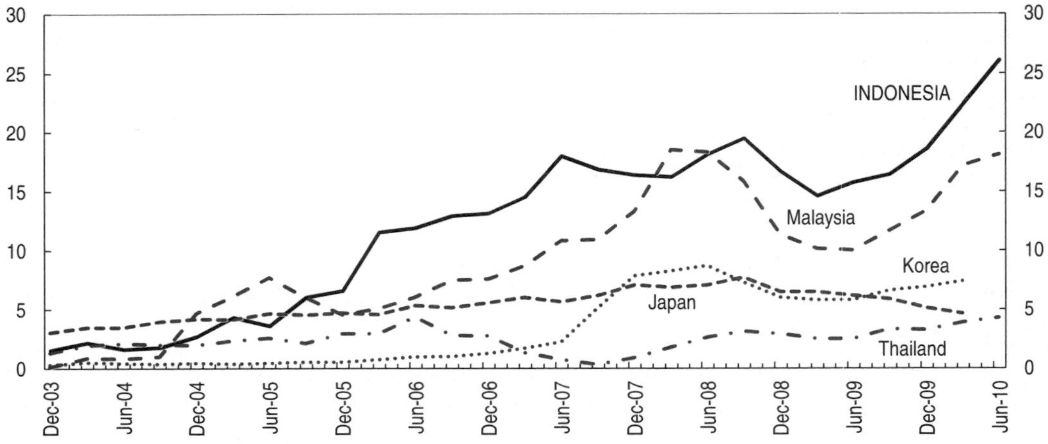

Source: AsianBondsOnline.

StatLink http://dx.doi.org/10.1787/888932341252

cumulative amount of between 25 and 125 basis points from their trough. Some monetary tightening has already taken place through the increase in the primary reserve requirement since November 2010. BI will have to be extremely vigilant and act in a forward-looking manner to prevent consumer prices from rising above the end-2011 inflation target of 4-6%. This is likely to require BI to raise interest rates before the end of 2010.

The central government budget balance is projected to be moderately negative in 2010 and 2011. The government expects budget deficit to amount to 1.8% of GDP in 2011 (after 2.1% in 2010). Total spending would remain broadly stable in terms of GDP at around 18%, while the country's tax ratio would rise slightly and exceed 12% of GDP. Because of implementation bottlenecks, especially concerning capital outlays, the fiscal balance is likely to be better than projected by the authorities.

Key challenges over the longer term

What are the prospects for long-term growth?

Potential output growth has recovered but is still below its pre-1998 pace

The Asian crisis ended the period of sustained growth since the 1980s, during which productive capacity rose by 6-6.5% on average per year (Table 1.5). After having collapsed during the Asian crisis and its immediate aftermath, potential output growth gradually recovered after 2000. It has been little affected by the global crisis and is estimated to have been slightly above 5% in 2009.

Capital accumulation and to a lesser extent labour input growth have been the main drivers of potential output in the past. By contrast, gains in total factor productivity (TFP) – the efficiency with which the factors of production are used to produce output – accounted for less than 20% of potential output growth before the Asian crisis. The contribution of TFP appears to have risen steadily since 1998, reaching almost 40% in the 2006-09 period. These estimations are consistent with other empirical analyses using either national-accounts or sectoral data (World Bank, 2010b; Alisjahbana, 2009; Van der Eng, 2007; Aswicahyono and Hill, 2002).

Table 1.5. **Actual and potential output growth and contributions to growth**

	GDP growth Per cent	Potential GDP growth Per cent	Contributions to potential output growth Percentage point		
			TFP	Capital	Labour
1980-89	6.4	6.4	1.0	3.5	1.9
1990-97	7.6	6.0	0.9	3.8	1.3
1998-99	–6.2	1.9	–0.5	1.2	1.2
2000-09	5.1	4.0	1.2	1.7	1.0

1. Potential output is estimated using a production-function approach (see Annex 1.A2).
Source: OECD calculations.

In this context, the rapid per capita income convergence of Indonesia during the early 1990s was halted in 1998, and average income has yet to recoup its relative pre-crisis level when compared with the OECD, despite some recent progress. Indonesia's relative income gap continued to improve in 2009 but remains high at about 90%, smaller only than India's among the OECD's Enhanced Engagement countries (Figure 1.8). This illustrates the scope for catching up in relative standards of living in the future.

Figure 1.8. **Income gap *vis-à-vis* the OECD countries in OECD's Enhanced Engagement countries**[1]

GDP per capita (thousands PPP, constant 2005 USD), per cent

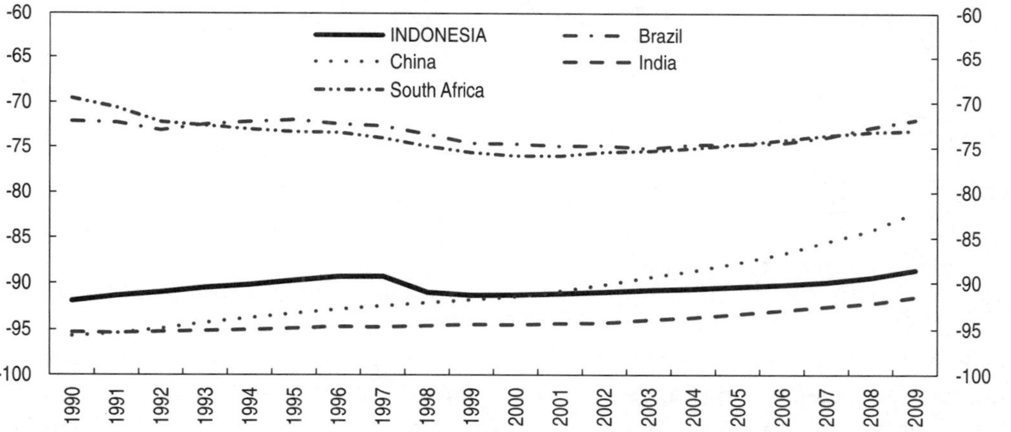

1. OECD excludes Chile, Israel, Mexico, Poland, Slovenia and Turkey.
Source: OECD calculations using World Bank (*World Development Indicators*) data.
StatLink http://dx.doi.org/10.1787/888932341271

Prospects for potential growth in the medium and long terms

Real GDP expanded by around 5% on average per year over the last decade, with rates being on an upward trend during most of the period. This is lower than the 7.0-7.7% objective for actual GDP growth which features in the government's Medium Term Development Plan for 2014 (Box 1.5).

Beyond that, ageing is also going to play an important role, as Indonesia will enter a decade of important demographic changes. The dependency ratio fell steadily from 1970 to 2009, as declines in fertility reduced the number of children and the number of elderly increased only very marginally. However, population projections point to a stabilisation followed by a decline in the working-age population and a rise in the dependency ratio starting over the next decade (Figure 1.9). Assuming capital and trend

Figure 1.9. **Projections of population and potential output growth**

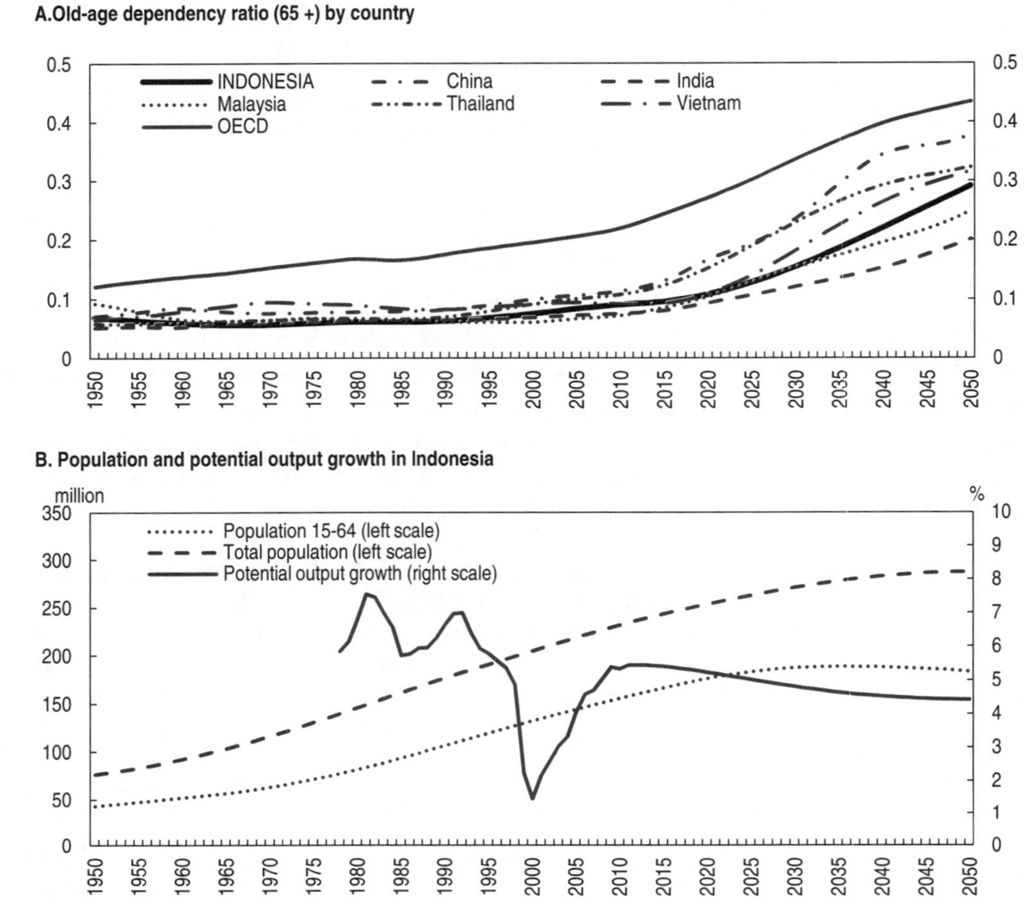

Source: United Nations and OECD calculations.

StatLink http://dx.doi.org/10.1787/888932341290

TFP grow at rates observed in 2008-09, structural unemployment gradually converges to its long-term average and no change in policy, potential output growth could slow to around 4½ per cent in the long term. These point estimates are sensitive to the calibration of the production function, as well as the TFP and capital-input projections, and are surrounded by large uncertainties. Still, changes to these assumptions would not modify the diagnostics of an expected slowdown in potential-output growth over the long term spurred by population ageing (see Annex 1.A2).

Ageing is going to bear on saving over the long term

Changes in the age structure are likely to affect potential growth through a slowdown in private saving resulting in increasing borrowing or lower capital accumulation, all else equal. Indeed, saving patterns are expected to alter when the elderly become a larger proportion of consumers and savers, with widespread implications for capital and goods markets. Panel-based estimations from Furceri and Mourougane (2010a) suggest that the old-age dependency ratio depresses private saving in Asia-Pacific countries, and the age structure is estimated to lower Indonesia's private saving-to-GDP ratio by around 1.6 percentage points on average from 2015 to 2050 (Figure 1.10). This is in the range of

Figure 1.10. **The effect of age structure on the ratio of private saving to GDP**

Percentage point

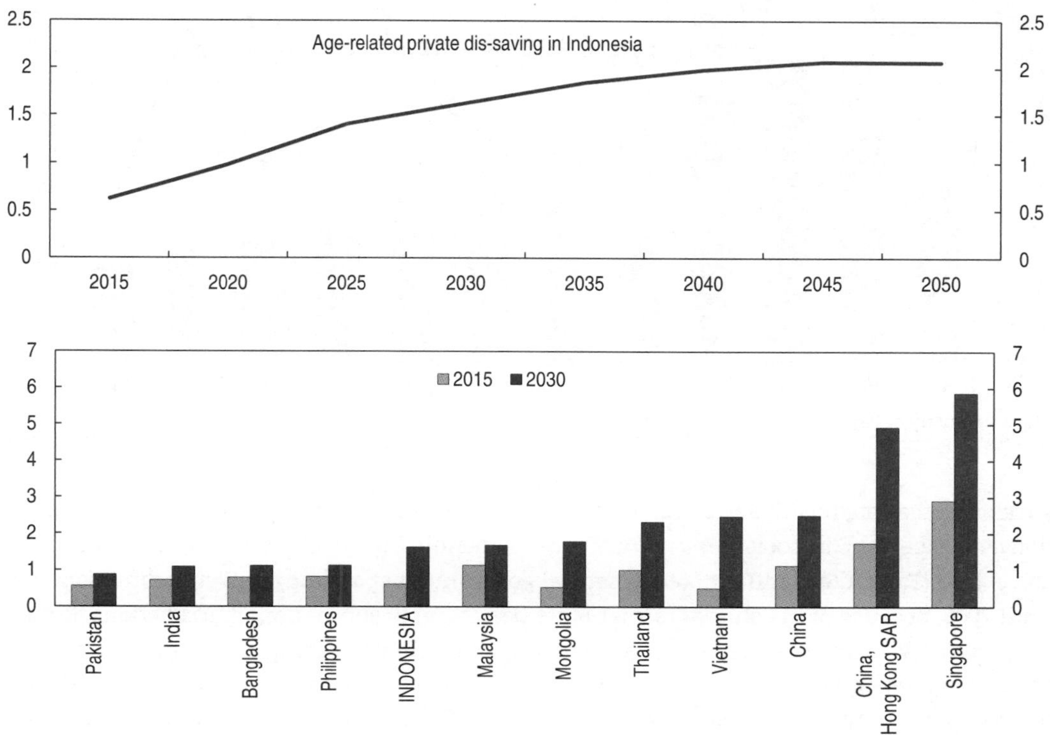

Note: Private saving is expressed as a per cent of GDP.

Source: OECD calculation using data from the United Nations and Furceri and Mourougane (2010a).

StatLink http://dx.doi.org/10.1787/888932341309

what is expected for other countries in the region. The effect is foreseen to steadily increase at least up to 2050.

Macroeconomic policy framework

The fiscal framework is sound, but there is room for improvement

Fiscal performance has progressed over the years

Indonesia's fiscal achievements have been enviable by international standards. The government budget deficit was gradually reduced from 2001 to 2005 (Figure 1.11). It subsequently deteriorated but has stayed below 2% of GDP since 2002. Gross debt as a percentage of GDP has been lowered at an impressive rate from its post-Asia crisis peak in 2000 to a preliminary estimate of 28% in 2009. Recent performance reflects not only an overall prudent framework but also substantial windfall revenues. In addition, the ratio of total government external debt to GDP declined sharply to 29% in 2009, from 47% in 2005 and 89% in 2000. The public deficit is now exclusively financed from domestic sources.

Responsibilities are shared between the central and regional authorities

Since the implementation of the decentralisation law in 2001, the conduct of fiscal policy involves the central and the regional governments (provinces and local governments). The central government controls tax policy by setting tax bases and permissible ranges for local tax rates. It also retains control in areas related to investment programmes, in particular in sectors

Figure 1.11. **Gross debt and fiscal balance**
In per cent of GDP

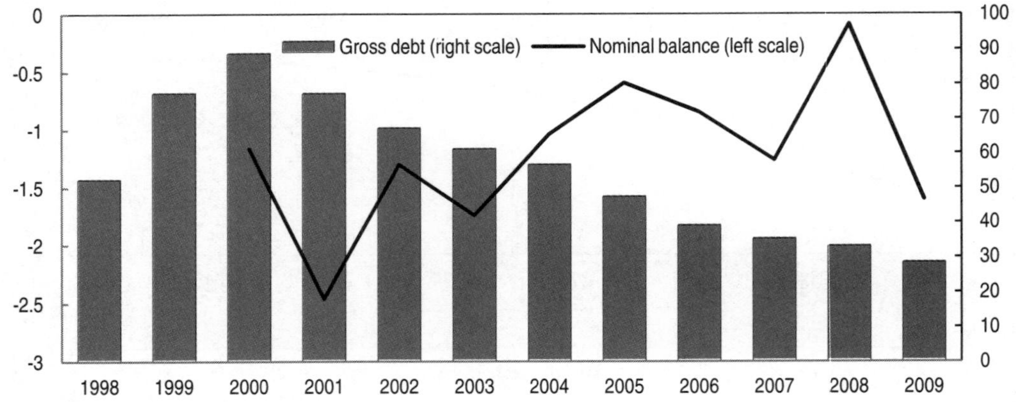

Source: Ministry of Finance and Debt Management Office.

StatLink http://dx.doi.org/10.1787/888932341328

such as education, health and infrastructure. Local authorities are responsible for most service delivery, especially in social areas. The share of spending by local governments has doubled since 2000 (Table 1.6). Simultaneously, central government spending on payroll diminished up until 2005, because of the shift of former State personnel to sub-national jurisdictions. But the trend was reversed thereafter. Local governments have limited taxing autonomy, and most of their revenues come from central government transfers in the form of Balance Funds and Special Autonomy and Adjustment Funds. Balance Funds consist in Revenue Sharing Fund (DBH), Special Purpose Grant Funds (DAK), and General Allocation Funds (DAU), the last one being the largest component of budget transfers to the regions. The amount of these

Table 1.6. **Government budget outcomes, 1990-2009**
Per cent of GDP

	1990	1995	2000	2005	2006	2007	2008	2009
Revenue and grants	18.1	14.2	14.8	17.9	19.1	17.9	19.8	15.1
Tax revenues	9.4	9.7	8.3	12.5	12.3	12.4	13.3	11.0
Income tax	3.5	4.2	4.1	6.3	6.3	6.0	6.6	5.7
Value added tax	–	–	2.5	3.7	3.7	3.9	4.2	3.4
International trade taxes	–	–	0.5	0.5	0.4	0.5	0.7	0.3
Non-tax revenues and grants	–	–	6.4	5.3	6.9	5.4	6.5	4.1
Government expenditures	17.1	13.0	15.9	18.4	19.9	19.2	19.9	16.7
Central government expenditures	–	–	13.6	13.0	13.2	12.8	14.0	11.2
Personnel	3.0	2.6	2.1	2.0	2.2	2.3	2.3	2.3
Goods and services	0.8	1.0	0.7	1.1	1.4	1.4	1.1	1.4
Interest payments	2.1	1.3	3.6	2.4	2.4	2.0	1.8	1.7
Subsidies	1.5	0.0	4.5	4.4	3.2	3.8	5.6	2.5
of which: oil	1.5	0.0	3.9	3.8	1.9	2.1	2.8	0.8
Transfers to sub-national governments	3.0	3.1	2.4	5.4	6.8	6.4	5.9	5.5
Overall balance	1.0	1.2	–1.1	–0.5	–0.8	–1.3	–0.1	–1.6
Memorandum items:								
Financing								
Domestic sources	–1.4	–0.2	0.4	0.8	1.7	1.7	2.1	2.7
Foreign sources	0.3	–1.0	0.7	–0.4	–0.8	–0.6	–0.4	–0.3

Note: For 2008 the sum of domestic and foreign sources significantly differs from the actual budget balance because of low utilisation of the budget by line ministries and lower energy subsidies than expected.
Source: Ministry of Finance.

allocations has steadily increased over the years. The use of the fund is fully autonomous based on the discretion of the local government. Finally, there are constraints on local-government borrowing and debt management.

Decentralisation is reported to have damaged the business climate, by increasing the number of local levies (many of them were subsequently annulled by the central government) and creating regulatory uncertainties. User charges are imposed for a variety of often unclear reasons, such as transporting certain type of commodities or trespassing sub-national jurisdictional borders. The financial burden imposed by local taxes and user charges is especially heavy for small firms since they pay more per employee or as percentage of sales than larger companies (KPPOD, 2008). These charges, in addition to being expensive, impose intra-national trade barriers. A 2009 law on local taxes and local levies was issued to address these problems. The law fosters regional competition to attract investors by increasing local governments' discretion in determining tax brackets. Second, it introduces a "closed-list" system defining all forms of levies that can be collected by local governments. All taxes and user charges not included in this list are considered as illegal, such as the levy on transporting certain types of goods. Third, it introduces the concept of a "benefit-tax link" whereby resources from some taxes are earmarked. Finally, the law puts in place a new monitoring system, which will take effect before the regulation is ratified.

The overall strategy of the government is presented in its Medium Term Development Plan (Box 1.5). Annual budgets are consistent with this strategy. Central government budgets rely on prudent macroeconomic projections. Budgets are revised in mid-year to account for major changes to the international environment, notably movements in oil and other commodity prices. Fiscal authorities also have the flexibility to stimulate the economy promptly in case of severe downturns. This is particularly important, as automatic stabilisers are likely to be weak because of the absence of unemployment insurance and the paucity of cyclically sensitive tax revenues (at least compared to OECD countries). Local governments also publish budgets, but they need to be submitted to and approved by the central government. Fiscal rules were introduced in 2003 but both fiscal balance and public debt are currently well below their legal limits of 3% and 60% of GDP, respectively.

Box 1.5. **The Medium Term Development Plan**

The Medium Term Development Plan (*Rencana Pembangunan Jangka Menengah Nasional*, RPJMN) 2010-14 describes the government's strategy to guide Indonesia's development for the next five years and outlines national priorities. It is the second phase of the Long Term Development Plan 2006-25 and will serve as a basis for the annual budget over the next five years. It is composed of three books. Book I outlines the strategy, Book II sectoral development plans and Book III regional development plans by island. Eleven national priorities are spelled out in Book I: bureaucracy and governance reform; education; health; poverty reduction; food security; infrastructure; investment and business climate; energy; environment and disaster management; least developed, frontier, outer and post-conflict areas; and culture, creativity and technological innovation.

Box 1.5. **The Medium Term Development Plan** *(cont.)*

Key development targets have been set (see Table 1.7 for a selection).

Table 1.7. **Key development targets**

	2008-09	2014
Macroeconomic environment		
Economic growth (per cent)	4.6	7.0-7.7
Inflation (per cent, end-year)	2.8	3.5-5.5
Social indicators		
Unemployment rate (per cent)	7.4 (2010)	5.0-6.0
Poverty rate (per cent)	13.3 (2010)	8.0-10.0
Education		
Gross enrolment rate for upper secondary education (per cent)	64.3	85
Gross enrolment rate for tertiary education (per cent)	21.3	30
Health		
Life expectancy (years)	70.7	72
Infant malnutrition (per cent)	18.4	< 15
Infrastructure		
Highway construction (2010-14)		19 370 km
Electrification rate	Around 60%	80%
Electricity generation capacity		Additional 3 000 MW per year

Source: Medium Term Development Plan 2010-14, BPS.

The priorities are a mix of existing and new programmes. Indeed, most measures related to poverty reduction, education and health care appear to be a continuation or expansion of existing programmes. By contrast, new programmes on infrastructure improvement have been announced. The government estimates it will cost IDR 1 287.6 trillion for the next five years (22.5% of 2009 GDP on average per year) to implement these priorities.

Revenue and spending reflect the stage of development of the economy

About two-thirds of government revenues are currently collected through taxes. Tax revenue has risen steadily, reflecting mostly increases in income tax, and to a lesser extent, value added tax. These two revenue sources now represent the bulk of government receipts, as the steady reduction in import tariffs has gradually diminished the importance of international trade taxes. Environment-related taxation is limited to the corporate income tax raised from the energy sector, which represents 5% of total revenue, part of the 10% VAT applied to all products and a 5% motor tax levied on the sale of gasoline and automotive diesel fuel. Despite the overall increase in tax revenues, the tax-to-GDP ratio remains low by international standards but is in line with Indonesia's real income position (Figure 1.12). This ratio will probably have to rise if the country is to develop its social protection system in the future and to cope with increasing health and education spending (see Chapter 4). Non-tax revenues have been stable over the years and come mostly from the natural resource sector, of which oil and gas are the main contributors.

Strengthening tax administration could also increase the tax-to-GDP ratio. Tax administration is complex, inefficient and involves high compliance costs. It is hindered especially by inaccurate and inefficient registrations of taxpayer accounts and documents management, along with still deficient IT infrastructure. Indonesia ranks poorly (126th out of 183 countries) on the paying taxes sub-index of the World Bank's Doing Business indicator, which seeks to capture the complexity of the tax system (World Bank, 2010c). Its

Figure 1.12. **Tax-to-GDP ratio and GDP per capita, 2007**

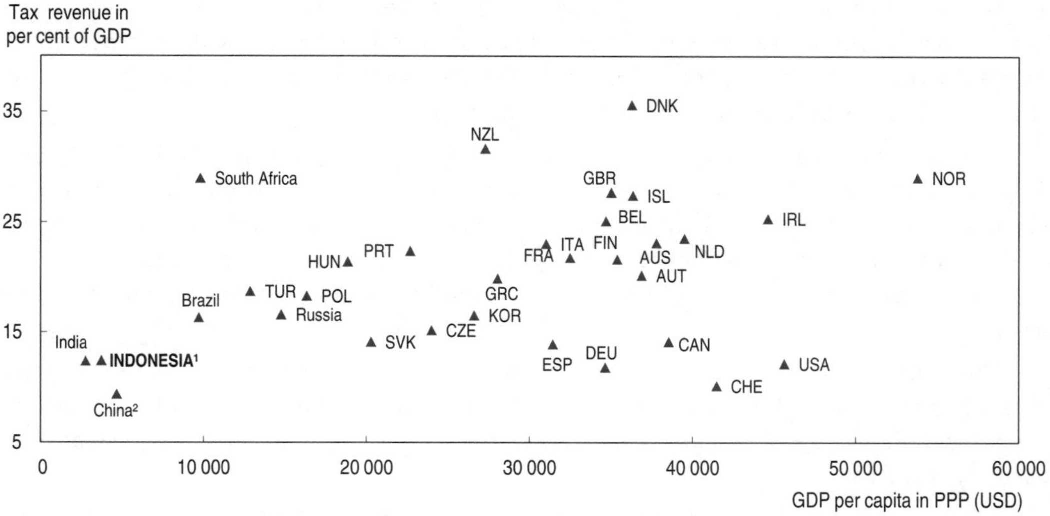

1. The Indonesia's tax ratio-to-GDP includes tax and customs duty revenues but does account for other sources such as revenues from natural resources and local taxes.
2. 2006.

Source: World Bank, Indonesia Ministry of Finances.

StatLink http://dx.doi.org/10.1787/888932341347

poor performance is attributable mostly to the compliance cost of the large number of tax payments firms have to make each year. A landmark tax administration law was passed in 2007, rendering tax collection more predictable and less arbitrary towards business and citizens. One of the major changes concerns the provision allowing taxpayers to file a tax objection or appeal without paying in advance the amount of tax which they dispute.

There have been important changes in the composition of expenditure. A reduction in interest payments has created fiscal room to finance capital ("development") spending. Energy subsidies continue to weigh heavily on the budget, despite successive reductions (see Chapter 2). Other subsidies (mainly for food) have also grown rapidly over the past decade. Spending on education has gradually increased, especially for primary education and is required to comprise at least 20% of government total expenditure. By contrast, health and infrastructure expenditure remain very low by international standards and below the country's needs (see Chapters 3 and 4). Slow disbursement rates, particularly for capital spending have compounded these problems.

A number of tax expenditure is granted to firms, especially in the energy sector, in the form of government-backed loans, exemptions from value-added tax and import duties or accelerated depreciation and amortisation on assets to reduce taxable income (Chapter 2). Information on these tax instruments is however scarce so that their cost-effectiveness is hard to gauge (Koplow *et al.*, 2010).

Policy considerations

Indonesia's fiscal framework is sound and has put the public finances onto a sustainable path. Refinements will nonetheless be needed to prepare the economy for the structural changes it will experience in the coming decades.

The government's strategy rightly focuses on economic and social development over the medium term, and the Medium Term Development Plan contains some useful indications of intended policy directions. The targets are ambitious and will need the government to work in close co-operation with its regional counterparts, which are responsible for service delivery in the social sector. In this regard, it will be important to clarify the role and functions of the different levels of government in the implementation of the Medium Term Development Plan-related programmes.

The 2009 clarification of local authorities' taxing powers is welcome and will certainly help to reduce uncertainties by decreasing their discretion in the choice of tax brackets. The law also includes earmarking of some local tax revenues, which is intended to increase the accountability of local governments. Earmarking may nevertheless render the budgeting framework rigid and ill-suited to a rapidly changing economy and should be revoked.

The government has recently identified several bottlenecks to disbursement ranging from administrative delays to appoint key personnel to a lack of capacity to plan or manage a project. Building up capacity, particularly at the local level, is likely to address at least partially these issues.

Efforts to focus on medium- to long-term analysis in budgeting and planning documents should be pursued. In addition to the Medium Term Development Plan, which runs to 2014, there is a plan to publish five-year macroeconomic and public-finance projections. These projections will help the authorities to communicate the key challenges facing the economy in the medium term. They will also highlight the importance of population ageing on productive capacity and savings in the long term (see above), issues that are currently absent from the policy debate in Indonesia. In addition, undertaking further analysis on the sources of potential growth and ways of improving social inclusion will encourage policy makers to favour measures that are consistent with stronger sustainable growth.

Tax and spending structures have evolved over the years to adapt to the needs of a fast evolving economy. Further changes are required to achieve the targets in the Medium Term Development Plan and accelerate Indonesia's economic development. *First*, inefficient spending such as energy subsidies should be phased out (Chapter 2). This will create further room in the budget to reallocate appropriations in favour of growth-enhancing programmes. In particular, it will be important to increase spending on infrastructure and education at the secondary level, which, if directed to more efficient uses, will boost potential growth in the medium term. There will be also a need to finance the increase in coverage of formal social protection and health insurance (Chapter 4). The draft 2011 State Budget appears to be consistent with these proposed changes. To avoid a wasteful use of resources, it is also essential to assess the efficiency of existing and new programmes and redirect spending to those areas that will have the most beneficial effect on long-term growth. A thorough assessment of existing tax expenditures and their relative cost-efficiency is also warranted with a view to phase out inefficient measures. *Second*, the adoption of a broad-based carbon tax is also an efficient way to reduce GHGs emissions and would help to achieve the government climate-change objectives. Revenues from this tax could be recycled to finance programmes in priority areas.

Finally, a better enforcement of tax collection will help to raise revenues. The authorities are well aware that the tax administration needs to be strengthened and made more effective so as to reduce inequities and bolster confidence in the system. Reforms started in 2001 around the principles of promoting voluntary compliance among taxpayers, enhancing the efficiency of administration and restoring taxpayers' trust in the tax administration system. Plans for further changes around the same concepts were laid out in the so-called Project for Indonesian Tax Administration Reform (PINTAR) programme for 2009-13. The Ministry of Finance has also put forward plans to separate tax collection and policy-making functions before the end of the year. The government should continue to strive to root out corruption from tax offices and review the VAT refund system, which has been shown to be vulnerable to large-scale fraud. As mandated by the 2009 Tax Law, a Taxation Supervisory Committee has been established as an independent entity within the Ministry of Finance. It is staffed with tax experts from outside the government, and its responsibilities include supervising tax revenues, receiving complaints from the public about tax officials and providing the minister with policy recommendations on how to improve tax collection. The Committee is still in its early days. The government should focus on providing it with the necessary financial and structural support to make it effective and then on implementing its policy recommendations.

Monetary policy is satisfactory, but the inflation target could be more ambitious

The monetary policy framework is based on flexible inflation targeting

The current framework combines inflation targeting (IT) with a flexible though not completely free-floating exchange rate and has been in place since July 2005. In 1999, BI was granted independence, although the inflation target range is officially chosen by the government based on BI's recommendations. BI's mandate is to ensure *rupiah* stability in addition to keeping end-year inflation within the inflation target range. The inflation targets for 2008-10 were initially set at 5% in 2008, 4.5% in 2009 and 4% in 2010 with a permissible deviation of ±1 percentage point. In September 2010, the 2010 target was revised to 5% and kept at this level for 2011, and slightly decline to 4.5% in 2012. For the subsequent years, the authorities have opted for a gradual decline in the target range to 3.5-5.5% in 2014 in the Medium Term Development Plan.

A recent review points to progress in the institutional and operational framework over the years (Bank Indonesia, 2009). The monetary policy communication process was generally judged satisfactory, and BI's transparency was classified as reasonably high in the 2010 *Financial Sector Assessment Programme* of the IMF (IMF, 2010). In addition, market surveys and empirical studies indicate that monetary policy credibility has doubled since 2005 but there is still room for improvement (Bank Indonesia, 2009).

Consistent with its mandate, BI intervenes in exchange markets to smooth excessive volatility but does not target a specified exchange-rate level. Throughout 2009, BI only partially offset the effect of capital inflows on the *rupiah* through foreign exchange interventions. Much of these interventions were sterilised through open-market operations using *Sertifikats Bank Indonesia* (SBIs). In 2009, BI accumulated around USD 14.5 billion of foreign reserves whereas the amount of outstanding SBIs increased by USD 11 billion. Sterilisation is potentially costly as the return on reserves is much lower than that of SBIs issued to absorb liquidity. However, this cost appears to have been fairly contained, notwithstanding the large interest rate differential between the US government bonds and SBIs. Assuming foreign reserves are invested in three-month US Treasury bills, whose average interest rate for 2009 dropped to 0.19%, and considering that the average interest rate paid on SBIs in the same year was 7.29%, sterilisation cost around USD 50 million or around 0.01% of GDP. Making the assumption that reserves are invested in five-year US treasury bonds will lead to a cost of a similar order of magnitude. Given the absence of a counter-factual scenario, it is difficult to assess the effect of sterilisation on interest rates. Although interest rates on maturities of one to six months have remained broadly stable, sterilisation may simply have prevented a more pronounced decline than would have happened in its absence. At the same time, sterilisation has limited the impact of reserve accumulation on the amount of money in circulation. Overall, sterilised foreign-exchange interventions have been found to be effective (World Bank, 2010a).

Indonesia's IT framework and macroeconomic stability appear to have contributed to a reduction in the level of inflation since 2007 (Figure 1.13). Still, Indonesia's inflation was substantially higher than that of OECD and regional peers on average over the last decade (Figure 1.14). Thailand, Singapore and Malaysia were able to keep inflation in check between 2001 and 2009, at around 3%. The Philippines experienced higher average price increases, at about 5.5%, but this was still considerably lower than Indonesia's outcomes. To address the issue of persistently high inflation rates, BI has set up an Inflation

Figure 1.13. **Inflation and monetary policy target range**

Annual percentage change

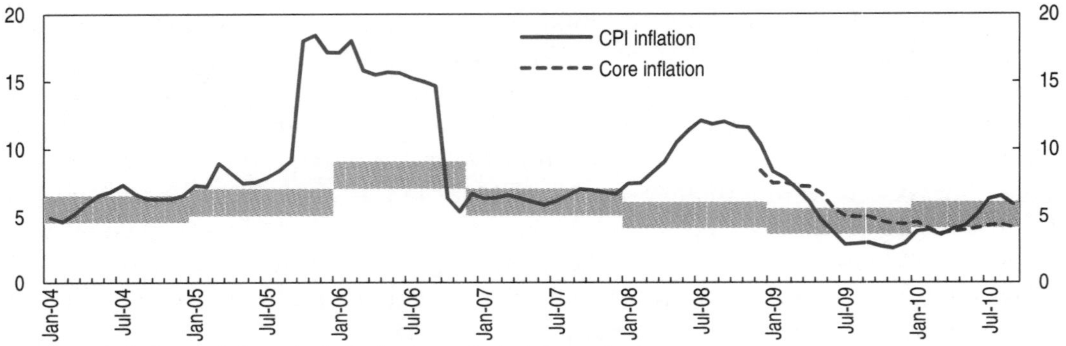

Note: Core inflation excludes volatile food price and administrated prices.

Source: Bank Indonesia, BPS.

StatLink http://dx.doi.org/10.1787/888932341366

Figure 1.14. **CPI inflation rate and volatility, 2001-09**[1]

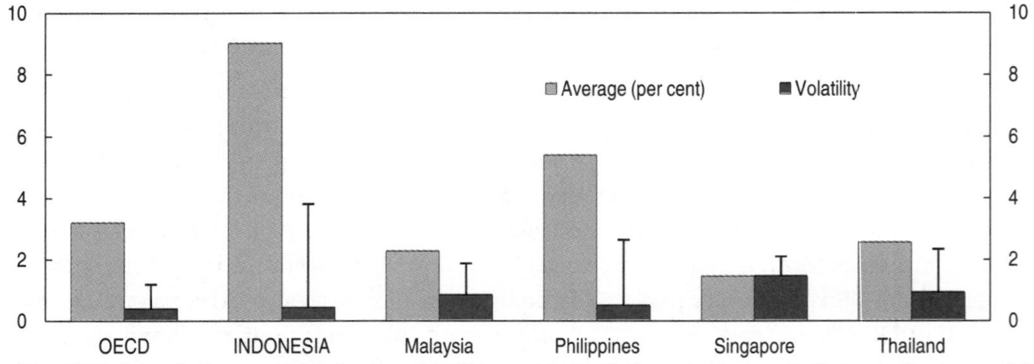

1. The OECD figure is the unweighted mean of OECD countries' inflation rate. Average inflation is the mean of the year-on-year monthly inflation rate from 2001 to 2009. Volatility refers to the coefficient of variation of the inflation rate (*i.e.* standard deviation over average inflation). The black line shows inflation volatility measured by its standard deviation.

Source: OECD and IFS.

StatLink http://dx.doi.org/10.1787/888932341385

Monitoring and Control Team to assess the sources of inflationary pressure on both supply and demand sides in addition to favouring coordination at the regional level.

Indonesian inflation dynamics are heavily affected by exchange-rate developments and activity (Table 1.8, Annex 1.A1). By contrast, cost-push factors, proxied by the international oil price, explain little of one-year-ahead inflation dynamics. Indeed, generous energy subsidies lower the pass-through from international price onto domestic prices (Chapter 2). Nonetheless, a large part of inflation remains unexplained. Administered price adjustments, which are not captured in this calculation, may have contributed to high headline inflation during some specific periods, such as in 2005 and 2008.[3] However, the impact of a one-off rise in administrative prices is likely to be short-lived.

Table 1.8. **One-year-ahead headline CPI inflation and contributions**[1]

	One year headline inflation	Contributions				
		Lagged inflation	Activity	Exchange rate	Oil price	Residual and constant
Average 1996Q2-1998Q4	12.9	–0.1	11.1	1.8	0.2	–0.2
Average 1999Q1-2005Q2	–5.8	0.0	–4.6	1.1	–0.1	–2.3
Average 2005Q3-2008Q4	–0.6	0.0	–2.1	0.4	–0.3	1.4
Average 2009Q1-2010Q2	–4.3	0.3	–5.9	0.7	0.0	0.6

1. Difference between average inflation over four quarters minus average inflation in the preceding four quarters. The first period corresponds to the pre-Asian crisis period. 2005 marks the beginning of inflation targeting.

Source: OECD calculations.

Policy considerations

High inflation has several costs and can be detrimental to long-term growth. *First*, rapid price increases generate uncertainty and can distort both consumption and investment decisions, and ultimately harm productivity. *Second*, high inflation can also have an impact on income distribution by lowering the purchasing power of those who have to live off fixed incomes. To a lesser extent, price increases can materialise in the form of menu costs faced by firms to change price labels or reprint price schedules and reprogramme computers.

The authorities plan to reduce the inflation target range gradually from its current level to 3.5-5.5% in 2014. Although this lower target range will prove beneficial to the economy, it is still above the inflation level recorded by regional peers. Lowering the inflation target even further over the medium term would demonstrate BI's commitment to price stability by anchoring inflation expectations to a lower and less distortionary level. In addition, moving from an end-year to a year-average inflation target would render the framework less sensitive to exceptional events.

The policy of adjusting inflation target each year has been introduced to account for changes in the international economic environment. This flexibility appears to be unnecessary in a context where monetary policy decisions are forward-looking and rely on a wide range of economic and financial indicators and lowers the credibility of the Central Bank's commitment. Reconsidering this policy would have the advantage of anchoring inflation expectations and will reduce the inflation bias from incomplete credibility by reaffirming the stringency of the commitment.

BI uses SBIs as the main tool to conduct monetary policy. With a high return-to-risk ratio and no collateral requirement, SBIs have been extremely attractive investment vehicles for banks and other institutional investors, such as local governments. This has complicated the task of BI and detracted from the effectiveness of monetary policy. In a policy package announced in June 2010, BI has taken action to buttress the monetary transmission mechanisms through the decision to stop the issuance of one-month central bank SBIs, to focus on three-, six- and twelve-month tenor SBIs and extend SBI auctions from a weekly to a monthly schedule. In addition, a one-month holding requirement for SBIs has been introduced. These measures seek to enable the formation of a short-term interest rate structure and are expected to induce banks to manage their liquidity more actively, relying more on the interbank market instead of rolling over their excess liquidity in SBIs, as they have routinely done so far. Other measures consist in the creation of a term-deposit facility and the widening of the policy-interest-rate corridor and may also help to develop open-market operations. Monetary transmission mechanisms could be strengthened further by using repurchase agreements instead of SBIs as a main tool for open market operations. This is common practice in OECD countries and in many Asian economies. This change could enhance the effectiveness of monetary policy transmission by focusing on a pure short-term liquidity-management instrument. If implemented, these changes are likely to lower the usefulness of SBIs, whose issuance could be gradually scaled back.

The large role portfolio investments play in total capital inflows and the ensuing risks of asset price bubbles pose challenges for inflation control, especially in case of sudden capital reversals. Capital inflows and in particular, portfolio investments, should be vigilantly monitored to safeguard the stability of the currency. Precipitous and unexpected capital outflows would result in *rupiah* depreciation and heightened inflation expectations. Managing risks related to capital flows is likely to require an array of policy instruments. The prudent monetary and fiscal policies that the authorities have undertaken thus far, along with a flexible exchange rate and resilient financial structure, are the most robust measures to deal with the potential negative consequence of sudden stops. In addition, the development of the interbank money market will address, at least partially, the risks generated by short-term capital inflows. Financial deepening could offer further investment opportunities to non-residents, in addition to domestic investors, thereby lessening the probability of sudden capital outflows. Bank Indonesia has taken steps to strengthen monetary and financial stability and support sustainable medium to long-term economic growth. Its policy package covers a range of measures aiming at enhancing the effectiveness of instruments and regulations both in *rupiah* and foreign exchange money markets, improving bank prudential regulations as well as deepening financial markets. The recent initiative by BI of imposing a minimum one-month holding period for SBIs for foreign and domestic investors, will also help to curtail the inflow of short-term speculative capital into a monetary instrument. However, its effects will need to be monitored carefully to assess its effectiveness and its effects on portfolio investments. Finally, while neither the theoretical nor the empirical literature has provided definitive conclusions thus far as to the appropriateness and effectiveness of *ad hoc* capital controls, they are sometimes found to distort markets and can lead to unintended consequences (Prasad *et al.*, 2003).

Financial markets

Substantial progress has been made since the Asian crisis, both in terms of developing financial markets and enhancing their resilience. Still, these markets are at an early stage of development.

Financial markets are shallow

Indonesia's capital markets are smaller and less liquid than in other ASEAN countries and OECD members (Figure 1.15). Market capitalisation of listed companies rose in 2009 to recoup its 2007 level, but still appears to be lower than in regional peers. Domestic credit to the private has remained sub-par in relation to OECD countries but also to regional peers. Financial-sector shallowness in Indonesia is attributable to low capital market utilisation to finance investment. It also reflects limited intermediation performed by non-bank financial institutions, with in particular modest hedging and insurance facilities. Equities and securities markets are still relatively underdeveloped, with almost no venture capital and a very small corporate bond market. Financial intermediation is overall less advanced in Indonesia than in OECD members, the other Enhanced Engagement countries and regional peers. The larger value of bank assets in Indonesia than bond market capitalisation shows that financial activity is still largely bank dominated. The bank industry appears to be fairly concentrated, with the largest 14 banks holding 80% of the total assets of the banking sector (World Bank, 2010a).

Access to financial services by the population is limited. Formal access to finance (*i.e.* having an account with a financial intermediary) is similar to what is observed in Brazil, South Africa and China (World Bank, 2008). Indonesia is also reported to have lower levels of financial access than Malaysia, Thailand and Sri Lanka but is better placed than Bangladesh and Philippines (World Bank, 2010b). Indonesia counts only five cash machines

Figure 1.15. **Indicators of financial market depth**

Per cent of GDP

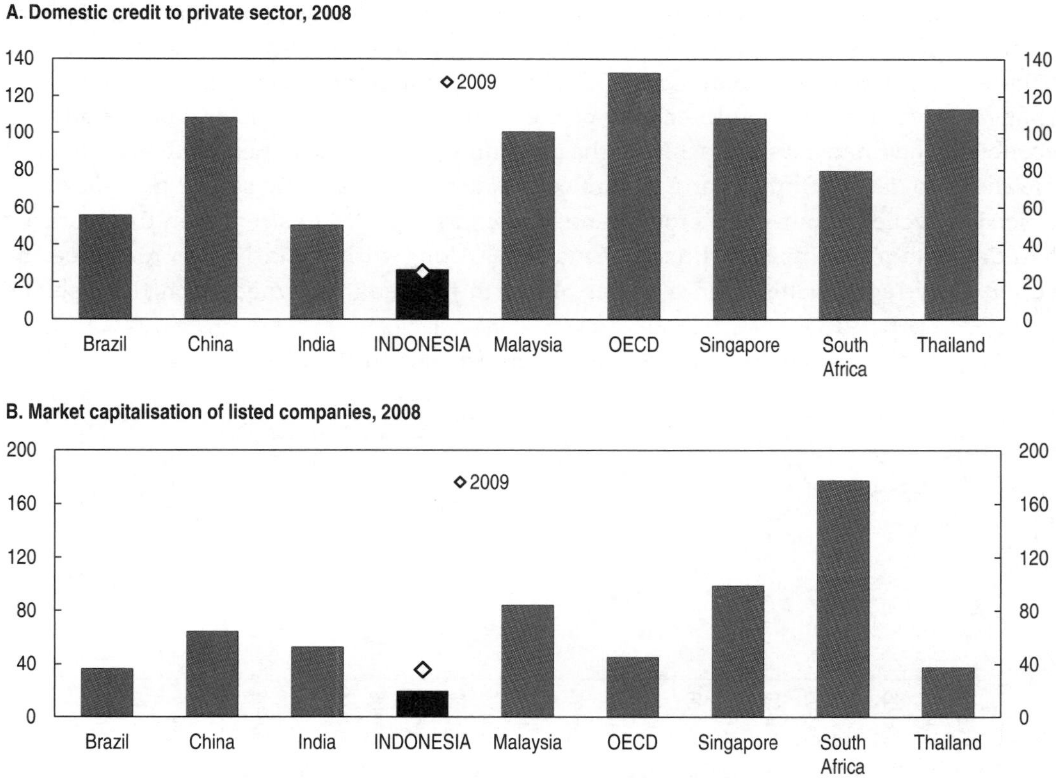

Source: BAPEPAM, Bank Indonesia and World Bank (*World Development Indicators*).

StatLink http://dx.doi.org/10.1787/888932341404

for every 100 000 people, against an average of 13 for Brazil, South Africa and China, even though Indonesia compares more favourably in terms of geographic penetration of cash machines (Beck *et al.*, 2007).

Even though the recent crisis has shown the risks and limits of unregulated financial liberalisation, financial-market deepening could bring considerable benefits to Indonesia. It would facilitate access to credit by SMEs and households in addition to widening investment opportunities and attracting more foreign investors. Money-market products could be developed to support short-term liquidity management and help absorb excess liquidity in the economy, minimising the risk of financial-system instability that can emanate from exchange-rate and stock-market volatility. Short-term instruments would also create competition in real-sector financing, lowering borrowing rates.

Evidence at the aggregate level shows that access to finance, usually measured by the credit-to-GDP ratio, has a positive effect on long-term growth (Beck *et al.*, 2000; Love, 2003). In addition to making the economy more dynamic by allowing small firms to grow faster and increase innovation rates, deep financial markets can contribute to diversification and reduce its susceptibility to sector-specific shocks. Besides benefiting firms, available empirical evidence suggests that a higher level of financial development is associated with lower income inequality and poverty in the long run (Honohan, 2004; Beck *et al.*, 2007).

Financial-sector reform is underway

The Asian crisis underlined the importance of well functioning financial markets and adequate regulations and prompted a radical reform of Indonesia's financial regulatory and prudential framework. BI launched reforms requiring banks to observe stricter risk-management criteria and strengthen their balance sheets. This seems to have already born fruit in the form of improving non-performing loans and capital-adequacy ratios (Figure 1.16). Overall, the soundness of the banking system has risen markedly, and these changes have strengthened the ability of the banking sector to withstand recent adverse economic and financial shocks. BI and the government were able to take swift and effective measures to deal with them and restore confidence in the banking sector. In addition, BI officials unveiled a four-point programme in late January 2010 to strengthen the country's banking sector and deepen financial markets. Along with initiatives to reinforce the supervisory regime and build a better platform for bank intermediation through the

Figure 1.16. **Banking soundness indicators**[1]

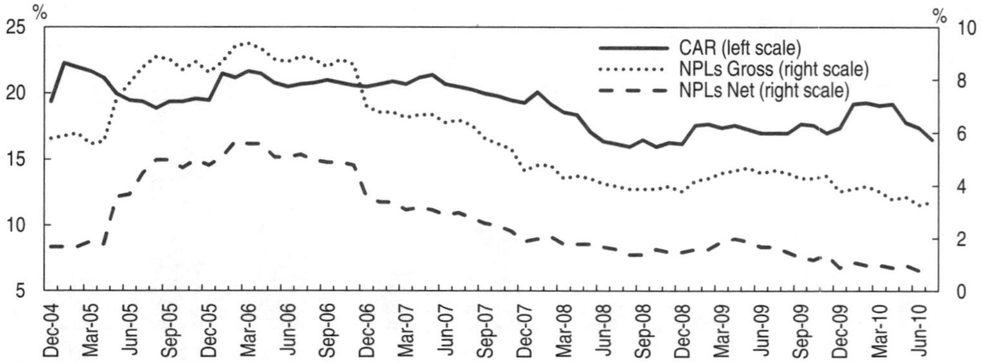

1. CAR refers to the capital-adequacy ratio and NPL to the share of non-performing loans.

Source: Bank Indonesia.

StatLink http://dx.doi.org/10.1787/888932341423

improvement of regulation, the objective was also to develop and enhance rural banks' role in micro-finance and to raise the profile of Islamic banking in the economy.

The Asian crisis also triggered a rethinking on the supervisory framework, and the country has opted to move toward a unified-supervisor model. Currently, Indonesia's financial supervision system comprises two separate supervisors: BI deals with the banking industry and Bapepam-LK with capital markets and insurance. According to Law 3/2004 a new entity, namely the Financial Services Authority (OJK), created in 2007, is scheduled to consolidate all financial supervising activities under a single roof and become operational by the end of 2010 (BT Partnership, 2007). Transition costs in moving from one model to another are likely to be important, even though temporary. The establishment of OJK is based on the following principles: *i)* independence in the management and supervision of the financial sector; *ii)* consistency and fairness towards all financial institutions, excluding any discrimination; and *iii)* transparency in its decision-making and implementation process. Such a model can be justified on the ground that the activities of modern private institutions span various financial activities, involving a plethora of financial products. In addition, financial innovation has rendered the traditional categories of financial activity obsolete. The drawback of the single-regulator model is that it requires the regulator to be staffed with experts in a range of areas.

National and super-national financial institutions and governments are currently focused on finding the best ways to address concerns in this area. It is to be expected that national approaches will differ. A new bill specifying the governance structure of the OJK and the division of work between the OJK and BI is under discussion. According to this new legislation, BI would have access to banking sector information gathered by OJK. A programme would be created to facilitate the exchange of information between the two institutions. Finally a joint inspection programme would be put in place allowing BI officers to take part on banking supervisory activities involving OJK banking inspectors. Until the OJK bill is passed and implementing regulations are issued, it is unclear what the precise relations of OJK with BI, will be. The risk of rising uncertainty in financial markets is clear.

Policy considerations

The modernisation of the financial system is crucial to raising the long-term GDP potential growth rate and curbing poverty. Indonesia has already made some notable progress in developing its financial system, and the authorities should persevere in their intent. BI's four-points programme, announced in January 2010, provides a template for restructuring the banking sector, which will need to be followed through by concrete measures. This process will have to move in line with the ongoing decisions on reforming financial markets at the G20 level.

BI has launched reforms requiring banks to observe stricter risk management criteria and improve their balance sheets. This seems to have already resulted in better non-performing-loans and capital-adequacy ratios. The Indonesian authorities have also initiated policies to encourage access to financial services such as the launch of new saving product, *Tabunganku* (my savings). Further progress could be achieved by accelerating the establishment of a credit registry with up-to-date information on the credit history of borrowers. Credit registries facilitate lenders' routine task of verifying borrowers' repayment record and make delinquency more costly, thus diminishing moral hazard. Furthermore, they can be used to build credit scores predicting repayment probability on the basis of borrowers' characteristics, thereby decreasing loan losses. The use of such registries is well advanced in developed countries, and there is evidence that credit scoring has resulted in increased credit disbursements for smaller and innovative firms, even by those large banks that had previously not served these companies (Berger *et al.*, 2005). Although the use of credit registries is less common in less developed countries, it is expanding and there is evidence that their introduction is associated with easier access to finance.

The current state of transition generated by the requirement to establish a new single financial authority (OJK) by the end of 2010 appears to have created undue uncertainty. In this respect, it would be helpful to specify roles, functions and the degree of autonomy of OJK as soon as possible. It will also be important to ensure that it will benefit from open and effective communications with BI so that the latter can conduct its operations with full knowledge of the current state of the banking system. Some of these aspects will be clarified by the OJK bill currently under discussion, as soon as it is passed. The bill will need to be also complemented by implementing regulations to specify how the OJK and BI will operate and collaborate in practice.

Labour markets

A dual labour market

Indonesia is characterised by a dual labour market, with a rigid formal market and a widespread informal sector. The unemployment rate in the formal sector had been trending up since the 1980s, reaching around 11.2% in 2005. It has declined since then to 8% in 2009. Nevertheless, statistical estimates point to a still very high level of structural unemployment at around 9.5% in 2009 (Figure 1.17). One possible explanation of the contrasting recent trends between actual and structural unemployment would be that rigid institutions have hampered factor allocation and slowed the structural unemployment adjustment process.

In the aftermath of the Asian crisis, Indonesia's labour code was strengthened to provide social protection for the most vulnerable workers. Provisions have become more restrictive over time, especially after enactment of the Manpower Law of 2003, as described in details in the 2008 *Economic Assessment*. Severance payment entitlement is generous, in part because of the lack of any system of unemployment insurance. The standard severance pay is calculated as one month of salary per year of service (capped at nine months). In the case of dismissals for economic reasons, retirement, death or disability, entitlement is doubled. A long-term service compensation also imposes an additional financial burden on employers.[4] Total compensation is capped at 10 months'

Figure 1.17. **Actual and structural unemployment rate**

Percentage of labour force

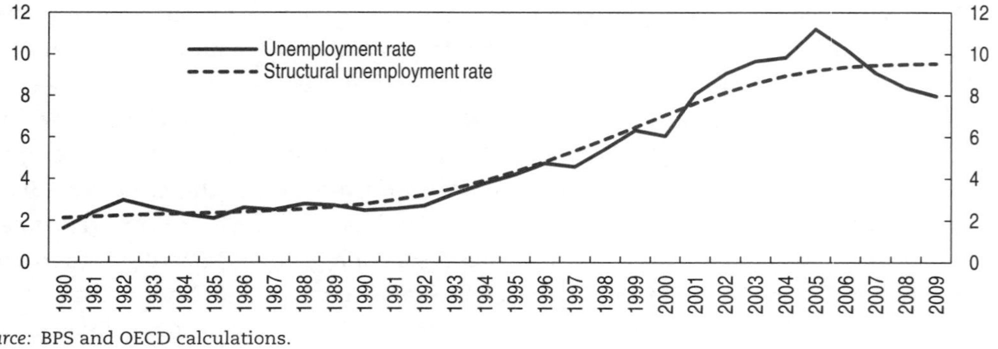

Source: BPS and OECD calculations.

pay after 24 years of service, because compensation for over 21 years of service is calculated as two months' pay for every three years of service.

In addition, employment protection legislation (EPL) is currently more restrictive in Indonesia than in OECD countries and slightly more stringent than in China and India (Figure 1.18). The cost of individual dismissal is in fact higher in Indonesia than in any other country for which the OECD EPL indicator is constructed.[5] This reflects bureaucratic dismissal procedures for individuals that make it extremely lengthy to terminate regular contracts.[6] There is also a lack of flexibility in the use of temporary and fixed-term contractual arrangements in Indonesia.[7] This deters firms from hiring and can encourage informality. Higher costs stemming from onerous labour legislation can also adversely impact the trade competitiveness of labour-intensive sectors.

Minimum-wage provisions have also become increasingly onerous, especially since decentralisation in 2001 when they became the prerogative of local governments. Indonesia has one of the highest relative minimum wages in the world, equal to 65% of the average wage of salaried workers (Figure 1.19). Minimum wages can vary by a factor of two across provinces (Figure 1.20). High minimum wages are likely to have a detrimental

Figure 1.18. **Employment protection legislation, 2008**

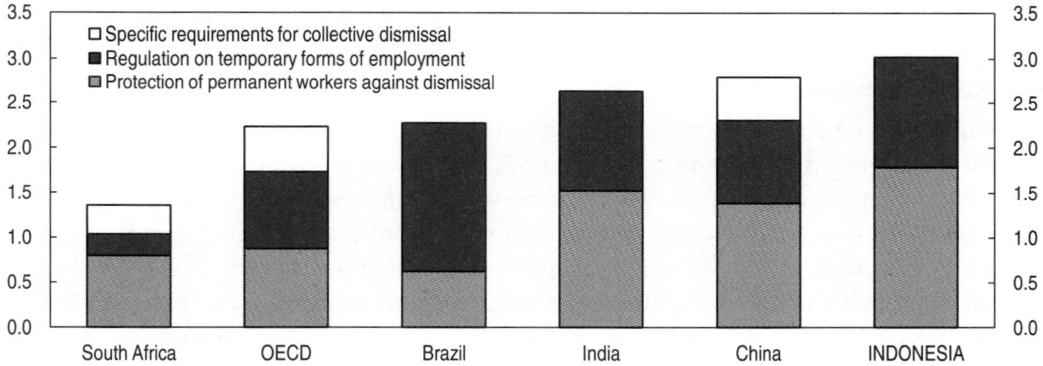

Note: See Venn (2009) for details. The scale of the indicator ranges from 0 to 6, from least to most restrictive.

Source: *OECD Employment Outlook Database.*

StatLink http://dx.doi.org/10.1787/888932341442

Figure 1.19. **Ratio of minimum wage to average wage by country, 2008**

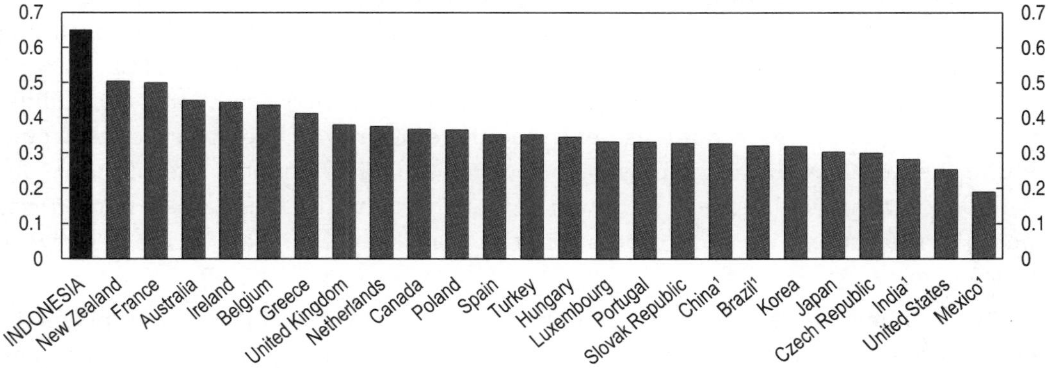

1. Data for China, Brazil, India and Mexico are for 2005.

Source: *OECD Employment Outlook* and BPS.

StatLink http://dx.doi.org/10.1787/888932341461

Figure 1.20. **Average and minimum monthly wage by province, 2008**

Million *rupiah*

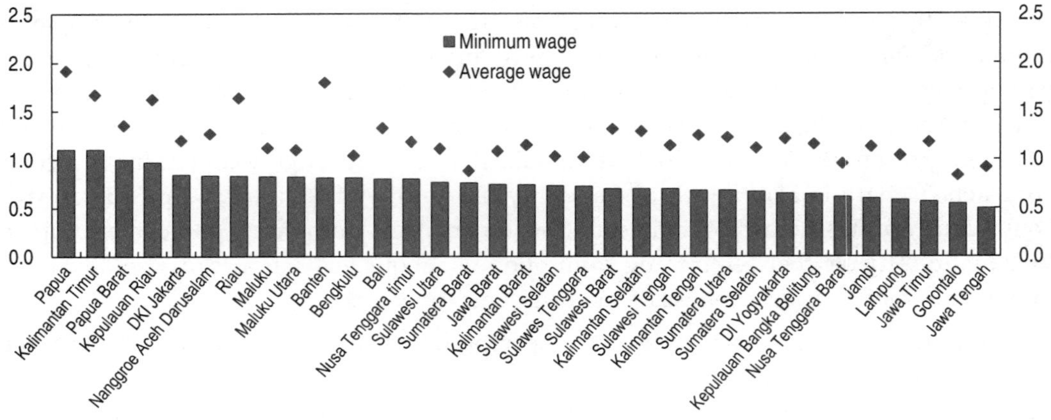

Source: BPS.

StatLink http://dx.doi.org/10.1787/888932341480

impact on the labour market, especially for groups with weak labour-market attachment, and to reinforce a high degree of informality (Suryahadi *et al.*, 2003). It is also an inefficient instrument to fight poverty, as it is not of course binding in the informal sector.

Policy considerations

Reforming labour market institutions will help Indonesia to make the most of its current demographic dividend and the rapid growth of its workforce. The restrictive Indonesian labour code is detrimental to growth as it impedes factor reallocation, lowers trade competitiveness and perpetuates labour informality. It provides a safety net for formal-sector workers, but to the detriment of informal-sector workers or vulnerable workers such as women and youths with low labour-market attachment. Thus, it does not achieve its objective of providing adequate protection against adverse economic shocks.

Indonesia has currently a unique opportunity to build an effective social protection system, by introducing some form of unemployment insurance, which is currently non-existent. The design of a future unemployment insurance system will need to be adapted to Indonesia's social preferences, with the underlying objective of encouraging workers to seek formal-sector jobs. Although several options are available for consideration, OECD experience suggests that unemployment insurance should be time-limited, declining during the spell and conditional on a minimum duration of employment (OECD, 2006). A "mutual obligations approach", whereby unemployment benefit is conditional on fulfilling job-search requirements, would also enhance the efficiency of the measure but would require the development of employment services to deliver support and monitor job-search behaviour.[8] Obviously, this will take time to materialise. In this context, unemployment benefits should be at first modest to prevent an increase in work disincentives.

By shielding workers against unemployment risks, introducing an unemployment benefit system could help overcome resistance to reforming the labour code. The establishment of unemployment insurance would make generous severance payments unnecessary. They could be reduced, for instance, by imposing a cap on the level of severance pay at a lower number of workweeks. Further increases in the minimum wage should be resisted to alleviate the adverse impact of a high minimum wage on employment, especially for low-skilled workers. One option would be to cap increases in real minimum wages so as not to exceed trend labour productivity gains. As already stated in the 2008 *OECD Economic Assessment*, the labour code could be made more flexible for regular contracts by simplifying procedures. Work arrangements could also be made less stringent by extending the maximum duration of temporary and fixed-term contracts. Finally, sharing the cost from long-term service between employers and employees would lower the burden imposed on employers.

Climate change and deforestation

Deforestation is the main source of GHG emissions

Being an archipelago, Indonesia is highly vulnerable to climate change, whose impact is likely to fall disproportionally on the poorest households. With 4.7% of the world total, it is the world's fourth largest GHG emitter (following China, the United States and Brazil) due to land use change, deforestation and peat fires. CO_2 emissions per capita are increasing faster than GDP growth, indicating that the current growth path relies on increasing contribution from emission-intensive sources (Indonesia Climate Investment Fund, 2010), and were higher in 2005 than in the OECD and other Asian countries (Figure 1.21). There is also evidence that Indonesia's forestry resources are being unsustainably depleted (Box 1.6).

Figure 1.21. **CO_2 emissions intensity by country, 2005**

Million tonne CO_2 equivalent per GDP in PPP (billion 2000 US dollars)

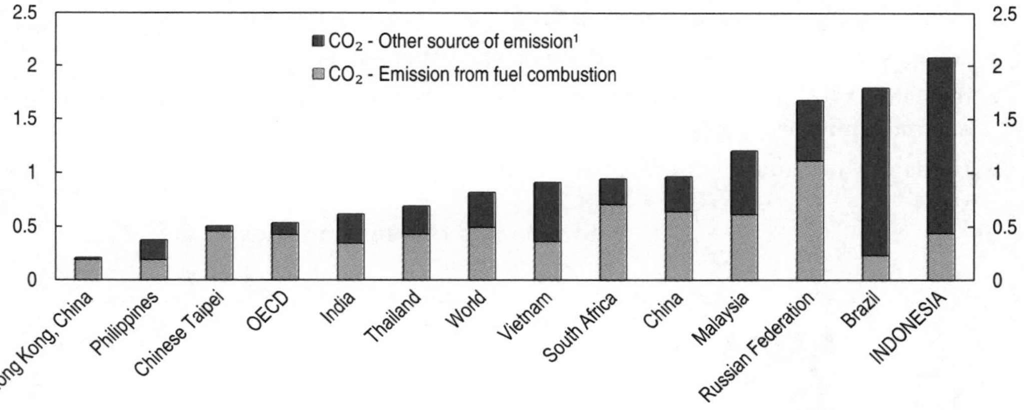

1. Includes deforestation.

Source: IEA.

StatLink http://dx.doi.org/10.1787/888932341499

Box 1.6. **Forest losses**

Deforestation rates in Indonesia are amongst the highest in the world, second only to Brazil (FAO, 2010). The rate of deforestation appeared to have slowed from 2000 to 2005, although estimates vary depending on the definition of forest and methods used. Overall, the rate of deforestation is estimated to be about half the average rate in the late 1990s. Recent analysis suggests that the period before 2000 was also characterised by more forest fires. The rate of deforestation is estimated to have risen again since 2005 (Figure 1.22).

Box 1.6. **Forest losses** *(cont.)*

Deforestation has been particularly prevalent in Sumatra and Kalimantan. Most forest losses have occurred on production and conversion forests – forests that can be converted to industrial timber or agricultural plantation – rather than protected and conservation forests. These areas have been allocated for economic exploitation through selective harvesting or through liquidation and conversion to agricultural or plantation uses. Heavy losses in production forests are likely to be related to poor forest-management practices, illegal logging and insufficient or ineffective law enforcement. Considerable deforestation is also occurring outside state forests. Plantation crop expansion is the main driver of deforestation in these areas, driven by permits granted by local governments. In contrast, protection and conservation forests have been relatively less damaged (World Bank, 2009a).

High rates of forest conversion and the widespread incidence of peat fires mean that emissions from forest lands are very large in Indonesia. According to the National Council on Climate Change, deforestation and forest degradation amounts to about 84% of the nation's total GHG emissions. In addition, forest losses can entail several costs to society, including watershed degradation, drying of land, erosion, increased social conflicts and rural poverty, and lost opportunities for receipts of carbon market payments.

According to Ministry of Finance (2009), options for cutting carbon emissions stemming from deforestation and land conversion include:

- the development of a revised national forest conservation strategy;
- better enforcement of laws against illegal logging and the fostering of alternative sources of log supply;
- incentives for better management practices in production forests;
- changes to regulatory settings in the pulp and paper industry;
- regulations to improve the management of palm plantations, including zero burning and more intensive production; and
- regulatory measures to improve the management of peat lands.

Figure 1.22. **Deforestation rates in Indonesia**
Per cent per year

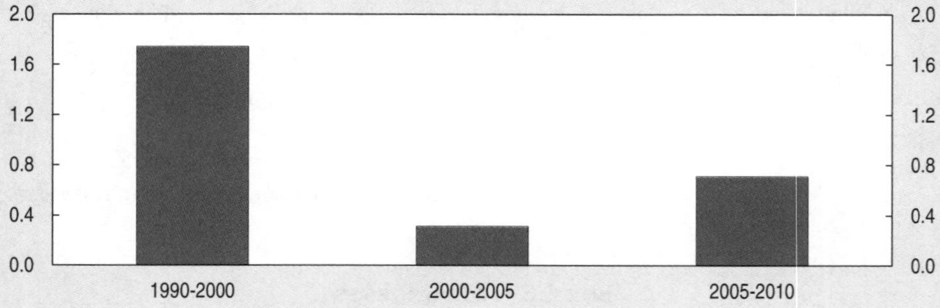

Source: FAO (2010).

Environmental sustainability has become a national priority. The President has announced GHG emission reduction targets at the national level (26% by 2020 compared to a Business As Usual scenario, 41% with international support), which have been supplemented by targets at the sectoral level. The government intends to codify this commitment through a presidential decree. The Medium Term Development Plan provides the basis for budgeting and implementation.[9] In addition a 2009 green paper put forward recommendations on the design of an economic and fiscal strategy for climate change mitigation in Indonesia.[10] The removal of energy subsidies features prominently in this strategy, together with the introduction of a small carbon tax (Chapter 2). This will complement a range of existing measures to foster the deployment of cleaner energy sources (such as the introduction of renewable-energy targets) and to improve energy efficiency.[11] A newly established National Council on Climate Change with representation from 15 ministries is co-ordinating climate-change activities. In addition, the government has created the Indonesia Climate Change Trust Fund (ICCTF) to support adaptation and mitigation activities with the help of government and international donor contributions.

Policy considerations

Despite laudable efforts, Indonesia's green economy strategy is still at a very early stage, and, except for the geothermal sector, it is often limited to first-principles considerations. This is particularly the case for forestry for which recent policies have sent mixed signals. A recent regulation allows open-cast mining in production forests and underground mining in both protection and production forests. Furthermore, there have been some discussions to increase the role of the private sector in the protection of conservation forests, where no human activity except education and research is allowed. At the same time, Indonesia has committed to a two-year moratorium on new concessions to convert forest and peat land into plantations in the context of a recent broader agreement with Norway, which will finance progress in Indonesia's programme on Reducing Emissions from Deforestation and Degradation through a USD 1 billion grant. In addition, a timber legality standard and verification system was introduced to address some governance issues behind deforestation. The overall aggregate impact of these measures on forests and ultimately GHG emissions remains unclear. It will be crucial to review in depth the factors explaining high deforestation rates and identify the most cost-efficient measures to slow its pace and reverse recent trends. In particular, it will be important to ensure that the timber legality standard is enforced, as illegal logging is likely to be an important factor of rapid deforestation.

Climate change policies involve many areas and are under the responsibility of several ministers. The National council on Climate Change has been established to co-ordinate climate change activities. Achieving policy coherence is important, as it enables to exploit synergies across policy domains and prevents the introduction of measures that would go counter the emission-reduction objective. For instance, the development of coal-powered generation is at the moment encouraged through government-backed loans to the state-owned electricity supplier. Such a policy is inconsistent with the overall climate-change strategy.

Governance

The quality of governance is low

By shaping the economic environment and influencing the behaviour of economic agents, governance is a key determinant of long-term growth. It is also associated with good development outcomes, in particular poverty reduction. As yet, the literature has not reached a firm conclusion on the direction of causality between governance and economic developments. Most probably, institutions and economic performance reinforce each other, creating a virtuous circle capable of raising citizens' welfare.

Measuring governance is notoriously difficult. Most of the available indicators are perception-based, not comparable over time, and some of them can provide only a country ranking rather than an absolute measure of governance (Furceri and Mourougane, 2010b). They should thus be interpreted with caution, and cannot be used to monitor changes in governance levels for a given country. Indonesia, as the other Enhanced Engagement countries, scores extremely low when compared to OECD countries along different dimensions of governance (Figure 1.23).[12]

Fighting corruption is one of the government's main stated priorities.[13] From 2002 to 2008, Indonesia improved from the 8th to the 31st percentile in the distribution of the Governance Matters' control of corruption indicator. This progress is at least partly attributable to the adequate financial resources agencies fighting corruption have received and the freedom they have in recruiting staff. Despite recent progress, corruption is still a particularly acute problem, especially in the natural resource sector. Many existing laws and regulations are rarely enforced, and violations are widely ignored (International Energy Agency, 2008). In 2009 the government expressed the intention to participate in the Extractive Industries Transparency Initiative (EITI), comprising oil, gas and mining industries. This is a worthwhile initiative, likely to enhance the governance of extractive industries as the government will be obliged to publicly disclose all payments made to, and revenues received from, companies in these industries. To date, however, Indonesia has not reached the stage of official candidate country.

Deficiencies in the rule of law are reported to be one major obstacle hampering investment. The weakness of the enforcing-rule formal mechanisms is also manifest in the large share of the population still relying on village heads to settle disputes though traditional resolution systems, which are not necessarily consistent with state laws (World Bank, 2009b). The country's *court system* is considered one the weakest links in Indonesia's governance and accountability system (OECD, 2008). The court system has suffered from inadequate funding and cumbersome procedures, which have led to inconsistent decision-making and legal uncertainty.

Access to information that should be in the public domain remains limited in some areas. Budget information is hardly accessible to the public, even though the law specifies that budgetary documents are subject to public scrutiny and parliamentary budget deliberations should be open to the public (Budlender and Satiro, 2008). Furthermore, although high ranking officials have to fill in personal wealth declarations, the impact of these declarations has been limited, since the public does not have full access to them and the current legislation does not specify adequate sanctions for failing to fill in the personal wealth declarations and illicit enrichment (World Bank, 2009b).

Local governments have enacted a plethora of business-licencing requirements as a means of revenue collection. They are costly, lengthy and complicated, are not accompanied by specific services and are operated, in many districts, solely as a rent-seeking instrument (KPPOD, 2008). Although national regulations set the maximum time to obtain a business registration at seven days, a survey among firms show that this is hardly the case, with the average time being 14 days (KPPOD, 2008). This explains the poor performance of Indonesia in the World Bank's Doing Business exercise, which ranks Indonesia 161st out of 183 economies for the ease of starting a business, far worse than Malaysia (55th) and Thailand (88th) (World

Figure 1.23. **Governance indices and GDP per capita in OECD and Enhanced Engagement countries**

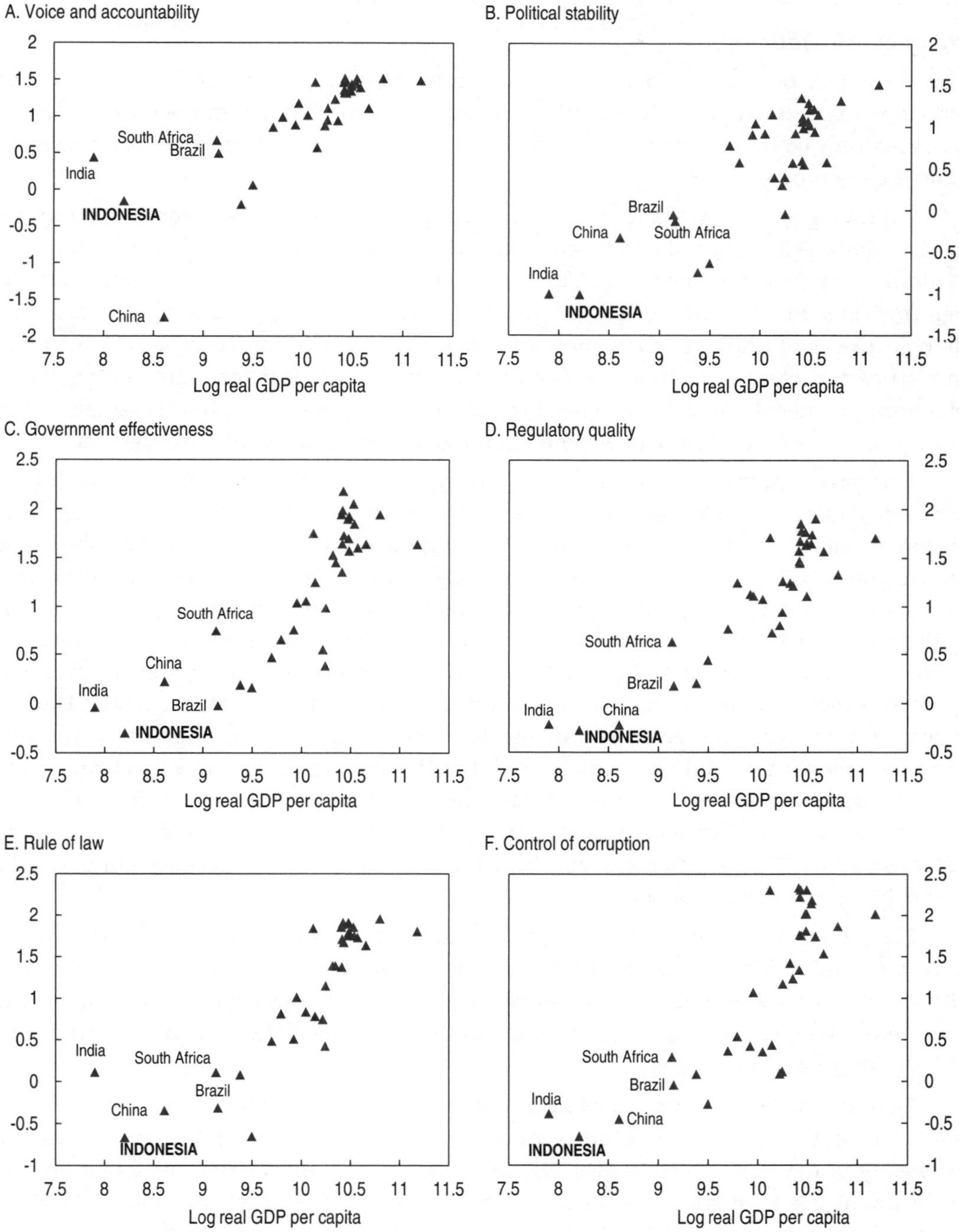

Note: GDP per capita is measured in 2000 USD in PPPs and refers to 2008.

Source: World Bank (*Governance Matters*).

StatLink http://dx.doi.org/10.1787/888932341518

Bank, 2010c). In addition to forcing many enterprises to remain informal, these barriers hamper entrepreneurship and small firms' growth (Klapper *et al.*, 2006).

Policy considerations

Further institutional reforms to improve governance are a pre-requisite to meet the government's economic development objectives. Recent macroeconomic achievements are no reason for complacency. Current efforts to strengthen governance are welcome and should be reinforced.

Improving governance and combating corruption have featured prominently in the government's reform agenda and have been included as one of the main objectives in its Medium Term Development Plan. The recent establishment of a National Bureaucratic Reforms Direction Committee, headed by the Vice-President, is a promising new initiative. Its objective is to improve government effectiveness through bureaucratic reforms in all ministries and state institutions. However, in addition to a clear mandate and an action blueprint, the new Committee will need the power to oversee reform implementation and to impose some form of sanctions, when necessary, to achieve quantifiable results.

The government is also seeking to strengthen village-level dispute resolution processes, raise people's legal awareness and improve out-of-court mediation services. However, reforms to the general Court system have slowed in recent years and should be stepped up (OECD, 2008). In the initial years of the *reformasi* period, ambitious reforms were approved to enhance the judicial system, by creating numerous independent institutions with judicial review and oversight responsibilities, such as the Judicial Commission, Prosecutorial Commission and Policy Commission. Furthermore, the Supreme Court was granted responsibilities for court administration from the Ministry of Justice and Human Rights. However, in more recent years progress in reforming the judicial system has slowed considerably. Entrenched interests in maintaining the status quo have weakened the political support for such reforms. In addition, as a result of initial reforming zeal, numerous institutions with judicial review and oversight roles were created with contested responsibilities. This is slowing down the establishment of an effective system of checks and balances and accountability.

The passage of the 2008 Freedom of Information Law has the potential to ease public access to public information that has been so far difficult to obtain. The government should concentrate on building the necessary support and framework to implement the Law's provisions adequately, such as allocating clear responsibilities to public institutions for providing such information.

The system of business licensing is complicated, lengthy and costly and acts as a barrier to entry. Cumbersome entry procedures represent corruption opportunities, especially in developing economies (Djankov *et al.*, 2002). To improve this situation, the government has mandated the setting-up of one-stop shops in all Indonesian districts; they are supposed to consolidate the processing of all common business licenses into one single location. However, several districts still lack one-stop shops and their establishment needs to be accelerated. Furthermore, the authorities need to enforce the national legislation setting the time limit (seven days) to obtain business licences issued by local authorities. The 2009 law on regional taxes, limiting the type of taxes and user charges local governments can rightfully impose, is likely to greatly improve the local business climate. However, the government needs to swiftly issue the implementing regulations so that it can issue guidelines on setting licences to limit the size of fees local governments are allowed to charge.

Summary of policy recommendations

A summary of policy considerations is presented in Box 1.7. With growth likely to remain weak in developed economies over the next few years, growth prospects will be determined by the country's ability to allow domestic sources to play a more dynamic role. The following chapters examine some areas where reforms would spur long-term growth. Reforming energy subsidy policy (Chapter 2) will create substantial fiscal space, which could in turn be used to foster investment in infrastructure (Chapter 3) and finance expanded social programmes (Chapter 4).

Box 1.7. **Summary of policy recommendations: Macroeconomic and structural policies**

Fiscal policy

- Change the tax and spending mix. Phase out inefficient spending such as energy subsidies and increase spending on growth-enhancing programmes. Assess the cost efficiency of new and existing spending programmes, as well as of tax expenditure. Introduce a carbon tax. Continue efforts to improve enforcement of tax collection.
- Pursue efforts to focus on medium- to long-term analysis in budgeting and planning documents.
- Revoke the earmarking clause in the 2009 law on regional taxes and levies.

Monetary policy

- Increase the policy interest rate before the end of the year to achieve the 2011 end-year inflation target.
- Stick to the commitment of lowering the inflation target range to 3.5-5.5% by 2014, and move from an end-year to a year average inflation target. Reconsider the policy of re-adjusting inflation target for a given year the following year. Use short-term repurchase agreements (repos) as the main tool for open-market operations.

Financial markets

- Accelerate the establishment of a credit registry with up-to-date credit histories of borrowers.
- Pass and implement the OJK bill as soon as possible in order to specify the roles, functions and degree of autonomy of the Financial Services Authority (OJK) and take measures to insure open and effective communications between OJK and Bank Indonesia so that the latter can conduct its operations with full knowledge of the current state of the banking system.

Labour markets

- Introduce a two-pronged strategy whereby some form of unemployment insurance will be introduced while increases in minimum wages would be capped so as not to exceed trend labour productivity gains and generous severance payments would be reduced, for instance by imposing a cap on the level of severance pay. Simplify dismissal procedures for regular contracts and extend the duration of temporary and fixed-term contracts. Share the burden imposed by long-term service between employers and employees.

Box 1.7. **Summary of policy recommendations: Macroeconomic and structural policies** *(cont.)*

Deforestation and climate change

- Follow up on the Ministry of Finance green paper and swiftly review the most cost-efficient measures to slow deforestation rates. Make sure the timber legality standard is enforced.
- Ensure energy policies are consistent with the objective of emissions reduction.

Governance

- Pursue efforts to fight corruption and strengthen governance. Step up reforms to the court system.

Notes

1. BI intervened in the foreign-exchange market in late 2008, after the *rupiah* depreciated against the USD by around 30% from September to November 2008, and again in 2009.
2. In late 2008, the government recapitalised Bank Century as it breached reserve requirements. In 2009, Bank IFI and a small rural bank were liquidated.
3. The contribution of administered prices amounted to 9.6 percentage points of the 17.1% CPI inflation rate in 2005 and 3 percentage points of the 11% inflation rate in 2008.
4. Long-term service pay is calculated as one month of salary for every three years of service, starting with two months' pay for the first three years of service.
5. The EPL indicator is constructed for all OECD members, accession and Enhanced Engagement countries.
6. Employers are required to seek authorisation for dismissals from the local Manpower Department. In the case of dismissals due to violations of work rules, bargaining agreements or the terms of individual contracts, employers must issue three warnings within six months of each other before applying for a dismissal authorisation. Unlike a number of OECD countries, the Indonesian code does not impose additional requirements for collective dismissals. See Chapter 3 of OECD (2008) for more details.
7. Temporary work is allowed for three months, which is the statutory duration of probation of long-term contracts. Fixed-term contracts are limited to three years, comprising an initial two-year contract plus a single one-year extension. Sub-contracting is also limited to three years and to workers performing non-core activities. It is also allowed for workers performing one-off tasks or engaged in seasonal work or in jobs related to the introduction of new projects or products.
8. An elaborate version of this strategy (often labelled "flexicurity") has played a central role in achieving greater mobilisation of resources in some OECD countries (OECD, 2006). Governments have assumed a duty to provide jobseekers with effective re-employment services, counselling, training and financial incentives to enable them to find a job. This is the "rights" side of the approach. Beneficiaries, in turn, have had to take active steps to find work or improve their employability, or else face the risk of moderate benefit sanctions. This is the "obligations" side of the approach.
9. The Plan follows up on the 2007 National Action Plan, the 2008 Development Planning Response to Climate Change and the Climate Change Roadmap for the Medium Term Development Plan, which translates the government's orientations into a set of measures.
10. A white paper describing the policy mix necessary to reach the emission targets as well as a National Action Plan and a Regional Action plan for reduction of GHG emissions from 2010 to 2020 are under preparation.
11. In 2008, Indonesia announced the 10 000 MW Crash Programme Phase II, which aims to increase renewable generating capacity, particularly from geothermal and hydro-electric sources. Targets have been set to boost the capacity of micro-hydro power plants, geothermal plants, wind power, solar power and biomass by a total of 14 GW by 2025. By comparison, total generation capacity amounted to just below 40 GW in 2007 (IEA, 2009). Since January 2009, the transport, industry and

power-generation sectors and fuel distributors in Indonesia have been obliged to use biofuel blends. The government has set a goal that biofuels should contribute 3% of the energy mix by 2015 and 5% by 2025. To boost the development of biomass, the Indonesian government plans to open 6 million hectares of new plantation areas for sugar cane, cassava, palm and jatropha by 2025.

12. These indicators are based on expert assessments and surveys on firms and are updated every year. They are constructed in such a way that their average across all countries is a zero and the standard deviation is one. As a result, their scale is arbitrary. Moreover, these indicators are subject to very large measurement errors.

13. The Commission for Eradication of Corruption (KPK) was established in the wake of the Asian financial crisis when the parliament passed new anti-corruption legislation. Additional institutions and mechanisms have been created to combat corruption, such as the Indonesia Financial Transaction Reports and Analysis Center (PPATK) and the temporary (from 2005 to 2007) Corruption Eradication Co-ordination Team. Efforts to fight corruption were renewed in 2004 when additional measures were taken by granting greater autonomy to KPK and the Anti-Corruption Court. The record of these institutions is overall positive. KPK has initiated a number of high profile cases and never lost a single one. Recently, however, much public attention seems to have been diverted toward the Bank Century scandal, and the overall pace of reforms appears to have slowed.

Bibliography

ADB (2010), *Clean Technology Fund Investment Plan for Indonesia*, Asian Development Bank, Manila, *www.adb.org/Documents/Reports/Others/INO-CTF-Investment-Plan.pdf.*

Alisjahbana, A. (2009), "Revisiting Indonesia's Sources of Economic Growth and its Projection Toward 2030", *Working Paper in Economics and Development Studies*, No. 200905, Padjadjaran University, Bandung.

Atkeson, A. and L.E. Ohanian (2001), "Are Phillips Curves Useful for Forecasting Inflation?", *Federal Reserve Bank of Minneapolis Quarterly Review*, 25(1), 2-11.

Aswicahyono, H. and H. Hill (2002), "'Perspiration' vs 'Inspiration' in Asian Industrialisation: Indonesia Before the Crisis", *Journal of Development Studies*, 38(3), 138-63.

Bank Indonesia (2009), *Review on the Inflation Targeting Framework (ITF) Implementation in Indonesia*, December, Jakarta.

Bank Indonesia (2010), *2009 Economic Report on Indonesia*, Bank Indonesia: Jakarta, *www.bi.go.id/web/en/Publikasi/Laporan+Tahunan/Laporan+Perekonomian+Indonesia/lpi_09.htm.*

Beck, T., R. Levine and N. Loayza (2000), "Finance and the Sources of Growth", *Journal of Financial Economics*, 58 (1), 261-300.

Beck, T., A. Demirgüç-Kunt and M.S. Peria (2007), "Reaching Out: Access to and Use of Banking Services across Countries", *Journal of Financial Economics*, 85(1), 234-66.

Beffy, P.O., P. Ollivaud, P. Richardson and F. Sédillot (2006), "New OECD Methods for Supply-Side and Medium-Term Assessments: A Capital Services Approach", *OECD Economics Department Working Paper*, No. 482.

Berger, A.N., W. Scott Frame and N.H. Miller (2005), "Credit Scoring and the Availability, Price, and Risk of Small Business Credit", *Journal of Money, Credit, and Banking*, 37 (2), 191-222.

BT Partnership (2007), "Indonesia: New FSA", *International Financial Law Review*, February 2007, *www.iflr.com/Article/1977347/New-FSA.html.*

Budlender, D. and H.A. Satriyo (2008), *Budget Advocacy in Indonesia, Country Report: Indonesia*, International Budget Partnership and the Ford Foundation.

Cotis, J.P., J. Elmeskov and A. Mourougane (2005), "Estimates of Potential Output: Benefit and Pitfalls from a Policy Perspective", in L. Reichlin (ed.), *Euro area business cycle: stylized facts and measurement issues*, CEPR, London.

Djankov, S., R. La Porta, F. Lopez-De-Silanes and A. Shleifer (2002), "The Regulation of Entry", *Quarterly Journal of Economics*, 117(1), 1-37.

FAO (2010), *Global Forest Resource Assessment: Country Report Indonesia*, *www.fao.org/forestry/62318/en/idn/* Roma.

Furceri, D. and A. Mourougane (2010a), "The Influence of the Age Structure on Saving and Social Spending", *Proceedings of a conference organised by the Asian Development Bank in December 2009*, forthcoming.

Furceri, D. and A. Mourougane (2010b), "Structural Indicators: A Critical Review", *OECD Economic Studies*, forthcoming.

Honohan, P. (2004), "Financial Sector Policy and the Poor", *Working Paper*, 43, World Bank, Washington, DC.

IMF (2010), *Financial Sector Assessment Programme: Indonesia*, Washington DC.

International Energy Agency (2008), *Energy Policy Review of Indonesia*, IEA, Paris.

Kaid, A. and N. Swindi (2009), "Is There a Relationship between the Openness of an Economy and Economic Growth? A Descriptive Study on the ASEAN 10", *Business e-Bulletin*, 1(1), 15-24.

Kaufmann, D., A. Kraay and M. Mastruzzi (2009), "Governance Matters VIII: Aggregate and Individual Governance Indicators: 1996-2008", *World Bank Policy Research Working Paper*, No. 4978.

Kiyota, K., M. Molnar and R.M. Stern (2008), "Storm in a Spaghetti Bowl: FTAs and the BRIICS", in OECD (eds.), *Globalisation and Emerging Economies: Brazil, Russia, India, Indonesia, China and South Africa*, OECD, Paris.

Klapper, L., L. Laeven and R. Rajan (2006), "Entry Regulation as a Barrier to Entrepreneurship", *Journal of Financial Economics*, 82(3), 591-629.

Koplow, D., A. Jung, M. Thöne and L. Lontoh (2010), "Mapping the Characteristics of Producer Subsidies: A Review of Pilot Countries", *The Global Initiative Untold Billions: Fossil-Fuel Subsidies, the Impact and the Path to Reform*, August.

KPPOD (2008), *Local Economic Governance in Indonesia*, *http://kppod.org/ind/datapdf/rating/2007/LEGI2007.pdf*.

Love, I. (2003), "Financial Development and Financing Constraints: International Evidence from the Structural Investment Model", *Review of Financial Studies*, 16 (3), 765-91.

Ministry of Finance (2009), "Economic and Fiscal Policy Strategies for Climate Change Mitigation in Indonesia", Paper written in the context of the Australia Indonesia Partnership.

OECD (2006), *Revised Job Strategy*, OECD Publishing, Paris.

OECD (2008), *Indonesia Economic Assessment*, OECD Publishing, Paris.

Prasad, E., K. Rogoff, S.-J. Wei and A. Koseet (2003), "Effects of Financial Globalisation on Developing Countries: Some Empirical Evidence", *Economic and Political Weekly*, 38(41), 4319-30.

SMERU (2009), "Monitoring the Socio-Economic Impact of the 2008/2009 Global Financial Crisis in Indonesia: Monitoring Update July-October 2009", *SMERU Research Institute*, *www.smeru.or.id/crisismonitoring_reportintro.php?id=4*.

Stock, J.H. and M.W. Watson (1999), "Forecasting Inflation", *Journal of Monetary Economics*, 44(2), 293-335.

Stock, J.H. and M.W. Watson (2007), "Why Has US Inflation Become Harder to Forecast?", *Journal of Money, Credit and Banking*, 39(1), 3-33.

Suryahadi, A., W. Widyanti, D. Perwira and S. Sumarto (2003), "Minimum Wage Policy and Its Impact on Employment in the Urban Formal Sector", *Bulletin of Indonesian Economic Studies*, 39(1), 29-50.

Van der Eng, P. (2009), "Total Factor Productivity and Economic Growth in Indonesia", *Working Papers in Trade and development*, No. 2009/01, The Australian National University, Canberra.

World Bank (2008), *Finance for All: Policy and Pitfalls of Expanding Access*, World Bank, Washington, DC.

World Bank (2009a), *Investing in a More Sustainable Indonesia: Country Environmental Analysis*, World Bank Office, Jakarta.

World Bank (2009b), *Indonesia Development Policy Review*, World Bank, Washington, DC.

World Bank (2010a), *Indonesia Economic Quarterly: Continuity amidst Volatility*, World Bank Office, Jakarta.

World Bank (2010b), *Indonesia Economic Quarterly: Looking Forward*, World Bank Office, Jakarta.

World Bank (2010c), *Doing Business 2010 Indonesia*, World Bank, Washington, DC.

ANNEX 1.A1

Explaining inflation in Indonesia

This annex presents estimates of backward-looking Phillips curves in Indonesia and selected Asian economies to uncover the main inflation dynamics' determinants. In the case of Indonesia, the relative forecasting performance of the Phillips curve is also assessed against alternative models.

Methodology

A backward looking Phillips curve model, developed by Stock and Watson (1999) and used, among others by Stock and Watson (2007) and Atkenson and Ohanian (2001), is estimated:

$$\pi_{t+h}^{h} - \pi_{t}^{h} = \alpha^{h} + \beta^{h}(B)\Delta\pi_{t} + \delta^{h}(B)\Delta x_{t} + \varepsilon_{t}^{h} \quad (1)$$

where π_t^h is the h-period average (annualised) inflation rate defined by $\pi_t^h = h^{-1}\sum_{i=0}^{h-1}\pi_{t-i}$ (for $h = 2,4,8$) with the annualised inflation rate $\pi_t = 400\ ln(P_t/P_{t-1})$ and P_t is the quarterly headline consumer price index. α^h is a constant, β^h (B) and δ^h (B) and are lag polynomials expressed in terms of the backward operator *B* (The number of lags of the polynomials is selected using the Bayesian information criterion); Δx_t is a vector of variables including the annualised quarterly seasonally adjusted real GDP growth rate and its lags, the current output gap, the annualised quarterly exchange rate change and its lags and the change in the annualised quarterly oil price inflation; ε_t^h is an error term. The output gap is computed as residual of the regression $\ln y = \tau + \sum_{i=1}^{5} t^i + \varepsilon$ where y is real GDP, τ a constant and t a linear trend and i goes from one to five (higher order terms were dropped because of collinearity). The use of alternative commodity prices does not significantly change the results.

To assess the forecasting performance of this model and following Stock and Watson (2007), the Phillips curve is compared against alternatives:

- *Naive*. This is the base model; the forecast of h-quarter average inflation rate is the average rate of inflation over the previous h quarters:

$$\pi_{t+h|t}^{h} = \pi_{t}^{h} \quad (2)$$

with $\pi_{t+h|t}^{h}$ forecast the h-period average π_{t+h}^{h} with information available at time t.

- *Autoregression (AR)*. This is a univariate regression specified in terms of the change in average inflation. The *h*-step-ahead forecast is obtained from the following regression:

$$\pi^h_{t+h} - \pi^h_t = \alpha^h + \beta^h(B)\Delta\pi_t + \varepsilon^h_t \quad (3)$$

where α^h is a constant, β^h (B) is a lag polynomial and ε^h_t is an error term. The number of lags of the polynomial is selected using the Bayesian information criterion.

- *Backward-looking Phillips curve (PC)*. This is model (1). For the forecast comparison, different specifications of (1) are considered:
  - PC-ΔY, which includes the GDP growth rate and its lags;
  - PC-YG, which includes the output gap;
  - PC-ΔY-YG, with the GDP growth rate, its lags, and output gap;
  - PC-ΔFX, with the exchange rate change and its lags;
  - PC-ΔOP with the change in oil price inflation and its lags;
  - PC-ΔY-YG-ΔFX, which includes the GDP growth rate, the exchange rate change, their lags and the output gap;
  - PC-ΔY-YG-ΔOP, with the change in oil price inflation instead of the exchange rate change;
  - PC-ΔY-YG-ΔFX-ΔOP, the full model.

These models present the advantages of being nested into each other. The forecast from the AR model equals the one produced by the naive model when $\alpha^h = 0$ and β^h (B) = 0, whereas the PC models equals the naive model when $\alpha^h = 0$, β^h (B) and δ^h (B) = 0.

To compare the forecasting power of these models the pseudo out-of-sample forecast methodology is used. This involves using only the data available at time t to perform the lag selection and estimation of the different models and forecast the *h*-step ahead average inflation rate (*i.e.* average inflation from t+1 to t+*h*). The data are available from 1991Q1 for inflation and from 1993Q1 for the other variables to 2009Q1 and come from the IMF International Financial Statistics. The forecasting period starts from 2006Q1 and ends in 2009Q1. We compute the forecast two-, four- and eight-quarters ahead. The forecasting performance of the different models is evaluated through their root mean square forecasting error (RMSFE).

Results

The estimates of model (1) suggest that the variables considered have different explanatory power across countries and forecast horizons (Tables 1.A1.1-3). The output gap appears to be an important determinant of future inflation across all countries and forecast periods, but its effect appears to be more pronounced in Indonesia than other countries, especially for four and eight-step-ahead inflation. Exchange rate movements are significant only for Indonesia across all forecast horizons. Surprisingly oil-price changes do not appear to have significant effect on inflation for the countries and time periods considered, but for Indonesia on a short-term horizon.

It is of interest to compare the forecasting properties of model (1) for Indonesia with those of alternative models. The results are shown in Table 1.A1.4. The rows report the RMSFE of the different specifications relative to the naive model. A value less than one indicates that the model has a better forecasting performance than the naive model.

Table 1.A1.1. **Regression results of backward-looking Phillips curve (two-quarter-ahead inflation)**

	Indonesia	Malaysia	Philippine	Thailand
Change in inflation	–0.525**	–0.384+	–0.129	–0.23
	[0.15]	[0.22]	[0.13]	[0.18]
t-1	–0.610**	–0.912**	–0.714**	–0.989**
	[0.14]	[0.24]	[0.17]	[0.14]
t-2	–0.347**	–0.730**	–0.540**	–0.936**
	[0.11]	[0.26]	[0.16]	[0.23]
t-3			–0.573**	–0.753**
			[0.14]	[0.16]
t-4			–0.525**	–0.756**
			[0.13]	[0.18]
t-5			–0.387**	–0.568**
			[0.13]	[0.14]
t-6			–0.320**	
			[0.11]	
GDP growth	–0.520+	–0.024	–0.287*	–0.039
	[0.28]	[0.05]	[0.12]	[0.08]
t-1	0.025			
	[0.15]			
t-2	0.227			
	[0.21]			
t-3	0.352+			
	[0.19]			
t-4	0.585*			
	[0.22]			
t-5	0.141			
	[0.15]			
t-6	0.011			
	[0.13]			
t-7	–0.431**			
	[0.15]			
t-8	–0.15			
	[0.14]			
Change in FX	0.134*	–0.003	–0.019	0.014
	[0.05]	[0.03]	[0.04]	[0.02]
Output gap	1.371*	0.294+	1.319**	0.468**
	[0.57]	[0.15]	[0.38]	[0.16]
Change in oil price	0.039*	0.008+	0.007+	–0.011
	[0.01]	[0.00]	[0.00]	[0.01]
t-1	0.066**			
	[0.02]			
t-2	0.033*			
	[0.01]			
Constant	–2.599	–0.058	1.008	–0.3
	[2.00]	[0.34]	[0.78]	[0.53]
Adj. R-Squared	0.723	0.499	0.442	0.555
Observations	59	60	60	60

Note: +, * and ** denote 10, 5 and 1% statistical significance level.
Source: OECD calculations.

According to this exercise, the change in oil price and activity variables are the most important variables to forecast average CPI inflation rate over two quarters in Indonesia. For $h = 2$, the RMSFE of PC-DY-YG-DOP is the lowest of the models considered and is

Table 1.A1.2. **Regression results of backward-looking Phillips curve (four-quarter-ahead inflation)**

	Indonesia	Malaysia	Philippine	Thailand
Change in inflation	–0.192	–0.182	0.002	–0.220+
	[0.12]	[0.14]	[0.10]	[0.11]
t-1		–0.469*	–0.344**	–0.562**
		[0.18]	[0.11]	[0.10]
t-2		–0.611**	–0.448**	–0.781**
		[0.19]	[0.11]	[0.13]
t-3		–0.840**	–0.641**	–0.877**
		[0.27]	[0.12]	[0.13]
t-4		–0.686*	–0.557**	–0.764**
		[0.28]	[0.10]	[0.15]
t-5		–0.397*	–0.363**	–0.540**
		[0.19]	[0.10]	[0.10]
t-6		–0.277+	–0.257**	–0.369**
		[0.16]	[0.08]	[0.13]
t-7				–0.225+
				[0.13]
GDP growth	–0.461*	–0.054	–0.169	–0.076
	[0.18]	[0.04]	[0.11]	[0.06]
t-1	0.254+			
	[0.15]			
t-2	0.29			
	[0.23]			
t-3	0.341+			
	[0.17]			
t-4	0.350*			
	[0.15]			
t-5	–0.231+			
	[0.13]			
t-6	–0.198			
	[0.13]			
t-7	–0.448**			
	[0.14]			
t-8	–0.152			
	[0.13]			
Change in FX	0.085*	–0.011	–0.015	–0.005
	[0.04]	[0.02]	[0.02]	[0.01]
Output gap	2.767**	0.316**	1.472**	0.577**
	[0.72]	[0.12]	[0.30]	[0.12]
Change in oil price	0.019	0.003	0.002	0
	[0.02]	[0.00]	[0.00]	[0.01]
Constant	–0.571	0.097	0.394	–0.33
	[2.33]	[0.24]	[0.60]	[0.33]
Adj. R-Squared	0.767	0.44	0.562	0.629
Observations	57	58	58	57

Note: +, * and ** denote 10, 5 and 1% statistical significance level.
Source: OECD calculations.

around 30% lower than the naive model. Over four quarters the forecasting performance of PC-DY-YG-DOP deteriorates considerably and its forecast is not better than the one of the reference model. However, even over this forecast horizon the importance of the change in oil price inflation in forecasting average inflation is evident by the performance of the PC-DOP model, which has the lowest RMSFE. Over a longer forecasting period (eight

Table 1.A1.3. **Regression results of backward-looking Phillips curve (eight-quarter-ahead inflation)**

	Indonesia	Malaysia	Philippine	Thailand
Change in inflation	–0.335**	–0.058	0.032	–0.102
	[0.09]	[0.07]	[0.06]	[0.06]
t-1	–0.576**			
	[0.12]			
t-2	–0.642**			
	[0.14]			
t-3	–0.622**			
	[0.15]			
t-4	–0.439**			
	[0.11]			
t-5	–0.232**			
	[0.06]			
t-6	–0.206**			
	[0.05]			
t-7	–0.244**			
	[0.05]			
t-8	–0.096*			
	[0.04]			
GDP growth	–0.142	–0.029	0.032	0.050+
	[0.14]	[0.02]	[0.07]	[0.03]
t-1	0.098			0.03
	[0.14]			[0.02]
t-2	0.285+			0.04
	[0.14]			[0.03]
t-3	0.455**			0.070**
	[0.16]			[0.02]
t-4	0.333**			
	[0.09]			
t-5	0.301**			
	[0.09]			
t-6	0.173			
	[0.11]			
t-7	0.144			
	[0.11]			
Change in FX	0.023	–0.013+	–0.012	–0.012+
	[0.03]	[0.01]	[0.01]	[0.01]
t-1	0.076**			
	[0.03]			
t-2	0.096**			
	[0.03]			
t-3	0.108**			
	[0.03]			
t-4	0.070*			
	[0.03]			
Output gap	2.469**	0.314**	0.850**	0.326**
	[0.21]	[0.05]	[0.19]	[0.05]
Change in oil price	–0.007	–0.001	–0.001	0.002
	[0.02]	[0.00]	[0.00]	[0.00]
Constant	–10.808**	0.038	–0.46	–1.243**
	[2.35]	[0.18]	[0.32]	[0.19]
Adj. R-Squared	0.917	0.368	0.181	0.685
Observations	54	54	54	54

Note: +, * and ** denote 10, 5 and 1% statistical significance level.
Source: OECD calculations.

Table 1.A1.4. **Pseudo out-of-sample forecasting results for CPI inflation**

	2-quarter ahead	4-quarter ahead	8-quarter ahead
Relative RSMFE			
AR	0.96	0.9	1.47
PC-DY	1.01	1.37	2.47
PC-YG	1.07	0.98	1.18
PC-DY-YG	1.14	1.24	0.85
PC-DFX	1.15	1.37	1.74
PC-DOP	1	0.84	1.48
PC-DY-YG-DFX	1.08	1.26	0.71
PC-DY-YG-DOP	0.72	1.11	0.82
PC-DY-YG-DFX-DOP	0.78	1.11	0.53

Note: The relative RSMFE is the ratio of the root mean square forecasting error of the different models to that of the naive model.
Source: OECD calculations.

quarters), average inflation is best predicted by the Phillips curve including the real GDP growth, current output gap, exchange rate and oil price (PC-DY-YG-DFX-DOP). Overall, these findings suggest that movements in the oil price and exchange rate are passed onto the CPI relatively quickly, whereas over the long run inflation is best predicted by changes in real activity.

ANNEX 1.A2

Estimation and projection of Indonesia's potential output growth

This Annex estimates potential output growth in Indonesia using a production-function approach and derives long-term projections using United Nations population projections.

Methodology

Estimation of potential output

Potential output is calculated using a Cobb-Douglas production function. The methodology is similar to the one used by the OECD, which is described in Beffy *et al.* (2006), but has been adapted to account for Indonesia's data limitations.

Potential output is calculated using the following equation:

$$y_t^* = tfp_t^* + (1-\alpha) * k_t^* + \alpha(1-u_t^*) * lf_t^* \qquad (1.A2.1)$$

where all the variables are expressed in logarithms. y_t^* denotes potential output, k_t^* the optimal capital stock, u_t^* is the structural rate of unemployment, lf_t^* is trend labour force and tfp_t^* trend total factor productivity (TFP). Optimal capital is set to be equal to actual capital. Robustness tests using filtered capital are presented below. Structural unemployment, labour force and TFP have been filtered using a double-sided Hodrick-Prescott filter.

Data for GDP, gross capital formation, labour force and the unemployment rate are taken from national accounts and labour force surveys. The capital stocks were constructed using the perpetual inventory method (for investment series starting in 1960 and using a fixed depreciation rate of 5%). Missing values in the unemployment rate series were interpolated linearly. TFP data have been computed as a residual from the following equation using data on real GDP, actual capital, unemployment and the labour force: $tfp_t = y_t - (1-\alpha) * k_t - \alpha(1-u_t) * lf_t$. The share of labour in GDP, α, is set at 60% to fit the Indonesian data. This is consistent with Alisjahbana (2009). Changes to alternative plausible values of this parameter are presented below.

As underlined in Cotis *et al.* (2005), production-function based potential output estimates, as well as those derived from other approaches, should be interpreted with caution. They are in particular sensitive to the measurement errors in TFP. Moreover, factor quality is treated in the calculations as constant over time, whereas increases in the stock of human capital of the labour force are expected to affect the economy's overall efficiency.

Finally because of its simplicity the methodology does not account for the effects of structural reform on efficiency and input accumulation.

Long-term projections

The same methodology is used to derive long-term projections of potential output, relying on United Nations population projections (medium scenario). Capital and trend TFP are assumed to grow at rates observed in 2008-09 and structural unemployment to gradually converge to its long-term average.

Findings

Using the methodology described above, potential output is estimated to have grown at the hefty pace of around 6-6½ per cent from 1980 to 1997. The Asian crisis ended this period and potential output growth slowed to less than 2%. It recovered subsequently to around 4.0% during the 2000-09 period. This is consistent with OECD (2008), which also derives production-function-based estimates for Indonesia using different data. Population ageing is found to slow potential output growth from 2015 onward to reach 4½ per cent by 2050. Similar results would be obtained by computing potential output with actual rather than smoothed capital data (Figure 1.A2.1). Using a labour share of 50% rather than 60% would imply a stronger end point of 5% for potential output by 2050, but would not alter the diagnostics of a slowdown in potential growth stemming from population ageing.

Figure 1.A2.1. **Potential output growth in Indonesia**

In per cent

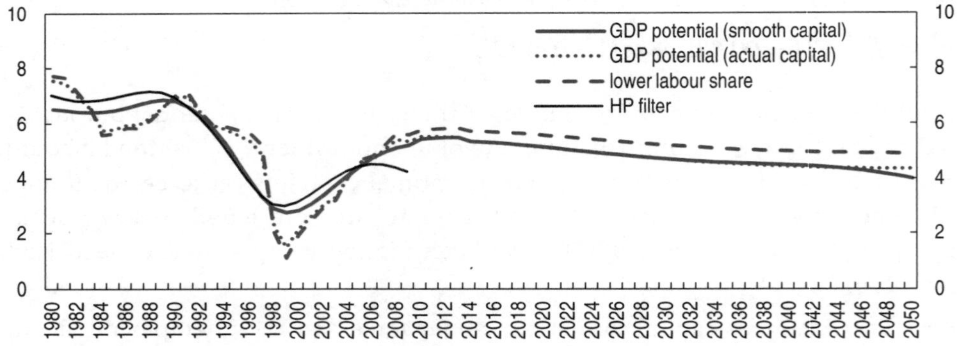

Source: BPS and OECD calculations.

StatLink http://dx.doi.org/10.1787/888932341537

Chapter 2

Phasing out energy subsidies

The oil price hike in 2007-08 underlined the vulnerability of Indonesia's energy subsidy policy to oil price volatility. In addition to entailing significant economic and environmental costs, energy subsidies put pressure on the public budget and benefit mostly rich households. Phasing them out would benefit both the economy and the environment. At the same time, past experience in Indonesia and elsewhere suggests that such a reform is likely to face stiff opposition and will therefore need to be carefully designed and communicated. Compensation in the form of targeted cash transfers will help to shield low-income households from attendant rise in energy prices.

The 2007-08 rise in oil prices renewed global interest in fuel subsidies and concerns about their fiscal costs, notably for G20 countries, which account for over 70% of such subsidies. This is particularly important for Indonesia, where energy subsidies touch upon each of the development challenges put forward by the government: enhancing economic growth, reducing poverty and favouring an environmentally friendly path to development by reducing GHG emissions and adopting cleaner sources of energy.

This chapter starts by describing the main features of the subsidy policy in Indonesia. It subsequently details the costs associated with this policy, reviewing in turn economic, fiscal, social and environmental burdens. Benefits of reforms, together with related political economy aspects, are then discussed. A final section sets out policy recommendations.

Energy subsidies are large by international standards

The Indonesian energy subsidy policy has focused on consumer subsidies in the form of under-pricing of energy, though producer subsidies in the form of tax expenditure also exist (Morgan, 2007). The central government subsidises the price of several energy products, including gasoline, kerosene and diesel, and it sets tariffs for electricity.[1] Compensation for the revenue loss is provided to the state-owned energy companies. It is determined administratively and is a function of the inputs used in the production process.

Subsidies were introduced in Indonesia for social considerations to make available a "basic need" at a price affordable to the poor.[2] This holds in particular for kerosene, which is the only fuel product consumed by the low-income urban population and is second to wood as an energy source for rural consumers. Originally, energy subsidies were available for all segments of the population, but coverage has shrunk over the years. The number of fuel products eligible for the subsidy was reduced in 2005. Since 2008, electricity subsidies are no longer available for larger industrial consumers. High-volume household customers benefit from the subsidised rate only up to a certain threshold.[3]

The overall amount of energy subsidies provided by Indonesia in 2008 was high by international standards. According to a price-gap methodology, whereby subsidies are measured as the difference between the regulated retail price and an agreed benchmark price that is an estimate of the "economic price", Indonesia featured among the ten non-OECD countries providing the most generous energy subsidies in the world, in particular for oil (Figure 2.1).[4, 5] By contrast, many OECD countries have reduced or eliminated direct subsidies to fossil fuels and lifted price controls over the past two decades, as part of a general move away from government intervention in the traditional part of energy sectors (IEA, 2008a).

The size of energy subsidies fluctuated widely over the past decade, following movements in international prices and the exchange rate and adjustments to the subsidy regime (Box 2.1). Subsidies increased markedly from 1997 to 2001, reflecting the sharp depreciation of the *rupiah* (Figure 2.2, Panel A). They fell drastically in 2002 due to a policy

Figure 2.1. **Energy subsidies in selected countries, 2008**

Billion dollars

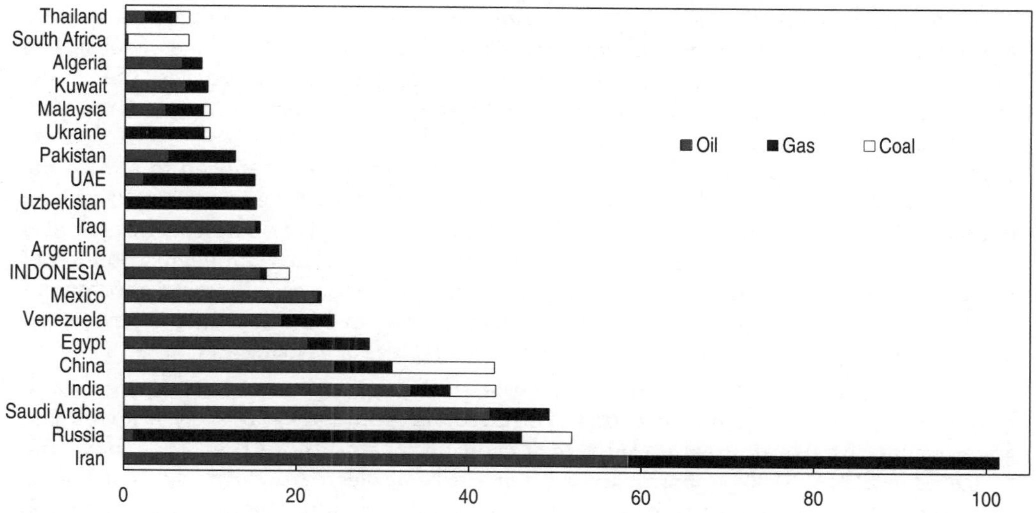

Source: IEA *World Energy Outlook*, 2010 (forthcoming), *www.worldenergyoutlook.org/subsidies.asp*.

Box 2.1. **Past reforms to energy subsidies in Indonesia**

The central government has been working towards reducing energy subsidies through energy price increases and other measures for several years. Many attempted reforms have faced public resistance, sometimes leading to their reversal.

Changes to subsidy policy since 1998

In 1998, a fuel price hike led to riots and is generally thought to have contributed to the downfall of the Suharto government.

In 2000, a National Development Programme (*Propenas*) stated that oil subsidies had to be eliminated by 2004. External factors (oil price fluctuations) and internal factors (a rise in poverty) prevented its full implementation. A "compensating programme for oil subsidy elimination" was also introduced. It covered many areas, including health, education and small business promotion.

In 2002, the government allowed fuel product prices to move in line with international prices. In early 2003, the government attempted to close the gap between domestic and international fuel prices by increasing fuel prices the same day that it increased various utility prices. However, this reform was poorly communicated and resulted in public protests. The government rolled back most of the increase and severed the link to world prices.

In 2005, the government undertook two large fuel-price hikes. The price of diesel fuel doubled and that of kerosene nearly tripled. To mitigate the impact of the reform on the poor the government introduced an unconditional cash-transfer system through the postal system. Monthly cash payments of USD 10 were distributed to 19 million low-income individuals.

Box 2.1. **Past reforms to energy subsidies in Indonesia** *(cont.)*

In 2008, the government ceased paying subsidies to larger industrial electricity consumers. In the same year the government announced that it would phase out the sale of subsidised fuel to private cars and restrict it to public-transport providers and motorcycles. The shift is expected to be fully implemented by 2014. In May 2008, the government increased gasoline and diesel prices by nearly 30%, and then in July 2008 it raised LPG prices by 23%. Compensation programmes in the form of cash transfers were introduced to reduce the burden on low-income households (*Bantuan Langsung Tunai*). They were directed at 19 million families, for a total amount of IDR 14 billion for the 2008 fiscal year. The government also relied on other compensation programmes (Food Sustainability Programme, distribution of rice and control of rice price, financial support for the education of children of government employees, subsidy increase for small-scale credit facilities). In December 2008, following the drop in world oil prices, the government reduced retail prices of gasoline and diesel.

In the Medium Term Development Plan, the government announced its objective to remove fossil-fuel subsidies by 2014. The 2010 State Budget explicitly allowed the government to raise domestic fuel prices if oil prices rise more than 10% above the budgeted level of USD 80 per barrel. In addition, the basic electricity tariff was raised by an average of 10% in July 2010, and by an average of 10-15% for industries. Smaller residential consumers, representing around 87% of all households, are estimated to have been shielded from the price hike (World Bank, 2010). The objective of the July increase was also to simplify commercial tariffs which previously depended on usage and supply agreement with the state-owned electricity provider by unifying them into one usage tariff for each connection capacity. A 15% increase in electricity tariff for 2011 was initially put forward in the 2011 Draft Budget. The increase has subsequently been postponed.

In June 2010, the government planned to limit fuel use for private cars with engine capacity of more than 2000 cubic centimeters. This plan was delayed to next year.

In September 2010, the House of representatives agreed to raise the quotas on subsidised fuel consumption in the revised 2010 State Budget. Such a move appears to be inconsistent with the authorities' will to curb the consumption of subsidised fuel. This suggests policy reacts asymmetrically to oil price changes. When oil price exceeds the level forecast in the State Budget, additional spending are allocated to finance energy subsidies. By contrast, when oil price is below the excess amount of subsidies initially allocated is not saved.

Changes to energy laws

Law No. 30/2007 stipulated that energy prices should be based on fair economic value and that the central government should create a subsidy fund for poor people. This law still needs implementing regulations. In 2009, a law allowed electricity suppliers to set different prices across geographic areas and classes of consumers. As of October 2010, however, that law still needed implementing regulations as well.

Programmes to lower and diversify energy consumption

In 2008, the Ministry of Energy proposed distributing a so-called "smart card" to households that would entitle the holder to purchase a limited quantity of subsidised fuel each month. This proposal was dropped around mid-year due to concerns about its technical feasibility.

Indonesia has a programme to phase out the use of kerosene, in favour of liquefied petroleum gas (LPG). LPG stoves and small LPG cylinders have been distributed, free of charge, to urban households using kerosene stoves, starting with households living around the capital. There are plans to expand this programme to other cities. The objective of this programme was also to reduce the pressure on the state budget as LPG is less subsidised than kerosene. LPG is also found to be more consistent with the nation environmental objective to move to a low-carbon environment. In 2008, 5.3 million households stopped using kerosene.

of incremental adjustment to oil price and the appreciation of the *rupiah*. Hikes in international prices led to a sharp rise in subsidies in 2004 and 2005. They declined thereafter as the government tightened its subsidy policy in March and October 2005. Increasing international oil prices and a recovery in consumption led to a peak in energy subsidies at 4.5% of GDP in 2008. By comparison, public capital expenditure and spending on social programmes amounted to only 1.5% and 1.2% of GDP respectively that year. Energy subsidies declined to 1.7% of GDP in 2009 and are expected to cost the government a total of IDR 144 trillion (USD 15.7 billion) in 2010, corresponding to 2.3% of GDP. Those estimates are based on an assumed oil price of USD 80 a barrel.

Oil subsidies account for the bulk of energy subsidies. Kerosene is the most heavily subsidised oil product and absorbs about half of the total.[6] Gasoline and diesel each represent roughly one quarter. Electricity subsidies were larger than oil subsidies in 2009 for the first time in five years and amounted to 0.9% of GDP in 2009 (Figure 2.2, Panel B).

Figure 2.2. **Evolution of subsidies and their composition over time**

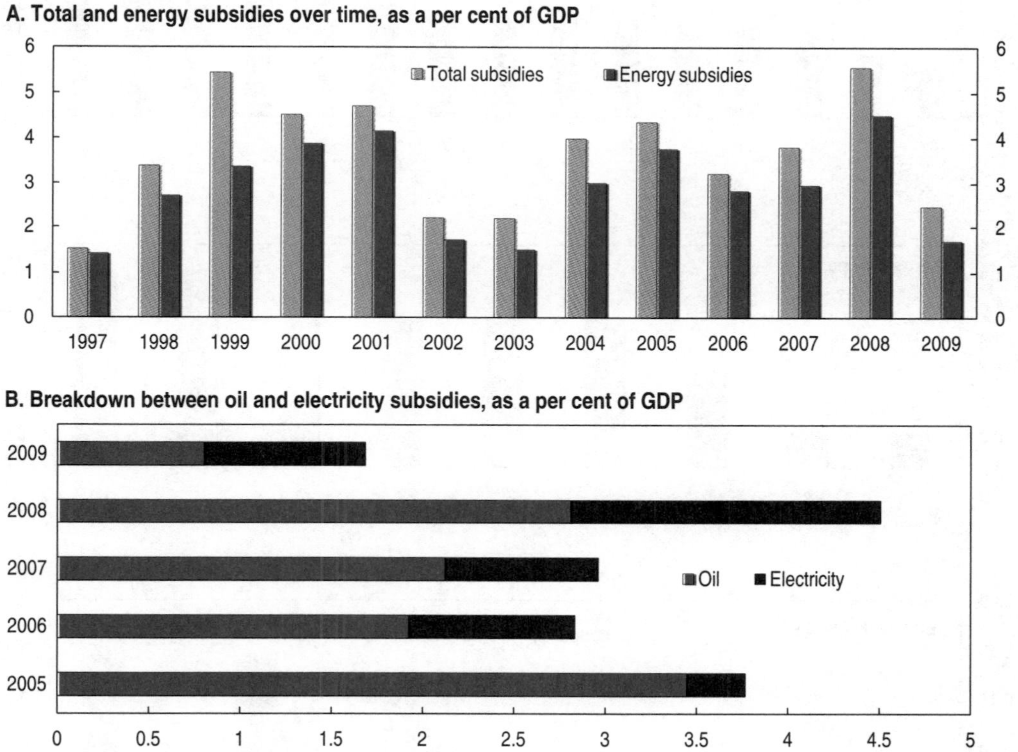

Source: Bank Indonesia and Ministry of Finance.

StatLink http://dx.doi.org/10.1787/888932341556

Because of these subsidies, fuel and electricity tariffs are much lower than the cost of provision and in particular lower than in regional peers (Figure 2.3). In addition, subsidies smooth the volatility of international prices by lowering the level of pass-through onto domestic retail prices. This pass-through is estimated to be significantly smaller in Indonesia than in peer countries for all types of fuels, especially kerosene (Table 2.1). The counterpart is that oil-price volatility is transferred to public finances.

Figure 2.3. **Retail gasoline, diesel and kerosene prices in USD, 2008 or latest available date**

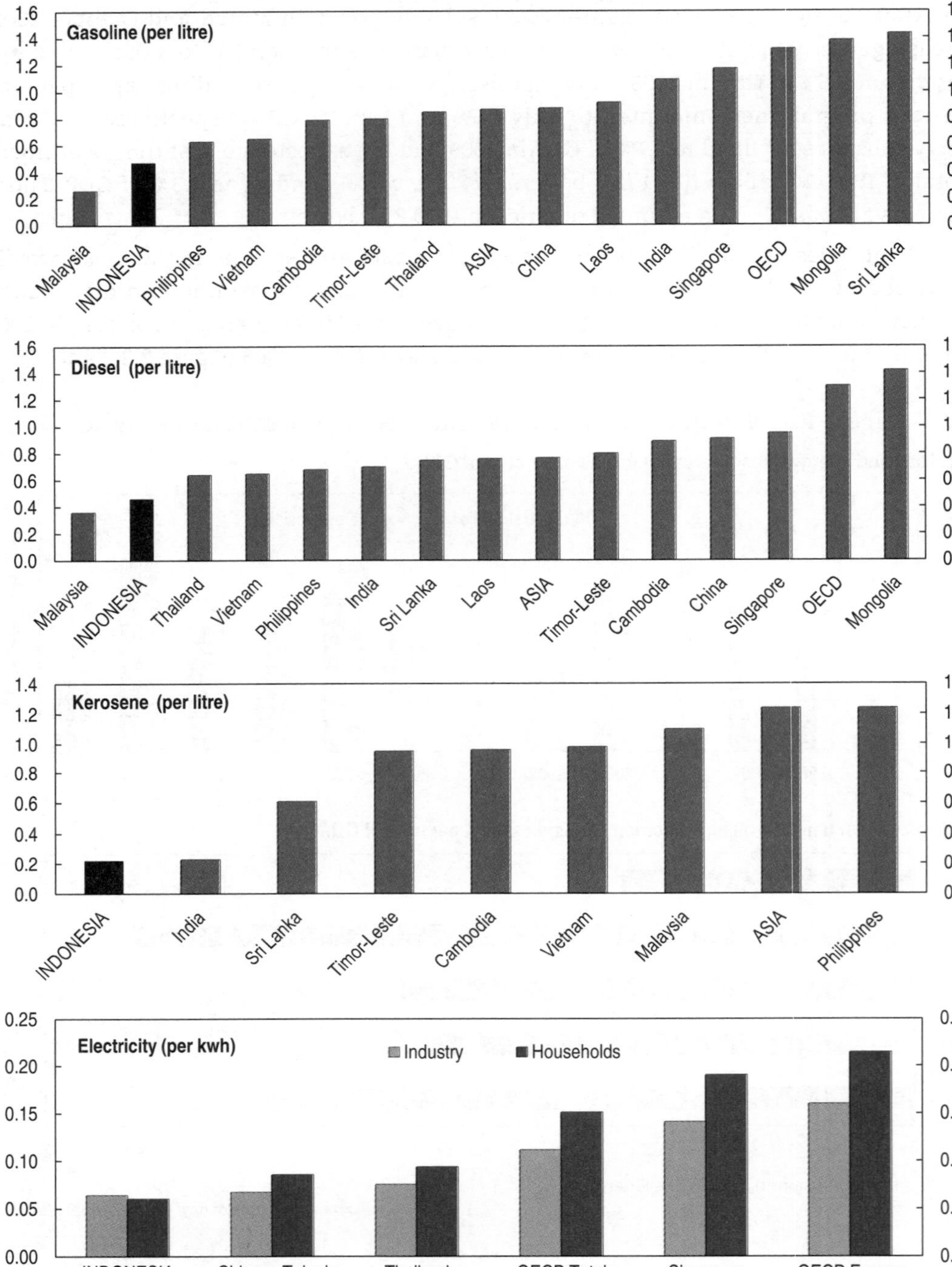

Source: Coady *et al.* (2010); IEA, *Energy Prices and Taxes.*

StatLink http://dx.doi.org/10.1787/888932341575

In addition to the direct price subsidies, Indonesia also grants implicit subsidies through a range of tax expenditures.[7] Capital costs are subsidised through government-backed loans to *Perusahaan Listrik Negara* (PLN), the state-owned electricity supplier, for the development of coal-powered generation. The government also provides subsidies for the

Table 2.1. **Pass-through of international prices to domestic retail prices (tax inclusive): 2004-08**[1]

	Gasoline	Diesel	Kerosene[2]
OECD	109.9	159.2	–
Asia[3]	83.0	99.4	97.3
Indonesia	**57.9**	**58.8**	**20.9**

1. The pass-through is estimated as the ratio of the absolute change in the domestic retail price to the absolute change in international price times 100.
2. The period is 2003-mid-2008 for kerosene.
3. Asia is an unweighted average of Cambodia, India, Indonesia, Malaysia, Philippines, Sri Lanka and India.

Source: OECD calculations using Coady *et al.* (2010) and US Energy Information Administration data.

production of renewable energy in the form of interest rate subsidies or funding for research and development. Total government allocations for biofuel development between 2006 and June 2008 are estimated to have been around IDR 1 793 billion (USD 197 million) (Dillon *et al.*, 2008).[8] In 2010, a ministerial decree encouraged investment in renewable energy, such as geothermal, solar and biofuels, including a 5% tax cut over six years for renewable energy producers, as well as exemptions from value-added tax and import duties on equipment. Another provision allows investors to use accelerated depreciation and amortisation on assets to reduce taxable income. Subsidies could also be provided through preferential treatments in production sharing contracts between the State, which owns all natural resources, and companies, which offer technical and financial services for oil exploration and development operations (IEA, 2008b).[9] However, little information is publicly available on this issue, and it is difficult to gauge the importance of this potential implicit subsidy (Koplow *et al.*, 2010).

Energy subsidies entail significant costs

Although policy-makers historically justified energy subsidies by public-policy objectives, subsidisation does not appear to be the most efficient policy to meet these objectives. In particular, energy subsidies entail significant economic, fiscal, social and environmental costs that are discussed in turn.

Economic costs

Efficiency costs arise because subsidies blur price signals, by setting prices at a lower level than opportunity costs, therefore potentially distorting consumption and investment decisions.

- The first mechanical impact is an over-consumption of subsidised energy. This leads to an increased demand for imports or a reduction in the amount of energy available for exports. Subsidies can thus result in a deterioration of the balance of payments and increase the country's dependence on energy imports. The resulting marginal negative effect on the value of the currency implies the country can enjoy fewer non-energy imports on a sustainable basis, however. If the country is economically small, like Indonesia, the effect of subsidies on world energy prices and consumption will be negligible. But when many countries engage in similar policies, world prices will be raised to the extent that supply is globally inelastic.
- The effect on energy prices propagates across sectors, in particular those which are energy-intensive, and affect their costs of production and in turn the prices of other goods. Relative price changes will also influence the competitiveness of goods on world markets.

- Subsidies diminish the ability and incentive to invest in new infrastructure and production processes. Subsidies also lead to a deterioration in the financial situation of state-owned energy companies and have resulted in under-investment in Indonesia. This is the case in the electricity sector, where *Perusahaan Listrik Negara* (PLN) has had to manage a large cross-subsidy programme across regions and consumers, which has impaired its financial condition. In 2009, the revenue from its sale of electricity on average amounted to only around IDR 654 per kWh, while the cost of supply reached on average IDR 1 300 per kWh. Compensation received from the State did not fill this gap. As a result, PLN has been unable to fund new investment, expand electrification in rural areas and sometimes even to conduct standard maintenance. The result has been a lack of development of its generating capacity and frequent blackouts.
- Distorted prices can also result in resource mis-allocation and inefficient investment choices. Subsidies to specific energy types or technologies inevitably undermine the development and commercialisation of other sources and technologies that might ultimately become more economically (as well as environmentally) attractive. In this way, subsidies can "lock in" technologies to the exclusion of other, more promising ones.
- Changes in energy prices can result in inter-factor substitution, whereby energy can be substituted for capital or labour. The importance of these substitutions depends in part on the share of energy in the total of production inputs and the substitutability of the different factor inputs. These mechanisms are likely to have played an important role in Indonesia, as energy was often substituted to labour in the country during episodes of increased fuel prices (Hope and Singh, 1995). Hence removing subsidies to producers is likely to increase employment in response to their more favourable relative prices.
- Subsidies hinder competition. State-owned energy company *Pertamina* is currently the only channel for fuel subsidies to flow to retail consumers. Other companies have been allowed to sell higher-octane fuels and other products, but their penetration remains very small, as their non-subsidised products can be more than 50% more expensive than Pertamina's subsidised output.
- Subsidies encourage corruption and smuggling of fuel products to neighbouring countries or to non-subsidised sectors where selling prices are higher.[10] Large administrative costs are incurred to monitor, prevent and deal with abuse.

Fiscal costs

Despite successive reductions, energy subsidies continue to weigh heavily on the budget. Indeed, the central government compensates the state-owned oil and electricity companies in the form of transfers for the losses they incur when the domestic price of fuel is kept below international prices. In 2008, energy subsidies represented 22% of government expenditure (comprising central government expenditure and transfers to regions). They fell to 9.9% in 2009 and are projected to reach 12.8 % in 2010 according to the 2010 revised State Budget. For 2011, the government has proposed to lower this ratio to 11%, with the bulk of the decline coming from an increase in electricity tariff. The planned 2011 rise in electricity prices has subsequently been postponed. By putting pressure on the budget, these subsidies run counter to the ongoing efforts to allocate a rising share of budgetary resources to more beneficial uses, such as infrastructure investment, human capital accumulation and social protection programmes.

The subsidy policy also renders the country's public spending particularly vulnerable to global energy movements.[11] As international energy prices are procyclical, spending on subsidies tends to rise when the global economy grows strongly and to fall during downturns. The effect of subsidies on the budget is only partially offset by revenues from the energy sector, even though these revenues accounted for almost 15% of the budgetary resources of the central government in 2009 (Figure 2.4). Indeed, over the last fifteen years, oil and gas revenues have increased far less quickly than other sources. They are predominantly non-tax revenues resulting from production-sharing contracts between the government and energy extractors.[12]

Figure 2.4. **Share of selected sources in central government revenue, per cent**

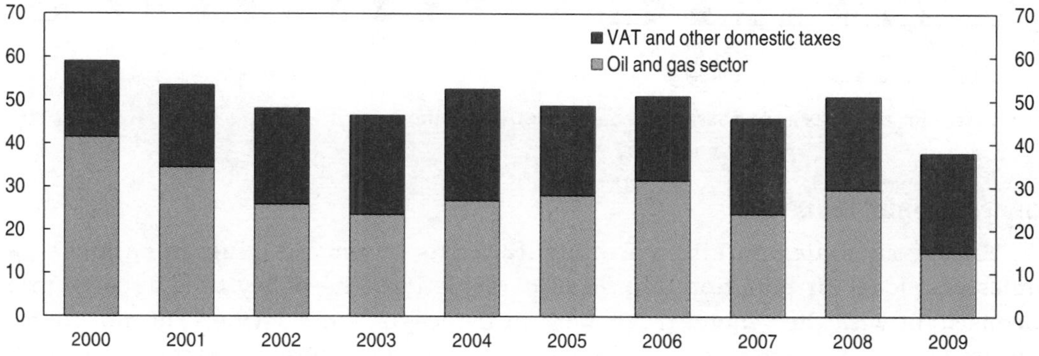

Note: Revenues include both tax and non-tax revenues.

Source: OECD calculations based on Ministry of Finance data.

StatLink http://dx.doi.org/10.1787/888932341594

Social costs

Energy subsidies have been introduced for social motives to make energy, a basic need, affordable to low-income groups. Energy subsidies affect household real outcomes both directly and indirectly. The direct effect is the gain in disposable income due to lower prices paid by households for consumption of fuel products. The indirect effect is seen in the lower prices paid by households for other goods and services stemming from the lower cost for fuel-based inputs of production.

In practice, however, benefits of fuel subsidies accrue mainly to high-income groups while their cost falls on the whole taxpaying population. As the subsidy per litre does not vary with household income, those who consume the most also receive the largest share of the subsidy. Surveys suggest that fuel consumption increases with income levels (Figure 2.5, Panel A). As a result, more than 90% of fuel subsidies benefit the 50% of the richest households in Indonesia (Agustina *et al.*, 2008). This is broadly in line with official views. In May 2008, the Co-ordinating Ministry of Economic Affairs advised that the top 40% of families receive 70% of the subsidies, while the bottom 40% benefit from only 15% of the subsidies. Electricity subsidies also appear to benefit mostly wealthier households. In 2005, the top decile received 44% more subsidies than the bottom decile (World Bank, 2006).

Accounting for income distribution, there is evidence that fuel subsidies are regressive. They represent less than 0.5% of poor-household incomes, as opposed to more than 1.5% for the most affluent incomes (Figure 2.5, Panel B).

Figure 2.5. **Fuel subsidies by income, 2007**

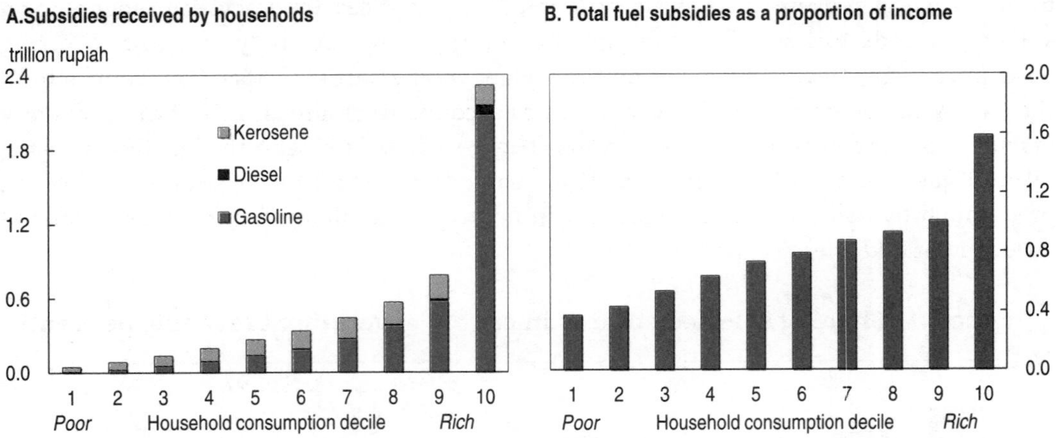

Source: Agustina *et al.* (2008), using Susenas 2007 and OECD calculations.

Environmental costs

Energy subsidies entail environmental costs by encouraging greenhouse-gas emissions, local air pollution and resource depletion. The policy thus appears to be inconsistent with the general trend, both in Indonesia and elsewhere, of moving to a greener economy. By keeping the price artificially low, fuel subsidies encourage wasteful consumption of polluting petroleum products. Subsidies can also lower incentives to improve energy efficiency. By blurring price signals, subsidies undermine the diversification toward existing cleaner energy sources and technologies. In the electricity sector, the compensation provided to the state-owned power utility PLN is a function of technology: PLN receives much more for electricity produced from diesel than for electricity produced from geothermal sources. Fuel subsidies also discourage innovation in the production and deployment of cleaner types of energy, such as LPG and renewables, even though Indonesia's endowment in these energy resources is substantial.[13]

Against this background, the removal of energy subsidies features as an important part of the government's strategy to move toward a low-carbon environment (Ministry of Finance, 2009). The objective to fully eliminate fossil fuel subsidies by 2014 has been announced, as well as the plan to reduce total energy subsidies (including fossil-fuel, electricity and biofuel subsidies) by 10%-15% on average per year during the period 2011-14. However, no precise timetable has been established for the removal of electricity subsidies and tariff hikes usually occur on an *ad hoc* basis. Given the political difficulties associated with the elimination of energy subsidies (see below), a pragmatic approach has been proposed, whereby a small carbon tax could be introduced simultaneously with a phasing out of energy subsidies over time.[14]

Removing subsidies will enhance Indonesia's long-term prospects

Removing energy subsidies is likely to benefit both the economy and the environment. The removal of energy subsidies is expected to have significant general-equilibrium effects, including on energy prices, consumption and trade. Efficiency gains are likely to benefit the economy as a whole, even though the indirect effects of higher energy prices can lead to higher production costs. In addition, the extent of support or protection in other parts of the economy could hinder the efficient reallocation of resources following a removal of subsidies. Environmental policies can also influence energy choices and change the GDP and environmental impacts of subsidy removal. Overall, estimates of reform benefits are hard to gauge, as many factors inter-play, and their impact will vary according to national institutions and endowments.

OECD empirical analysis suggests that a unilateral removal of subsidies would be beneficial for most economies, including Indonesia's, in the medium term and lead to moderate real income gains (Burniaux *et al.*, 2009; Table 2.2). These impacts depend to a large extent on whether the subsidy removal is compensated through an increase in spending or through tax cuts. These estimated gains are also likely to underestimate the

Table 2.2. **Selected studies on the impact of subsidy removal**

Authors and method	Scope	Effect on GDP	Effect on social costs	Effect on greenhouse-gas emissions
Burniaux *et al.* (2009) Multi-country general equilibrium model	World In this simulation, Indonesia is included in a group also comprising Middle East, Algeria-Libya-Egypt, Venezuela.	Indonesia, Middle East, Algeria-Libya-Egypt, Venezuela: Unilateral removal: 0.5% by 2050 Multilateral removal: –4.2% by 2050		Indonesia, Middle East, Algeria-Libya-Egypt, Venezuela: Unilateral removal: –20.2% CO_2 emissions by 2050 compared with BAU Multilateral removal: –37.4% CO_2 emissions by 2050 compared with BAU
Bulman *et al.* (2008)	Indonesia			Raising gasoline price by 500 *rupiah* per litre will reduce gasoline consumption by 2.5%. A 20% increase in the price of kerosene will lead to about 3.5% less consumption of kerosene.
Adam and Lestari (2008), Regression analysis	Indonesia		Increase in the price of oil correlates negatively with social welfare.	
Clement *et al.* (2007), Multi-sectoral general equilibrium model	Indonesia	Reduce real output by 2% in the short-term or no effect depending on the modelling assumptions. Aggregate price level increases by 1.1% as a result of a 25% increase in petroleum prices.	The poverty index increases modestly by 0.3-0.6%.	
IEA (1999), Static partial equilibrium analysis	Eight non-OECD countries, including Indonesia	In Indonesia, gain of about 0.24% of GDP per year from subsidy removal (compared with an average of 0.73% for the average of the examined countries).		–11% CO_2 emission per year from subsidy removal (compared with an average of –16% for the average of the examined countries)
Hope and Singh (1995), Case study from actual reforms in 1980s	Columbia, Ghana, Indonesia, Malaysia, Turkey and Zimbabwe	In Indonesia, energy prices were increased between 1982 and 1985 by 20 to 50% a year. GDP growth rates were higher during the times of energy-price increases, compared with the preceding two years. CPI was stable during the first three years. It is estimated that a shortfall of 18.5% in government revenues was avoided thanks to the price reforms.	The loss of income resulting from subsidy reform ranged from 1 to 3%, with urban poor being the most affected.	

Note: Past studies should be used with caution as they were undertaken at a time Indonesia was an oil exporter.
Source: OECD based on Ellis (2010).

true benefit of reforms, as they do not account for non-material gains, such as improvement in the quality of life through better health outcomes.

The effect of a subsidy phase-out on international trade would vary across sectors. Given current resource endowments, it is likely that Indonesia would reduce its imports of kerosene and of automotive diesel fuel and increase its exports of natural gas.

Past experience points to a short-lived effect of an increase in energy prices on inflation (Figure 2.6). Back-of-the-envelope calculations suggest that a 50% increase in energy prices could automatically boost headline CPI inflation by a maximum of about 2-3 percentage points, reflecting the relatively small weight of energy in the price index.[15] This is a lower bound, however, as higher energy prices are likely to spread to transport and other energy-intensive sector costs as well as to wages. The mechanical effect is nonetheless not markedly different from was observed in the past, when about 20-40% of the rise in fuel prices passed into headline inflation, suggesting second-round effects are small.

Figure 2.6. **Effect of fuel price increase on monthly rates of inflation**

Per cent

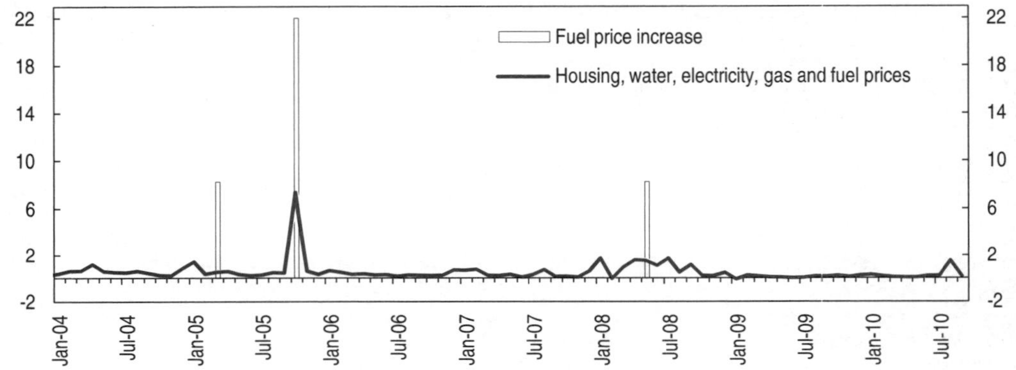

Source: MEI, BPS, Pallone (2009).

StatLink http://dx.doi.org/10.1787/888932341613

On the fiscal front, lowering the amount of fuel subsidies by one-fourth (this would correspond to a 15% rise in all subsidised energy prices) is estimated to generate savings of USD 2 billion per year (0.2% of GDP) (Agustina *et al.*, 2008). This decrease would also lower the public account's vulnerability to movements in international energy prices (Figure 2.7). Assuming no change in subsidy policy, the amount of fuel subsidies would exceed energy-related revenues when the oil price is above USD 110 per barrel. Lowering fuel subsidies by one-fourth would push this threshold to USD 135 per barrel, while a two-third decrease would insure that energy revenue are larger than subsidies even if the oil price were to reach USD 160 per barrel.

Even if energy subsidies are regressive, removing subsidies without any compensation entails the risk of an increase in poverty, as fuel spending represents about 5% of total spending of the poorest households. The effects of the reform on poverty will thus depend on the extent to which low-income households are compensated for the rise in prices and on the efficiency of such compensation policy. In the past, the Indonesian authorities have introduced compensation programmes to mitigate the loss of purchasing power. Lately, measures have targeted poor households (Table 2.3).

Figure 2.7. **Effect of a decrease in fuel subsidies on the differences between energy revenues and subsidies for different levels of oil price**

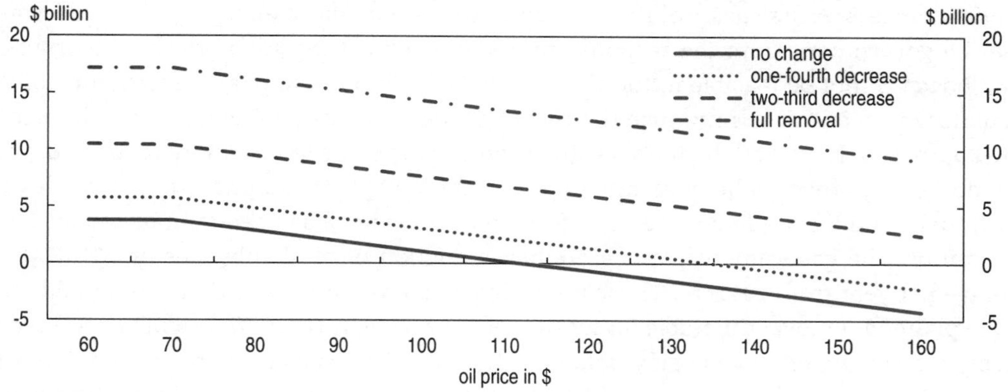

Note: Feed-back effects in the form of impact of rising price on household consumption are accounted for.
Source: Agustina *et al.* (2008) and OECD calculations.

Table 2.3. **Compensating programmes for fuel subsidy elimination**

Measures	2000	2001-04	March 2005	October 2005	2008
Cash transfers to poor households	●	●		●	●
Scholarships to finance education		●	●		
Health card for the poor		●	●		
Improving service quality in the transport sector		●			
Revolving funds for SMEs		●			
Clean water sanitation programme		●			
Support for elderly householders		●			
Empowerment programme for fisheries		●			
Scholarships for religious schools		●			

Source: OECD based on Adam and Lestari (2008).

On the environment side, the removal of energy subsidies, assuming that no other mitigation action is implemented, would markedly lower GHG emissions in Indonesia, as higher energy prices dampen energy use. Emission reductions could be doubled if multilateral action on removing subsidies is taken (Burniaux *et al.*, 2009). Alternative modelling assumptions could lead to more optimistic conclusions. Ministry of Finance (2009) reports that a full subsidy removal could double the gains in GDP and poverty reduction stemming from combining a USD 10 per tonne carbon tax and sales tax cuts.

Policy considerations

Phasing out oil and electricity tariffs would have a number of advantages. The resulting spare resources could be efficiently used through direct income support, for instance targeted cash transfers to protect low-income households from attendant energy-price rises. These transfers have been found to be more effective than subsidy policy in helping to boost incomes of the poorest segments of the population. Increasing subsidised energy prices would also facilitate the financing of additional spending on health, education and infrastructure (see Chapters 3 and 4), which are crucial to raising living standards in the longer term.

The Indonesian government is clearly aware of these issues and has expressed its intention to reform the system. A key to success will be to remove energy pricing from the political process. A first-best solution would be to fully liberalise energy prices. This would free the government from the responsibility of directly setting such prices. This solution may, however, not be feasible in the short term, as it would require a strengthening of the regulatory framework to minimise the risk of anti-competitive behaviour (see Chapter 3). The approach adopted by the Indonesian authorities appears to be a more realistic though second-best approach. The government joined the G20 pledge to phase out subsidies for fossil fuels, and a complete removal of fossil fuel subsidies has been announced for 2014. In addition, the government plans a gradual reduction of total subsidies by 10%-15% on average per year from 2011-14. These are welcome steps, and the authorities should stick to the planned removal timetable for fossil fuels. However, further effort will be required to deeply reform the energy-subsidy policy. As it stands, the current commitment could be met without making any change to electricity subsidies, which also entail significant economic, social and fiscal costs. Electricity subsidies are also detrimental to GHG-emission reductions to the extent that power is generated from coal-fired plants. Extending the current pledge to fully remove fossil-fuel subsidies by 2014 to a medium-term elimination of electricity subsidies would enhance the government's credibility and diminish uncertainties associated with *ad hoc* changes in electricity tariffs.

Subsidy reform must also go hand in hand with reform to establish a more rational structure of energy taxes. At the moment energy-related taxes are fairly small relative to total revenue collected. Greater emphasis on energy taxes could encourage a shift toward cleaner energy sources: the introduction of a carbon tax, as suggested in Ministry of Finance (2009), would go in the right direction. In addition to providing incentives for pollution abatement, it would also encourage innovation for new products and processes and reduce emission levels at a low economic cost as long as it is broad-based. Revenues from the carbon tax could be recycled to finance programmes in priority areas.

The vulnerability of the economy to oil-price developments could be further reduced by shifting the energy mix toward less-polluting sources of energy. The government has already taken measures to encourage the development of renewable energy, in particular geothermal power. A conversion programme from kerosene to LPG has also been implemented, with promising results. However, it is not clear whether the focus of current policies on certain energy sources, such as ethanol or biodiesel, is appropriate. Indeed, there is still a debate concerning the level of full-cycle energy savings associated with particular energy sources. When soil acidification, fertiliser use, biodiversity loss and toxicity of agricultural pesticides are taken into account, the overall harmful environmental impacts of ethanol and biodiesel can exceed those of petrol and mineral diesel (Doornbush and Steenblik, 2007). In the case of Indonesia, if palm oil is used for biodiesel production and palm-oil plantations are converted from forests the net environmental impacts are likely to be negative. The use of jatropha curcas in biodiesel production could be envisaged, but there is currently limited evidence on its energy efficiency and environmental impacts from a life cycle point of view.[16] There may be scope, however, for biodiesel to play a useful role in supplying energy in rural communities, where the cost of fossil fuel supply is high (Dillon *et al.*, 2008). Given the latest available knowledge on the development costs of biodiesel and ethanol and their life-cycle environmental impact, current support to ethanol and biodiesel needs to be reviewed.

As reforming energy subsidies would reduce the purchasing power of the poorest households, the authorities should introduce compensating measures that support their real incomes in more direct and effective ways. International experience shows that transition support must be well targeted, coherent with underlying broader policy settings of economies and carefully planned. Among all the available social policy tools, cash transfers present advantages. They distort markets and incentives less than other programmes, can be easily targeted and their cost is usually known with certainty. When properly implemented, most of the cash transfer funds can be channelled to the poor.[17] This would be a particularly relevant tool for Indonesia, which already has a long tradition of targeted cash-transfer programmes, using statistical information to identify beneficiaries. One obvious cost of this option is nonetheless that the large informal sector may discourage individuals from registering for the programme. Regarding electricity, another possible compensation measure would be to subsidise new connections for households that have no access to the grid.[18] This would complement the use of volume-differentiated tariffs for poor households that are already in place.

Handling the short-run social impacts of a dismantling of subsidies is challenging and has been the main reason for backlash against past reforms both in Indonesia and in other countries (OECD, 2006). Indeed, while the costs of subsidies are spread widely throughout the domestic economy, their benefits are concentrated disproportionately on certain segments of the population. The resistance to cutting subsidies can stem from: special interests with strong links to the political system (traditional rent-seeking behaviour); anxiety over the social consequences and dislocation from reform of subsidy programmes; "myths" surrounding either the need for subsidies or the costs of reform; absence of a well-accepted "justification" for reform (presumably relating to a lack of understanding of either costs of subsidies or benefits of reform). As a result, reforming energy subsidies in practice requires strong political will to take tough decisions that benefit society as a whole. The following approaches can help policymakers to overcome opposition to reforms (OECD, 2006 and 2007):

- Implementing reforms in a phased manner can help to soften the financial pain of those who will lose from the change and give them time to adapt. Nonetheless, the gradual removal of subsidies carries some drawbacks: the benefits are delayed, and the reforms run the risk of being reversed later.
- The role of transparency on subsidy objectives, impacts and costs is essential in motivating the reform process. Politicians need to disseminate information on the economic and fiscal costs of current subsidies in a transparent way. Indonesia appears to be more advanced than many other countries in this regard, as it explicitly records subsidies in the budget documents. However, very little information is currently publicly available on implicit subsidies that some firms may be granted through preferential treatment in production-sharing contracts in the oil sector (Koplow *et al.*, 2010). A National Energy Council (*Dewan Energi Nasional*) was set up in 2009 to analyse energy-policy issues.[19] Because of its composition there are reasons to believe that this body is not fully independent from the political process, despite its wide mandate and the partly democratic election of its governing board members. Moreover, the institution is still missing a balanced and transparent decision-making structure (Purra, 2010).
- As well, it will be important to rigorously estimate the overall benefits of subsidy reform and communicate them to the general public. In particular, an understanding of the

distribution of costs and benefits is essential to designing the optimal path of the reform process. OECD experience suggests that permanent and independent institutions to investigate the benefits of reforms often carry more weight than *ad hoc* working groups or commissions (Tompson and Dang, 2010). A well-known example is the Productivity Commission in Australia whose reports significantly influence the debate on reforms. Publishing specific subsidy reports and communicating broadly about the benefits of reforms in the media could also help raise public awareness.[20] In the case of Indonesia, these tasks could be conferred to an independent productivity commission. Such an institution could be created as a permanent body, which would be used subsequently to estimate the benefits of reforms in a wider range of areas.

- It is also very important to consult with stakeholders in formulating reforms. Co-opting opponents to reform in the decision making or mobilising counter-interests has been found to be successful in overcoming opposition to reforms, when the latter comes from private stakeholders.
- Policy coherence is a critical aspect of successful outcomes from subsidy reform. Indeed, whole-of-government partnerships are crucial, given the multidisciplinary nature of such reform.

Box 2.2. **Summary of policy recommendations: Energy subsidies**

- Stick to the commitment and the planned timetable to phase out fossil fuel subsidies by 2014 and extend the commitment to a medium-term removal of electricity subsidies.
- Introduce a carbon tax. Revenues from the carbon tax could be recycled to finance programmes in priority areas.
- Rely exclusively on targeted compensatory measures to protect low-income households from the rise in energy prices. These measures could take the form of cash transfers or subsidies to encourage connection to the electricity grid.
- Review support to biodiesel and ethanol.
- Mandate an independent productivity commission to investigate the size and costs of energy subsidies and the benefits of their removal, along with the associated distributional impacts, and disseminate the results broadly.
- Consult with stakeholders in formulating subsidy policy reforms and ensure policy coherence by involving all the Ministries dealing with energy subsidies.

Notes

1. The government also subsidises the cost of low-volume LPG cylinders (see Box 2.1), but the subsidy is small. Volumes are also low. In addition, the state-owned railway company receives a modest amount of subsidised fuel, but the total amount is small.
2. Another argument sometimes put forward is that kerosene subsidies help to slow the pace of deforestation. However, there is evidence, admittedly rather old, that the elasticity of demand for firewood with respect to the price of kerosene is very small in Java (Pitt, 1983).
3. The threshold amounts to 80% of the average household consumption and applies to customers consuming 6 600 volt-amperes (VA) and 10 500 VA of power. In January 2010, the state-owned electricity company proposed to lower this threshold to 50%, but so far this proposal has not been followed through.
4. For convenience, the economic price is the international commodity price. In Indonesia, it is set as the Mid Oil Platts Singapore price plus a factor to cover freight, taxes and margins for corporate

profit. The electricity subsidy is computed as the difference between the average sales prices (Rp/kwh) of each tariff category less the cost of electricity supplies multiplied by the electricity sales volume (kwh). The cost of electricity supplies is computed based on a formula, including the rate of transmission and distribution losses, which is determined by the Directorate General of Electricity and Energy Consumption in the Ministry of Energy and Mineral Resources.

5. This approach is much more narrowly defined than the WTO Agreement on Subsidies and Countervailing Measures (ASCM), as it does not cover producer subsidies, which are traditionally very hard to quantify. According to this Agreement, a "subsidy" exists when there is a public "financial contribution" that confers a "benefit". A "financial contribution" arises where: *i)* a government practice involves a direct transfer of funds (*e.g.* grants, loans, and equity infusion), potential direct transfers of funds or liabilities (*e.g.* loan guarantees); *ii)* government revenue that is otherwise due is foregone or not collected (*e.g.* fiscal incentives such as tax credits); *iii)* a government provides goods or services other than general infrastructure, or purchases goods; or *iv)* a government entrusts or directs a private body to carry out one or more of the above functions. A "benefit" is conferred when the "financial contribution" is provided to the recipient on terms that are more favourable than those that the recipient could have obtained from the market.

6. In 2006 the kerosene subsidy per litre was 202% of the sales price (after tax) as opposed to 27% for gasoline and 39% for diesel (Agustina *et al.*, 2008).

7. Tax expenditures are tax exemptions, preferential rates and other design features that differ from the standard tax regime.

8. This estimate includes the loss incurred by the state-owned enterprise *Petarmina*, which has been required to sell biofuels at the same price as subsidised petroleum fuels.

9. The firm bears the pre-production risk, and can recover its costs up to a specified limit of annual production. The remaining output is shared between the two parties at a pre-agreed production split in favour of the State.

10. A typical example of fraud would be to mix subsidised household fuel with other types to use the mixture for industrial purposes to avoid paying the unsubsidised price.

11. The central government's budgetary position is more exposed to a rise in energy prices than those of local governments, as it pays for all the subsidies, while receiving only part of the revenues. This vulnerability was particularly evident in 2007-08 when oil prices surged. By contrast, regions always benefit from a rise in oil prices through higher revenues.

12. Energy-related non-tax revenue amounted to about 15% of the total revenue collected in 2009. Income tax revenue from the energy sector represents 6% of total revenue and grants. Additional tax revenues from the sector come from a 10% VAT applied to all products and a 5% motor tax levied on the sale of gasoline and automotive diesel fuel.

13. In 2007, 39% of generated electricity came from coal, 25% from oil, 25% from gas, 10% from hydro-electric sources, and 3% from geothermal and other renewable-energy sources.

14. A low tax-inclusive carbon price is currently proposed relative to the prices that have applied in the European Union or that are planned in other countries. The carbon tax on fossil fuels would be set at IDR 80 000 per tonne of CO_2 (about USD 9) and rise at a rate of 5% (real) per year to 2020.

15. A weight of 4-5% has been used for this calculation. This range has been computed by using the weight of "housing and housing facility" (25%) in the CPI index, the share of consumption of "housing and housing facility" in household consumption (20% in 2008) and the share of electricity, gas and oil in "housing and housing facility" (around 20% according to Susenas).

16. Jatropha is a poisonous plant that can be cultivated in waste lands. Some studies have found that the production of jatropha-based biodiesel leads to less GHG emissions than diesel (see for instance Prueksakorn and Gheewala (2006) in the case of pilot plantations in Thailand). However, the variability of oil yields is found to be important and depends on the use of fertilisers or irrigation process. More research is necessary to get a good insight into the environmental sustainability of jatropha cultivation.

17. According to World Bank estimates, about 80% of the outlays under the US Food Stamps, the Brazilian Bolsa Familia or the Lithuania Social Benefit have benefited the poorest quintile of the population.

18. The current rate of electrification is low and estimated at around 60% in 2010. The government has announced a target to increase this ratio to 80% by 2014.

19. The Council was created by the 2007 Energy Law. It is mandated to design and formulate national energy policies; determine a master plan on national energy and responses to energy crisis and emergency conditions; and monitor the implementation of cross-sectoral policies on energy. The Council is composed of members of different ministries and the industry as well as academics and is currently headed by the former CEO of PLN. The Council is assisted by a Secretariat General headed by a Secretary-General appointed by the President. Expenses are funded by the State Budget.

20. Germany publishes bi-annual subsidy reports. Switzerland has implemented an online subsidy database.

Bibliography

Adam, L. and E. Lestari (2008), "Ten Years of Reforms: The Impact of an Increase in the Price of Oil on Welfare", *Journal of Indonesian Social Sciences and Humanities*, Vol. 1, pp. 121-139.

Agustina, C., J. Arze del Granado, T. Bulman, W. Fengler and M. Ikhsan (2008), "Black Hole or Black Gold? The Impact of Oil and Gas Prices on Indonesia's Public Finances", *World Bank Policy Research Working Paper*, No. 4718.

Bulman, T., W. Fengler and M. Ikhsan (2008), "Indonesia's Oil Subsidy Opportunity", *Far Eastern Economic Review*, June.

Burniaux, J.M., J. Chateau, R. Dellink, R. Duval and S. Jamet (2009), "The Economics of Climate Change Mitigation: How to Build the Necessary Global Action in a Cost-Effective Manner", *OECD Economics Department Working Paper*, No. 701.

Clement, B., H.-S. Jung and S. Gupta (2007), "Real and Distributive Effects of Petroleum Price Liberalization: The Case of Indonesia,"*Developing Economies*, Vol. 45(2), pp. 220-237.

Coady, D., R. Gillingham, R. Ossowski, J. Piotrowski, S. Tareq and J. Tyson (2010), "Petroleum Product Subsidies: Costly, Inequitable and Rising", *IMF Staff position note*, February.

Dillon, H.S., T. Laan and H. Setyaka Dillon (2008), "Biofuels: At What Cost? – Government Support for Ethanol and Biodiesel in Indonesia", *Global Subsidies Initiative of the International Institute for Sustainable Development*, Geneva.

Doornbush, R. and R. Steenblik (2007), "Biofuels: Is the Cure Worse than the Disease?", paper prepared for the OECD Round Table on Sustainable Development, September, Paris.

Ellis, J. (2010), "The Effect of Fossil-Fuel Subsidy Reform: A Review of Modelling and Empirical Studies", *Global Subsidies Initiative and International Institute for Sustainable Development Working Paper*, March.

Hope, E. and B. Singh (1995), "Energy Price Increases in Developing Countries", *World Bank Policy Research Paper*, No. 1442.

IEA (1999), *World Energy Outlook*, Paris.

IEA (2008a), *World Energy Outlook*, Paris.

IEA (2008b), *Energy Policy Review of Indonesia*, Paris.

Koplow, D., A. Jung, M. Thöne and L. Lontoh (2010), "Mapping the Characteristics of Producer Subsidies: A Review of Pilot Countries", *The Global Initiative Untold Billions: Fossil-Fuel Subsidies, the Impact and the Path to Reform*, August.

Ministry of Finance (2009), "Economic and Fiscal Policy Strategies for Climate Change Mitigation in Indonesia", Paper written in the context of the Australia Indonesia Partnership.

Morgan, T. (2007), "Energy Subsidies: Their Magnitude, How They Affect Energy Investment and Greenhouse Gas Emissions and Prospects for Reforms", *Report for UNFCCC Secretariat Financial and Technical Support Programme*, Bonn.

OECD (2006), *Subsidy Reform and Sustainable Development: Economic, Environmental and Social Aspects*, OECD publishing, Paris.

OECD (2007), *Subsidy Reform and Sustainable Development: Political Economy Aspects*, OECD publishing, Paris.

Pallone, M. (2009), "Indonesia's Oil Crisis: How Indonesia Became a Net Oil Importer", *Journal of International Policy Solution*, Winter.

Pitt, M. (1983), "Equity, Externalities and Energy Subsidies: The Case of Kerosene in Indonesia", *Center for Economic Research Discussion Paper*, No. 181, Washington, DC, August.

Prueksakorn, K. and S.H. Gheewala (2006), "Energy and Greenhouse Gas Implications of Biodiesel Production from Jatropha Curcas, L.", proceeding of the 2nd Joint International Conference on "Sustainable Energy and Environment (SEE 2006)", 21-23 November, Bangkok.

Purra, M. (2010), "The Indonesian Electricity Sector: Institutional Transition, Regulatory Capacity and Outcomes", Center on Asia and Globalisaton, National University of Singapore, Singapore.

Tompson, W. and T. Dang (2010), "Advancing Structural Reforms in OECD Countries", *OECD Economics Department Working Paper*, No. 758.

World Bank (2006), *Making the New Indonesia Work for the Poor*, Washington, DC.

World Bank (2010), *Indonesia Economic Quarterly: Looking Forward*, World Bank Office, Jakarta.

Chapter 3

Tackling the infrastructure challenge

Indonesia's infrastructure is in poor shape, having suffered from protracted under-investment since the Asian financial crisis of the late 1990s, and constraints growth potential. This chapter focuses on the current state of the regulatory framework and discusses different options for improvement in order to attract needed private investment. It recognises the ambitious reforms undertaken by the government thus far, but suggests that further efforts are needed. The authorities should establish a simple regulatory environment based on effective regulatory agencies resulting in lower regulatory uncertainty and realign prices to cost-recovery levels.

Boosting infrastructure will be key to raising Indonesia's long-term prospects in the years to come. Following the 1997-98 crisis, public and private investment in infrastructure plummeted from around 5-6% of GDP to about 1% of GDP in 2000 (World Bank, 2007). Although it has since increased to around 3.5% of GDP, the current rate of investment is insufficient to raise the GDP growth rate to the government's target range of 7.0-7.7% in 2014.

As a result of a decade of under-investment Indonesia's infrastructure is in dire condition. Road congestion poses significant problems and electricity supply has not kept pace with growing demand, resulting in frequent power outages. Retail tariffs for most infrastructure services are below cost-recovery levels, especially in power and water supply, thereby discouraging new investment. Land-acquisition procedures for infrastructure projects remain cumbersome and have significantly slowed down the extension of the road network.

The government is well aware of the stakes involved in improving infrastructure and has made it one its main policy priorities. In its Medium Term Development Plan 2010-14, it announced plans to invest IDR 1 429 trillion (USD 157 billion, around 25% of GDP in 2009) from 2010 to 2014 in infrastructure, of which around 64% would be privately financed. To entice private investment and close the financing gap, Indonesia needs to build on recently undertaken reforms and further improve the regulatory framework.

This chapter describes the state of Indonesia's infrastructure and compares the regulatory framework in different sectors with those of OECD countries. It then deals with issues in selected sectors, namely road transport, sea transport, electricity, telecommunications and water and sanitation.

The state of infrastructure

Indonesia has under-invested in infrastructure for about a decade, reflecting, *inter alia*, sharp capital spending cuts implemented in the wake of the Asian crisis, low private participation and administrative capacity constraints (World Bank, 2007). This has resulted in deteriorating infrastructure quality and quantity. The rise in the size of Indonesia's infrastructure sector from 2003 to 2008 is totally attributable to the telecommunications industry, which has benefitted from regulatory reforms started earlier than in the other sectors and now represents a much larger share of output than in the average OECD country (Figure 3.1). Excluding telecommunications, the shortfall with the OECD in terms of the value added share in transport, electricity and water actually increased during the period.

With the exception of its mobile cellular network, Indonesia is lagging far behind in infrastructure stocks compared to the OECD and regional peers (Table 3.1). The gap in access to the internet and mobile and fixed-line subscriptions with Southeast Asia and the OECD appears to have narrowed as has, to a lesser extent, that in electric power consumption. However, the divide has widened with respect to access to improved sanitation facilities and water sources, quality of roads, and fixed broadband and

Figure 3.1. **Size of infrastructure sectors**[1]

Sector share of GDP

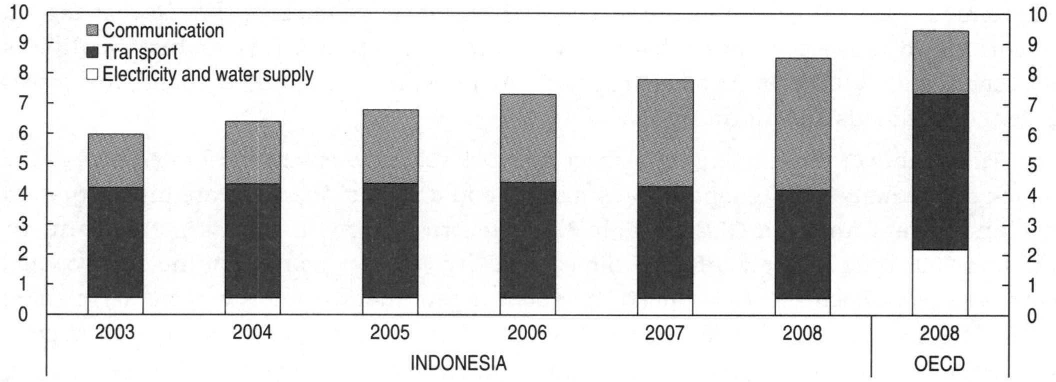

1. The figures for electricity and water supply sectors are aggregated, as many OECD members do not report separate figures. In Indonesia, water supply is the smallest among all infrastructure sectors, accounting for a stable share of GDP (0.5%) from 2003 to 2008. The share of the electricity remained at less than 1% of GDP during the same period. OECD excludes Chile, Israel, Mexico, Slovenia and Turkey.

Source: *STAN Database* and *BPS*.

StatLink http://dx.doi.org/10.1787/888932341632

Table 3.1. **Selected infrastructure indicators**

	Indonesia			Southeast Asia[1]	OECD[2]
	1995	2000	2008[3]	2008[3]	2008[3]
Water and sanitation					
Improved sanitation facilities (% of population with access)	51	52	52	83.3	99.9
Improved water source (% of population with access)	74	77	80	95.5	99.6
Energy and transport					
Electric power consumption (kWh per capita)	271.6	402.3	566.0	1 759.2	9 871.4
Electric power transmission and distribution losses (% of output)	11.7	10.9	10.6	7.9	5.9
Roads, paved (% of total roads)	52.4	57.1	55.4	79.8	79.0
Information and communication technologies					
Fixed broadband subscribers (per 100 people)	..	0.002	0.176	2.5	25.0
International Internet bandwidth (bits per person)	..	1.2	34.9	2 375.5	19 342.6
Internet users (per 100 people)	0.03	0.93	7.9	27.5	71.1
Personal computers (per 100 people)	0.5	1.0	2.0	13.3	69.9
Fixed broadband Internet access tariff (USD per month)	..	..	21.7	19.7	30.4
Mobile and fixed-line telephone subscribers (per 100 people)	1.8	5.0	74.9	98.0	149.5
Mobile cellular subscriptions (per 100 people)	0.1	1.8	61.6	86.4	103.4

1. Unweighted average of Malaysia, Thailand, Philippines and Vietnam.
2. OECD excludes Chile, Israel, Mexico, Poland, Slovenia and Turkey.
3. 2008 or latest available year.

Source: World Bank (*World Development Indicators*).

international internet bandwidth. Also, the efficiency of the electricity transmission and distribution network declined from 2000 to 2008. Power outages have also become more frequent in recent years since generation capacity has not kept pace with the growth in demand. Of particular concern is the state of the water and sanitation sector. It features poor access and service quality. The percentage of households connected to improved water sources and sanitation is low not only in comparison to OECD standards but also to regional peers.

Indonesia also compares poorly in terms of the quality of infrastructure, though the latter is notoriously hard to gauge. The Global Competitiveness Report of the World Economic Forum 2010-11 ranks Indonesia 82nd out of some 140 countries in that regard. According to these perception-based indicators, the gap in infrastructure quality as compared with Southeast Asia is particularly manifest in roads and ports and, to a lesser extent, in railroads and air transport.

The quality of the existing infrastructure stock seems to have deteriorated because of a lack of adequate maintenance. Transmission and distribution losses are higher than in regional peers and the OECD (Table 3.1). Electricity brown-outs are frequent. In autumn 2009 they severely affected the capital city, Jakarta, prompting the state-owned company *Perusahaan Listrik Negara* (PLN) to start urgent maintenance works. A large share of roads is also not in good condition. In 2006 the share of roads classified either as in good or medium condition, as opposed to damaged or heavily damaged, was 82% for national roads, 54% for provincial roads and 47% for district roads. As around 90% of the road network is under the responsibility of provincial or district authorities, only around 51% of all roads were in medium or good condition in that year (Figure 3.2). As regards water supply, non-revenue water (*i.e.* water that does not generate revenues, either because lost or stolen) is for many water-supply establishments well above 50% (Godman, 2005). In Jakarta, which has one of the most efficient water supply networks in the country, non-revenue water was still 50% in 2008 (Lanti *et al.*, 2009).

Figure 3.2. **Quality of national, provincial and district roads, 2006**[1]

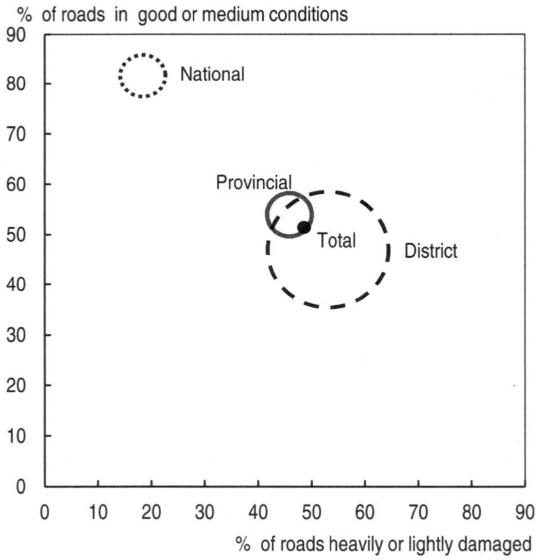

1. The size of the empty circles is proportional to the share of the total road network under the responsibility of the different levels of government.

Source: Ministry of Public Works.

StatLink http://dx.doi.org/10.1787/888932341651

A study by the Asian Development Bank estimated the maintenance costs for rural roads, irrigation and water infrastructure to be about 5% of the original investment annually (ADB, 2009). The collection of such a maintenance fee appears to be financially feasible in many communities and is already used for some water-supply projects.

There is evidence that the lack and poor quality of infrastructure are holding back investment and economic growth. A survey of Japanese foreign affiliates ranks underdeveloped infrastructure as the most important barrier to investment in the Indonesian manufacturing sector and the third most important in services (JETRO, 2009). In a survey by the Regional Autonomy Watch 27% of surveyed firms have identified infrastructure as the most important local constraints on their business activities (KPPOD, 2008).[1] The theoretical and empirical literature suggests that the positive effect of infrastructure on growth tends to be higher in less developed counties (Box 3.1). Therefore, Indonesia has potentially much to gain from improving its infrastructure.

Box 3.1. **Infrastructure and economic growth**

Although empirical estimates of the relationship between infrastructure and economic growth vary considerably, the consensus in the literature seems to have settled on the hypothesis that the impact of the former on the latter is positive and inversely related to the degree of economic development (Estache and Fay, 2007; Straub, 2008). The literature has identified several channels through which infrastructure might impact on growth, but their relative importance is unclear (Agénor and Moreno-Dodson, 2006):

- **Higher productivity of private inputs:** this effect results from the complementarity between inputs. In this case, a larger stock of infrastructure will increase the productivity of other inputs (Albala-Bertrand and Mamatzakis, 2004).
- **Higher private capital formation:** by raising the productivity of capital, along with that of the other private inputs, infrastructure is likely to increase marginal rates of return and private investment.
- **Lower adjustment costs of private capital:** this allows firms to adjust their capital stock to its optimal level in response to any shock.
- **Increasing the durability of private capital:** expanding and maintaining the quality of infrastructure might enhance the longevity and productivity of private capital and lower the maintenance costs of machinery and equipments.
- **Indirect positive effects on labour productivity:** better transport and communications infrastructure reduces commuting time, allowing workers to be geographically more mobile and productive.
- **Improving health and education outcomes and magnification of their impact on growth:** access to basic infrastructure impacts positively on education and health status; piped water and basic sanitation contribute to lower mortality and morbidity rates, especially among children, whereas electricity improves health and hygiene by lowering the costs of boiling water and cooking, in addition to improving educational outcomes (Warwick and Doig, 2004; Saghir, 2005).
- **Increasing the volume of trade:** Bougheas *et al.* (1999) show the stock of infrastructure and the volume of trade are positively related. Limão and Venables (2001) find that infrastructure is an important determinant of transport costs and conclude that poor infrastructure accounts for much of the different transport costs observed in coastal and landlocked countries. Djankov *et al.* (2006) find that each additional day of delay in shipping a cargo abroad reduces trade by more than 1%. Donaldson (2008) shows that the development of Indian railroads from 1861 to 1930 raised real income and welfare by allowing regions to specialise in their comparative advantage sectors and increasing trade among them.

Most delivery of infrastructure services has been corporatised, although the State still retains a major role in infrastructure development by providing services through Persero (*i.e.* profit earning and state-owned) enterprises. Many Perseros were created in the 1990s, and the performance of some of them has improved significantly since then to the point of not requiring government support anymore, as in telecommunications. By contrast, in many sectors, such as electricity and ports, SOEs have been unable to invest the necessary resources to improve the infrastructure network, even sometimes to maintain it. Furthermore, excluding telecommunications and toll roads, the level of competition in infrastructure sectors is still limited because of the regulatory environment, which has deterred private investment (OECD, 2010).

Infrastructure quality varies considerably across and within provinces with some of best districts being in East Java and the worst in North Sumatra (KPPOD, 2008). Decentralisation may have exacerbated differences in infrastructure services at local level. Local governments are now responsible for the provision of some infrastructure services, such as roads, water and sanitation, without however having the necessary planning and financing instruments to deliver them (KPPOD, 2008). The dramatic differences in infrastructure services across districts highlights that good performance is not always related to financial or natural endowments, but is primarily the result of sound political leadership and administrative capacities at local level.

Financing investment in infrastructure

Public spending and efficiency

After having collapsed in the wake of the Asian crisis, public spending on infrastructure increased in the last ten years, although it remains well below its pre-crisis levels. From 2000 to 2009 public spending on infrastructure increased from 0.8 to around 1.7% of GDP, although most of the increase took place before 2006 (Figure 3.3).

Figure 3.3. **Public infrastructure spending**

Percentage of GDP

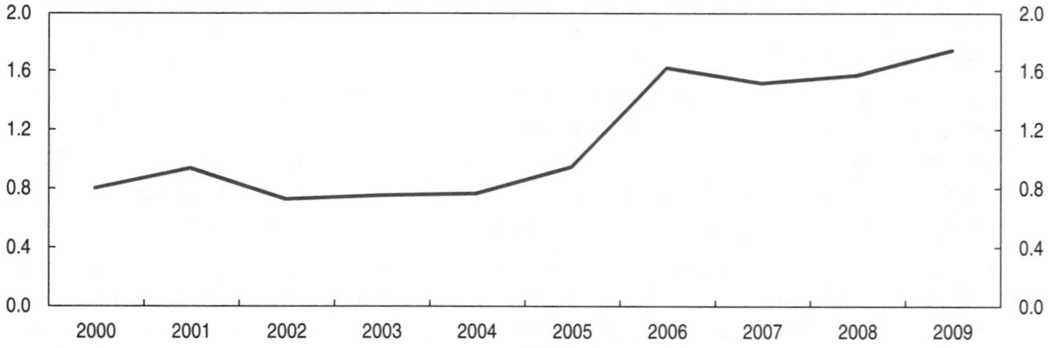

Source: Ministry of Finance and OECD calculations.

A large share of government's infrastructure budget is allocated to individual ministries (85% in 2009). The remaining part is spent on various programmes and funds not tied to any particular ministry, such as the Land Capping Fund and the Special Allocation Fund (*Dana Alokasi Khusus* or DAK).[2] The Ministries of Public Works and of

Transportation are responsible for most public spending in infrastructure channelled through ministries (40% and 19% in 2009, respectively).

The current allocation of responsibilities for infrastructure development is split among different ministries and agencies without any clear hierarchical authority. This arrangement is inefficient, as no agency provides the necessary degree of coordination, leadership and expertise to plan, execute and roll out infrastructure projects in a timely manner (Purra, 2010). The Ministry of Finance allocates the infrastructure budget to several other ministries. The Co-ordinating Ministry for Economic Affairs is supposed to coordinate overlapping activities, as in infrastructure projects, whereas the Ministry of National Development and Planning (Bappenas) is responsible for general development, planning policies and policy formulation. Lack of coordination and capacity is one of the reasons why the infrastructure budget is often under-spent, with spending concentrated at the end of the year. The government has tried to overcome this problem by creating inter-ministerial agencies, such as the National Committee for the Acceleration of Infrastructure Provision (KKPPI) and the National Energy Council, for energy policy (see Chapter 2), which should offer independent and expert advice on their areas of responsibility and improve coordination among other agencies. However, their lack of concrete powers to shape policies and make decisions, and their insufficient independence from line ministries, has jeopardised their effectiveness.

Co-ordination among the different ministries and agencies responsible for infrastructure development needs to be improved, either by giving more effective coordinating powers to the Coordinating Ministry for Economic Affairs or to Bappenas or by creating a new agency directly responsible for infrastructure development. In 2008, Australia established an agency, Infrastructure Australia, to coordinate infrastructure development by advising central and local governments on priorities and possible financing mechanisms. Although it is too early to evaluate it, its establishment signals the need to tackle the challenge of building and renewing infrastructure with innovative policy solutions so as to prioritise projects and overcome coordination problems.

In addition to low infrastructure spending in comparison with the country's needs, Indonesia suffers from persistent under-spending of budget resources allocated to infrastructure. Due to a lack of effective multi-year budgeting for investment projects, capital outlays tend to be concentrated at the end of the fiscal year, creating uncertainties regarding the successful completion of infrastructure projects spanning several fiscal years. Since 2003, a Medium-Term Expenditure Framework allows for multi-year budget appropriations and is scheduled to be implemented in 2011, with the first year being binding. The authorities should concentrate on using this framework to improve multi-year budget appropriations for infrastructure projects so as to avoid chronic under-spending and making spending more consistent over time.

Whereas several measures have already been taken to attract private investment in the sector (see below), their effects may take some time to materialise. At the same time, raising the amount of infrastructure investment the government intends to finance from 2010 to 2014 by even 10 or 20% per year will not have a dramatic effect on the budget. This suggests there could be the fiscal space to increase the public investment share from 36% to more than 40%. Considering OECD *Economic Outlook* projections for 2010 to 2012 and a nominal GDP growth rate of 12% per year from 2013 onwards, increasing public infrastructure investment by 20% from 2011 to 2014 will add around

0.2 percentage point to the yearly deficit-to-GDP ratio projected by the Medium Term Development Plan 2010-14 (Figure 3.4). This is probably an upward estimate as it ignores the direct effect of public infrastructure spending on GDP. To give an order of magnitude, the additional investment could be almost fully financed by the budget savings resulting from lowering fuel subsidies by about one-fourth (see Chapter 2).

Figure 3.4. **Central government budget deficit**[1]

Percentage of GDP

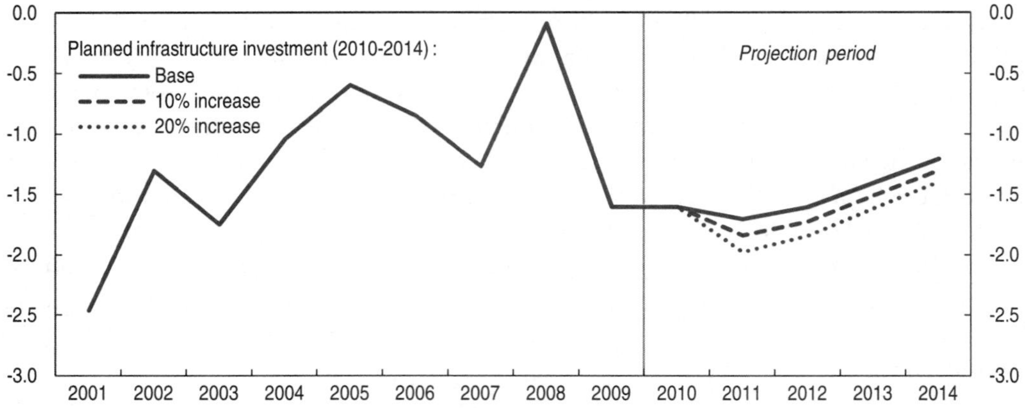

1. Scenarios are based on the assumption of a nominal GDP growth rate of 14.9, 16.4 and 14.2% per year for 2010, 2011 and 2012, and 12% for 2013 and 2014.

Source: Medium Term Development Plan, Ministry of Finance and OECD calculations.

The urgent need to launch new infrastructure projects should not come at the expense of maintaining and improving the existing infrastructure stock. Greater focus on maintenance is needed. However, maintenance expenses vary considerably across sectors and time according to demand and other sector characteristics. Sector studies are required to gauge the maintenance expenditure needed to preserve the quality of the existing infrastructure stock and to allocate budget resources accordingly.

Extent of private participation

The increase in infrastructure investment as laid out in the Medium Term Development Plan relies significantly on private financing. If the private sector has to cover around 64% of the planned investment spending over the 2010-14 period, it will need to sign around USD 20 billion of investment commitments each year. This figure is well above the peak PPPs reached in 1996 and highlights the scale of the challenge ahead (Figure 3.5).

Data on PPPs in Indonesia show that the number and investment commitments of PPPs collapsed after the Asian crisis, but have recovered in recent years. Before 1998 Indonesia used to attract more PPPs than its regional peers. After the crisis and the devaluation of the *rupiah* the number and value of PPPs plummeted. Subsequently, they started to recover in the middle of the decade, in response to improved macroeconomic conditions, ample liquidity in international markets, and a friendlier environment for private investment in infrastructure, as underlined in the OECD's *2008 Economic Assessment*.

The breakdown of PPPs by sector varies over time, with telecommunications accounting for the bulk of investment commitments. The share of energy is also

Figure 3.5. **Value and number of PPP projects over time**[1]

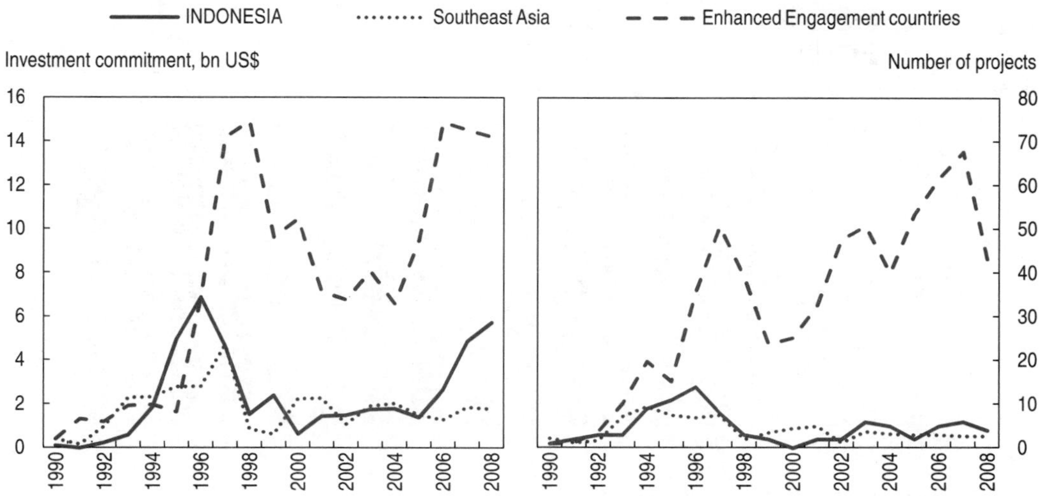

1. Southeast Asia refers to Malaysia, Thailand, Philippines and Vietnam; Enhanced Engagement countries refer only to Brazil, China, India and South Africa.

Source: World Bank and PPIAF (*PPI Project Database*).

StatLink http://dx.doi.org/10.1787/888932341670

important, particularly when measured in terms of number of projects (Figure 3.6). After the Asian crisis, PPPs concentrated even more on energy and telecommunications, whereas transport, because of land acquisition problems, and, to a larger extent, water and sewerage played more modest roles. Strong PPPs' investment commitments in telecommunications reflected a small number of large private investment projects.

PPPs present a number of advantages. They can potentially allow for an efficient allocation of risks to the party that is best able to manage them and draw on private project management expertise. In addition, they might allow governments to fund more infrastructure projects than traditional public capital spending allows, but this must not come at the expense of transparent fiscal accounting and a comprehensive disclosure of all fiscal risks (Box 3.2). However, PPPs achieve cost savings with respect to traditional public procurement methods only if their efficiency gains exceed their higher financing and transaction costs. The question on the long-run efficiency of PPPs has not been settled as, to date, insufficient research has been conducted (Hodge and Greve, 2009). PPPs' efficiency is likely to vary on case-by-case basis. A Public Private Partnership Center Unit and a Project Development Facility have been created in Indonesia, within the infrastructure inter-ministerial committee KKPPI and Bappenas respectively, as centres of technical expertise in project preparation.

The decision on which projects to finance with PPPs is fraught with difficulties. As stated in the *OECD Principles for Private Sector Participation in Infrastructure*, the choice between public and private provision should be based on cost-benefit analysis, taking into account all alternative modes of delivery, the full system of infrastructure provision, and the projected financial and non-financial costs and benefits over the project lifecycle (OECD, 2007). All risks need to be accounted for, and contingent liabilities in this respect should be included in cost-benefit analyses.

Value-for-money tests are admittedly difficult, and the experience of some developed countries with them has been far from satisfactory.[3] The international experience shows

Figure 3.6. **Sector share of total investment commitments and number of projects**

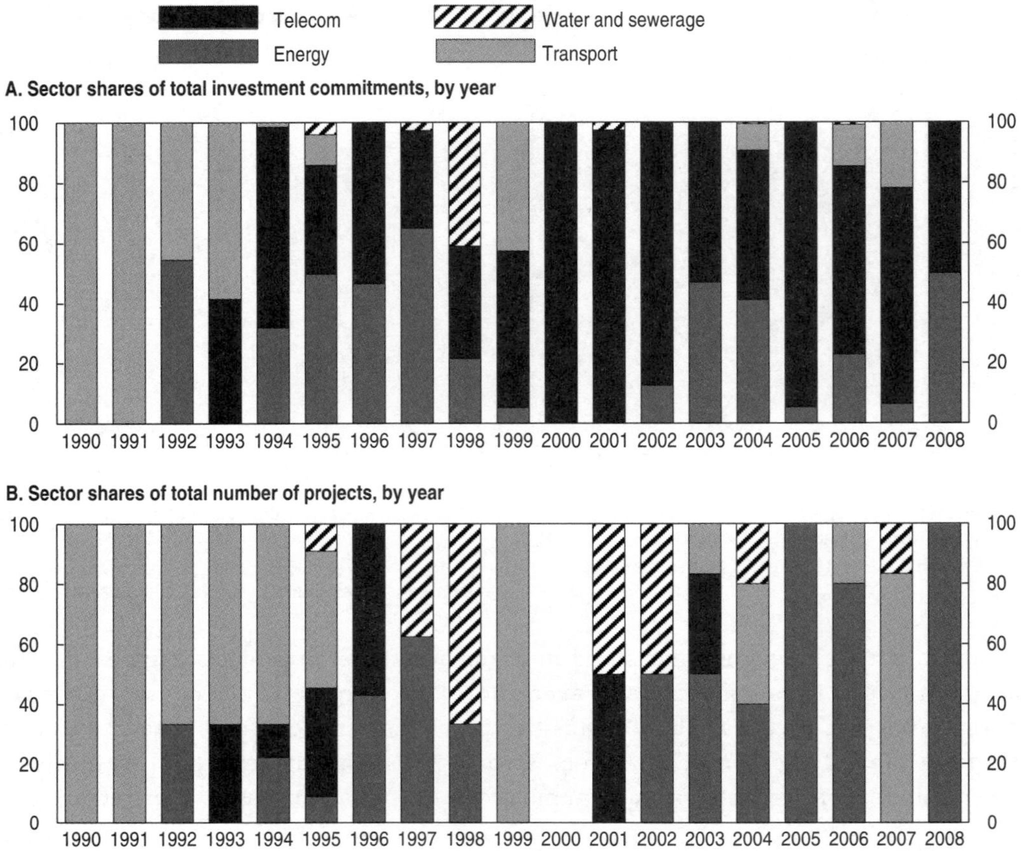

Note: The yearly number of projects is based on their financial closure year. Total investment commitments refer to projects whose financial closure is the same year or before.

Source: World Bank and PPIAF (*PPI Project Database*).

StatLink http://dx.doi.org/10.1787/888932341689

that, to be effective, value-for-money tests should be undertaken rigorously, without any bias in favour of any form of financing, and reflect the actual allocation of risks between parties. In addition, policy makers need to focus on the concept of "absolute affordability" of PPP projects. This refers to the threshold beyond which even projects offering good value for money may exceed budget constraints, thereby impairing long-term fiscal conditions (Posner *et al.*, 2009). This obviously calls for an appropriate treatment in the budget of all liabilities generated by PPPs.

The current legislation on the procurement process of PPPs in infrastructure requires the government to observe due diligence and focus on fiscal sustainability. Importantly, the legislation specifies that the government will not provide any blanket guarantee and that risks will be allocated to public and private parties on a case-by-case basis. In 2006, the Ministry of Finance specified that the government can cover the following risks:

- Political risk: related to unilateral action of the government, such as expropriation of assets, amendments to legislation, prohibition of fund repatriation and restrictions on currency conversion.
- Project performance risk: this is related to delay in or increased costs of land acquisition and changes by the government in project specifications.

Box 3.2. **Public Private Partnerships**

A fundamental difference between PPPs and public financing is their respective budget treatment. Broadly speaking, with the former, debt is incurred by the private sector, whereas with the latter the public sector incurs it, although accounting treatments vary substantially across countries. Reviewing the use of PPP practices in eight OECD countries (Australia, France, Hungary, Korea, Portugal, the United Kingdom, the United States and Chile) Posner *et al.* (2009) note how budget pressures were the prime reason for starting to use PPPs, at least in some of the countries. PPPs, however, can sometimes be used to simply circumvent spending controls and move debts off the balance sheet. In this case, the government is likely to bear most of the project risks and face potentially large liabilities in the medium-long term. In general, PPPs should not come at the expense of transparent fiscal accounting and a comprehensive disclosure of all fiscal risks. There are not universally accepted fiscal accounting and reporting standards for PPPs. Posner *et al.* (2009) suggest some measures on how to strengthen the budgetary review and deliberation processes for PPPs. These include:

- The upfront funding should be established for all PPP commitments in the budget-making process to make policy makers aware of the full cost consequences of their decisions.
- The upfront funding for PPP commitments should compete for limited budget resources with other competing claims so as to force decision makers to compare PPP costs and benefits with other programmes.
- All PPPs should be fully recorded in the budget, even if projects are deemed to be off balance sheet.
- The process for evaluating PPPs should be strengthened by defining explicit criteria to gauge affordability and conduct value-for-money reviews.
- Limits on the total level of PPP commitments undertaken in a given year can be used to assess affordability of PPPs. Limits can be measured on the basis of total net present value of long-term costs and/or total annual payments for approved projects.
- Government guarantees should be estimated at the time commitments are authorised. Accrual-based approaches to measure guarantees should be considered. Limits on total guarantees should also be explored.
- Strengthening longer-term budget frameworks could provide a more informed basis for evaluating the long-term affordability of PPP projects. Modelling long-term fiscal outlooks is the first step. Authorities should also consider developing their near- and medium-term fiscal targets consistently with the longer-term outlook.
- Full disclosure on future payment obligations for PPPs should be provided in budget documents. The United Kingdom and Portugal are two good examples of such transparency.

- Demand risk: where the realised revenue is lower than the minimum forecast revenue because of lower demand.

To manage such risks in a consistent framework, the government established the Indonesia Infrastructure Guarantee Fund (IGF) in 2009. It offers guarantees for government obligations for PPPs upon payment of a fee by the operator. It has been set up as a SOE with an initial capital of IDR 1 trillion, provided by the government, with additional capital expected to be injected by multilateral agencies and international donors. It will be commercially run with the objective of achieving an investment-grade rating. One of the main benefits of the IGF is that it will ring-fence government obligations arising from PPP projects. It will work as government's single window for appraising projects, structuring guarantees and processing claims. Moreover, IGF is expected to enhance the creditworthiness of insured infrastructure companies, thus allowing them to obtain private financing at more convenient terms. Its detailed operating procedures have yet to be established.

The government needs to pay special attention to demand-side risks, which is one form the government may guarantee. Assuming demand risks may have the advantage of creating a premium on bid prices. However, there could be a tendency to overestimate future demand to enhance the value of certain projects. This practice may impair the financial viability of the project in the long term and saddle the government with expensive compensation in the future. To diminish the likelihood of this occurrence, the government could rely on technical advisors to provide conservative and independent demand forecasts. This could limit the degree to which bidders can use overly optimistic demand assumptions in their project proposals and reduce opportunistic behaviour leading to contract renegotiation (APEC, 2009).

The lack of long-tenor local currency debt has been a major deterrent of private investment in infrastructure. Commercial banks, which are the main source of finance in Indonesia, are generally unable to provide long-term loans as a large share of their deposits has short maturity, one month or less, and lack the experience in assessing the creditworthiness of infrastructure projects. Indonesia authorities have long recognised this problem and taken steps to improve the situation. Recently, the government, in cooperation with the Asian Development Bank, the International Financial Corporation and the German Development Cooperation Agency, has set up the PT Indonesia Infrastructure Finance (IIF) with an initial equity capital of USD 60 million, plus additional USD 100 million of subordinated loans from the World Bank and Asian Development Bank each. IIF is a non-bank financial institution that will operate on a commercial basis and whose goal is to channel domestic private finance towards infrastructure projects. It will borrow from local institutional investors and banks looking for long-term placements delivering higher returns than sovereign and large corporate offerings and provide *rupiah*-denominated finance to creditworthy infrastructure projects. Its good credit rating will allow the IFF to borrow an estimated USD 2.7 billion (IDR 25 trillion) from the debt market. It will also provide advisory service to identify bankable projects and develop the infrastructure sector in general. In addition to channelling long-tenor local funds to long-term investments, IIF may help deepen Indonesian capital markets at long maturities through the issuance of long-dated and high-quality securities, which currently there is dearth of. Local currency financing is an especially welcome development as it will eliminate the exchange rate risk.

Comparing Indonesia's regulatory framework with OECD countries

A sound regulatory framework is of utmost importance for the development of infrastructure. Infrastructure investments are typically large and long lived and, as a result, uncertainty plays a disproportionate role in firms' investment decisions. Therefore, lower regulatory uncertainty and credible policy commitments on the part of the government are likely to result in higher private investment (Box 3.3). These include the presence of independent regulators, appropriate price regulations, calls for tender and permission, and FDI restrictions.

This section relies on information collected through an Infrastructure Investment Questionnaire sent to OECD national authorities in winter 2008 (Égert *et al.*, 2009). The

Box 3.3. Regulatory environment and infrastructure outcomes

The theoretical and empirical literature on the relationship among infrastructure regulations, uncertainty and infrastructure outcomes is scarce. However, the available evidence broadly suggests that a sound institutional setting improves infrastructure outcomes. Esfahani and Ramirez (2003) show in a growth model how institutions that lend credibility and effectiveness to government policies (*i.e.* low risks of contract repudiation) matter for infrastructure growth. Andres *et al.* (2007) report, for Latin America, that regulatory structure, framework and quality matter for aligning costs and tariffs, dissuading renegotiations, and improving productivity, quality of service, coverage, and tariffs. Henisz (2002), using a two-century-long panel dataset, shows that regulatory settings limiting abrupt policy changes, thereby reducing regulatory uncertainty, explain cross-national variation in the initial year of infrastructure adoption and infrastructure's subsequent rate of growth. Henisz and Zelner (2001) report that variation in the checks and balances on executive discretion, which arguably lead to credible policy commitments, explains the rates of basic telecommunications infrastructure across countries from 1960 to 1994. Serven (1997), employing a large cross-country time-series dataset of African countries, finds a negative association between investment performance and instability measures and concludes that uncertainty is an important factor explaining Africa's poor investment record. Keefer (1996) maintains that the high construction profits earned on Spanish railroads in the mid-nineteenth century arose as a consequence of poor credibility by the part of the State. The risk of government intervention was a strong incentive for investors to secure high rates of return in the construction process.

same questionnaire was sent to Indonesian authorities in autumn 2009. The information contained in the questionnaire needs to be interpreted with caution. Whereas it is likely to capture the *de jure* regulatory framework, it says little as regards the *de facto* situation. Stern (2007) underlines that what shapes the actual regulatory environment are the decisions of authorities, which in turn may or not discourage private investors. In addition, infrastructure regulation is complex since it has repercussion on several domains, such as pricing, service quality and environmental impact. Several OECD countries have adopted some form of regulatory impact analysis, to evaluate the effects and trade-offs of infrastructure regulation, although their full implementation can be administratively and technically challenging (OECD, 2009).

Sectoral regulator

The drive of the government to enhance the regulatory framework for infrastructure is evident from the "Infrastructure Policy Package" issued in 2006. The main objectives were to increase competition, eliminate discriminatory practices and unbundle the government's roles as policy-maker, regulator and service provider. Based on these principles, successive Indonesian governments have established a number of regulatory authorities, but not in all infrastructure sectors (Table 3.2). In particular, there is no independent authority regulating electricity, water supply and railway transport. This is in contrast with the vast majority of OECD countries, where regulatory authorities are more widespread (Box 3.4). In Indonesia, authorities for road, water and air transport are not independent from the executive branch of government (Table 3.3). This differs from OECD countries, where regulatory agencies are more often than not independent from the government.

Table 3.2. Presence of at the least one regulatory authority

	Indonesia	OECD countries[1]
Electricity	**No**	96%
Gas	Yes	96%
Water supply	**No**	84%
Railway transportation	**No**	92%
Road transportation	Yes	68%
Water transportation	Yes	76%
Air transportation	Yes	92%
Telecommunications	Yes	100%

1. Percentage of OECD countries that replied positively to the questionnaire (25 countries).
Source: OECD Infrastructure Questionnaire.

Box 3.4. The establishment of regulatory authorities

The most remarkable change in the infrastructure regulatory framework over the last 15 years has been the establishment of regulatory authorities in both developed and developing countries. More than 200 infrastructure regulatory entities have been created, not all of them autonomous from the government (Stern, 2007). Independence from the executive has generally come to be seen as an important requirement of effective regulatory entities, although not the only one. According to Melody (1997) independence means autonomy to execute policy and verifying its compliance without obstruction and undue interference from politicians or industry operators. This involves building the necessary skills to make impartial and informed decisions to achieve the stated policy objectives and to be accountable. Other characteristics as legitimacy and credibility are important elements of effective regulatory entities. Cubbin and Stern (2006) find, in a sample of developing countries, that even non-independent regulatory authorities established by a regulatory law, rather than government decrees, are associated with around 15-20% higher electricity generation capacity in the long term.

Recent trends suggest the number of independent regulatory authorities has been growing both in developed and developing countries. The independent regulatory agency model has become the standard recommended solution to the private investment problem in infrastructure sectors just as it is a way to handle commitment and time-inconsistency problems in monetary policy (Levine *et al.*, 2003). Estache and Goicoechea (2005) report that by 2004 around 64% of LDCs had established some kind of independent regulatory agency in telecommunications, 56% in electricity and 21% in water. Growing empirical evidence supports the hypothesis that higher-quality governance elements usually associated with independent regulators result in better industry performance. Cubbin and Stern (2006) – studying the reforms of the electricity sector in 28 developing economies from 1980 to 2001 – report that higher-quality regulatory framework is associated with 25-35% long-term increase in per-capita generation capacity. Gutierrez (2003) constructs an index of regulatory governance for telecommunications, in a sample of Latin American and Caribbean countries from 1980 to 1997, capturing the presence of a separate regulatory authority and its roles. He finds that a one percentage point increase in the index raises fixed mainlines per 100 inhabitants by about 20%. Also, the sequencing of regulatory reform appears to matter. Wallsten (2002) finds that establishing separate regulatory authorities prior to privatisation results in higher telecommunications investment, fixed telephone and cellular penetration. Moreover, investors are willing to pay higher prices for telecommunications firms in countries already having a regulatory body. This is consistent with the hypothesis that investors require a risk premium to invest, where regulatory rules remain unclear.

Table 3.3. **Independence of the regulatory authority**

	Does the regulatory authority receive instructions from the executive?		Can the executive overturn the decisions of the regulatory authority?	
	Indonesia	OECD[1]	Indonesia	OECD[1]
Operation of road infrastructure	Yes	44%	Yes	44%
Operation of air transport infrastructure	Yes	48%	Yes	44%
Operation of water transport infrastructure	Yes	40%	Yes	36%

1. Percentage of OECD countries that replied positively to the question (25 countries).
Source: OECD Infrastructure Questionnaire.

Indonesian regulatory authorities depend on the government or line minister and have a purely advisory role. This arrangement can be reasonably considered as a first step when reforming the institutional environment in order to give regulatory entities some time to gain expertise, credibility and authority and minimise the chance of regulatory capture by the private sector, but the time is now ripe to give them more autonomy.

In reforming its institutions in the infrastructure sector, Indonesia should establish effective regulatory authorities in sectors where they do not exist such as water supply and railway transportation. In addition, existing regulatory entities should be granted more independence, while carefully further enhancing the expertise they have gained thus far. Independent and effective regulatory authorities would lead to the separation of the dual role the government still plays in many infrastructure sectors as regulator and service provider through SOEs. This is consistent with the *OECD Guidelines on Corporate Governance of State-owned Enterprises*, that call for a clear distinction between the State's ownership function and other functions affecting service providers, especially with regard to market regulation (OECD, 2005).

Financial independence would be one way to give regulatory entities more leeway in some circumstances and soften short-term political pressures. This could be done by funding all or a substantial share of regulators' budgets with licence fees or other levies linked to service-provider turnover and using budget appropriations only in case these funds are insufficient. Specifically, the levy should be set out in law and can be seen as fees for regulatory services rather than taxes (Brown *et al.*, 2006). The government budget could fund regulatory entities only when they are asked to undertake specific tasks beyond their pre-specified responsibilities and for an initial period after their establishment.

Employing independent selection criteria to hire regulators based on merit and qualification alone would also go some way towards granting more autonomy to regulatory bodies besides strengthening their expertise. This implies moving away from the requirement to staff regulatory institutions with civil servants or employees of a particular ministry.

Indonesia authorities could confer more powers on regulators. In addition to be dependent on the government, Indonesian regulatory authorities have a very limited role when compared with the same kind of institutions in OECD countries (Table 3.4). In OECD countries, regulatory authorities are more likely to be responsible for implementing regulations, verifying compliance, and applying fines and sanctions, rather than designing specific rules. There is evidence that the power of regulatory authorities in overseeing contracts, by implementing regulations and verifying compliance, may lower the likelihood of firm- and government-led renegotiation (Guasch *et al.*, 2003 and 2007). Early negotiations might indicate opportunistic behaviour by the new operators during the bidding process

Table 3.4. **Powers of regulatory authorities in infrastructure industries**

	Design specific rules for the sector		Implement regulations and verify compliance		Power to apply fines and sanctions	
	Indonesia	OECD[1]	**Indonesia**	OECD[1]	**Indonesia**	OECD[1]
Electricity, consisting of:						
electricity generation	No	64%	No	68%	No	68%
electricity transmission	No	84%	No	92%	No	92%
electricity distribution and supply	No	88%	No	92%	No	92%
Gas, consisting of:						
gas production	No	28%	No	36%	No	36%
gas transmission	No	84%	No	92%	No	92%
gas distribution and supply	No	88%	No	92%	No	92%
Water collection, purification and distribution	No	40%	No	44%	No	44%
Railway transportation						
passenger transport	No	40%	No	52%	No	52%
freight transport	No	40%	No	48%	No	48%
operation of railroad infrastructure	No	36%	No	56%	No	56%
Operation of road infrastructure	No	44%	**Yes**	44%	No	44%
Operation of water transport infrastructure	No	44%	No	48%	No	48%
Air transportation, consisting of:						
air transport	No	44%	No	48%	No	48%
operation of air transport infrastructure	No	48%	No	48%	No	48%
Telecommunications, consisting of:						
fixed-line network	No	80%	No	96%	No	96%
fixed-line services	No	80%	No	96%	No	96%
mobile services	No	80%	No	96%	No	96%
internet services	No	76%	No	88%	No	88%

1. Percentage of OECD countries whose regulatory authorities are responsible for the specific issue (25 countries).
Source: OECD Infrastructure Questionnaire.

(through strategic underbidding) and after it (by successfully withholding critical information from the government in order to obtain a more advantageous distribution of rents).

The counterpart of strengthening regulatory bodies' independence and powers is to raise their public accountability by putting in place a system of checks and balances along with increasing transparency (Majone, 2006). Arguably, striking a balance between independence and accountability is difficult. Some measures have already been put in place in some sectors, as the publishing of annual reports and creation of forums where stakeholders can submit their views on issues under the purview of regulatory authorities (as in telecommunications). Public accountability could be further strengthened by allowing agencies' decisions to be reviewed by the courts or other non-political bodies when necessary, evaluating regulatory agencies at regular intervals by independent auditors or legislative committees, and establishing written procedures on how to remove regulators who act inappropriately.

Entrenching the regulatory authorities' general responsibilities in law, rather than ministerial decrees, could also reduce investors' perceived regulatory uncertainty. A ministerial decree is not a strong enough legal instrument to establish a regulatory agency, since it can be revoked or amended by the government ministry alone, without any consultation with parliament (Latifulhayat, 2008). In Indonesia there have been successful precedents in establishing effective regulatory bodies or independent commissions based on laws, such as the Indonesia Broadcasting Commission and the Indonesia Commission for Unfair Competition.

Price regulation

Price regulation of infrastructure services is an important policy instrument.[4] It affects the extent to which operators can recover their costs, make additional investment and adopt cost-saving technologies. Price regulation in infrastructure sectors can be broadly classified into two categories: rate-of-return regulation (or cost-based pricing) and price caps (or incentive-based pricing). In the rate-of-return regulation regime prices are set to cover production costs and allow a pre-determined rate of return to the capital invested. Its main drawback is that investors have incentives to overinvest and no reward from eliminating inefficiencies or adopt cost-saving technologies. By contrast, price-cap regulation simulates competitive conditions and offers strong incentives to adopt cost-saving technology and increase efficiency, but they have also be found to lead more often than cost-based pricing to contract renegotiation (Guasch *et al.*, 2003 and 2007). Incentive-based price regulation, such as price or revenue caps, if associated with independent regulators, has been found to boost infrastructure investment in OECD countries (Égert, 2009).

Determining the optimal price regulation regime for each sector is challenging. One size fits all measure is unlikely to be successful as the best pricing scheme depends on industry characteristics. However, both types of price regulation require effective and powerful regulatory authorities to monitor operators' behaviour and performance, and determine tariff increases. In this sense, the need to establish effective and independent regulatory entities is all the more compelling.

Indonesia differs from OECD countries as prices are regulated, at least partially, in all infrastructure sectors, except for the operation of road infrastructure (Table 3.5). Firms set tariffs following government's guidelines. In addition, these tariffs mainly ensure a pre-

Table 3.5. **Degree of price regulation in infrastructure industries**

	Are prices regulated?			
	Indonesia	OECD[1]		
		Yes, for all prices	Partially	No
Electricity, consisting of:				
electricity generation	Partially	0%	20%	64%
electricity transmission	Yes, for all prices	80%	12%	4%
electricity distribution and supply	Yes, for all prices	28%	68%	4%
Gas, consisting of:				
gas production	Partially	0%	8%	48%
gas transmission	Partially	68%	16%	4%
gas distribution and supply	Partially	36%	56%	4%
Water collection, purification and distribution	Yes, for all prices	32%	32%	12%
Operation of railroad infrastructure	Partially	32%	32%	12%
Operation of road infrastructure	No	32%	12%	16%
Operation of water transport infrastructure	Yes, for all prices	8%	20%	44%
Operation of air transport infrastructure	Yes, for all prices	8%	52%	16%
Telecommunications, consisting of:				
fixed-line network	Yes, for all prices	12%	68%	16%
fixed-line services	Yes, for all prices	0%	76%	20%
mobile services	Partially	0%	64%	20%
internet services	Partially	0%	24%	40%

1. Percentage of OECD countries that replied to the questionnaire (25 countries). Percentages may sum to less than 100 because of non responses.

Source: OECD Infrastructure Questionnaire.

determined rate of return or based on other cost-based regulation (*i.e.* a mark-up over costs). Only in telecoms, more specifically in fixed-line network and fixed-line services, are pure price caps used.

Permissions and calls for tender

An important issue for attracting private investment is whether permissions (such as planning permits, environmental licensing and local authorities' operating licences) are obtained before calls for tender are made. This bears particularly on the possibility of delays and ensuing cost overruns besides helping diminish uncertainty. Indonesia appears to be following best practice of obtaining this authorisation before calls for tender are made along with the majority of OECD respondents (Table 3.6). However, these responses need to be put in perspective. The lack of effective and expeditious land expropriation procedures has been the main obstacle to the development of toll roads. Thus, although the formal requirement of obtaining permissions and authorisations may already be in place, the lack of rule-enforcing procedures and administrative delays may hinder the development of infrastructure projects considerably (see Chapter 1).

Table 3.6. **Investment planning**

	Indonesia	OECD[1]
Does the contractor (a public body) usually obtain planning permission before calls for tender are made?	Yes	56%
As a principle, is environmental licensing obtained by the public body before calls for tender are made?	Yes	44%
If applicable, are local authorities' licenses obtained by the public body before calls for tender are made?	Yes	76%

1. Percentage of OECD countries that replied positively to the questionnaire (25 countries).
Source: OECD Infrastructure Questionnaire.

FDI restrictions

FDI legislation is an important factor behind the capacity of a country to attract private sector funding for PPPs and improve know-how through technological transfer. Foreign private investors may offer the financial resources and have the expertise to invest successfully in infrastructure. Despite renewed efforts to soften FDI barriers through the publication of a negative investment list, Indonesia's FDI regime remains quite restrictive by international comparison (Kalinova *et al.*, 2010).[5] Among infrastructure sectors, electricity is characterised by mild FDI regulatory impediments compared to transport and telecommunications. In these three sectors, among the five OECD's Enhanced Engagement countries, only China has more restrictive FDI regimes than Indonesia along with India in telecommunications (Figure 3.7).

Given their high level, there is scope to lower FDI restrictions in infrastructure, especially on foreign equity ownership in telecommunications and transport and, to a lesser extent, in electricity. Also impediments on equity acquisition could be lowered in electricity. Moreover, there is room to reduce regulatory impediments on foreign key personnel in these three sectors so as to facilitate the recruitment of directors and managers with the competences and skills necessary to improve the operations of infrastructure services. Besides providing additional capital injection, increasing foreign participation in infrastructure sectors has the potential to improve local know-how and raise the degree of competition, thereby accelerating the development of local infrastructure enterprises.

Figure 3.7. **FDI legislation in selected infrastructure sectors, 2009**[1]

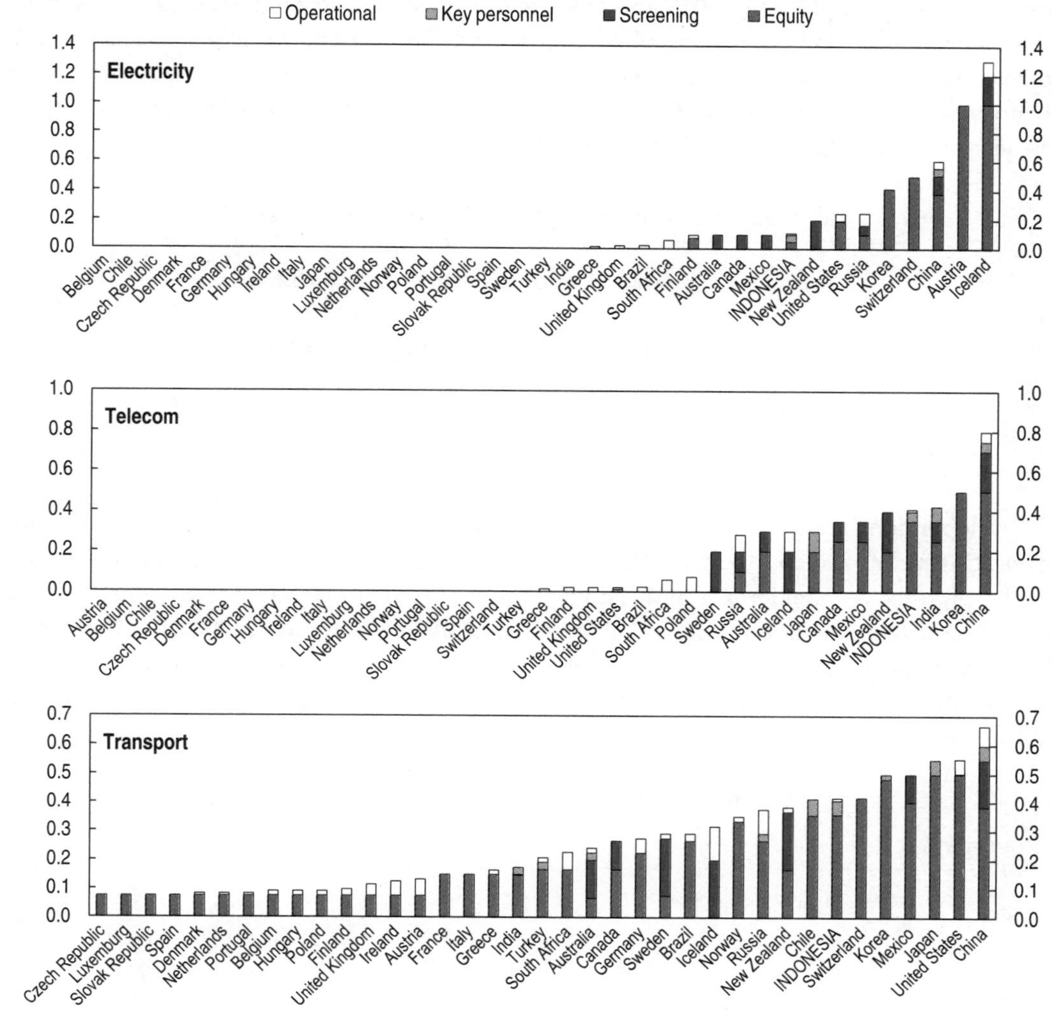

1. The indicator for each area (*i.e.* operational, screening, key personnel, screening and equity) ranges between 0 and 1. A higher score indicates more stringent FDI restrictions.

Source: Kalinova *et al.* (2010).

Selected infrastructure sectors

Electricity

The electricity sector is dominated by the state-owned company *Perusahaan Listrik Negara* (PLN). Historically, tariffs have been uniform across the country, and large consumers (mostly enterprises) have subsidised households. Because of this, PLN has had to manage a large cross-subsidy programme across regions and consumers. As a result of its impaired financial status, PLN has been unable to fund new investment, expand electrification in rural areas and sometimes even to conduct standard maintenance.

A large share of households does not have electricity connection, especially among the poor. However, the gap between the lowest and highest income quintiles, in terms of electricity supplied by PLN, narrowed sharply from 2005 to 2008 (Table 3.7). The government aims at increasing the electrification rate to 80% by 2014 and 90% by 2020. To achieve these targets the government has issued two 10 000 MW fast-track programmes, the first to be completed in 2013 and the second in 2015. The programmes also aim at increasing substantially the share of electricity produced from coal and gas, instead of oil, so as to reduce generation costs. To raise private investment in the electricity sector the government has eliminated import duties on equipment needed to build power plants in the second phase of its fast-track programme.

Table 3.7. **Sources of light by income levels, 2008**

	Lowest quintile	2nd quintile	3rd quintile	4th quintile	Highest quintile	Difference: Highest – Lowest	
						2008	2005
Electricity supplied by PLN	70.8	76.8	80.5	84.2	89.9	19.1	47.8
Torch	21.5	14.9	10.6	6.1	2.0	–19.5	–41.0
Other	7.8	8.3	8.9	9.8	8.1	0.4	–6.8

Source: Susenas and OECD calculations.

Independent power producers (IPPs) and captive power plants, which are electricity generating plants not connected to the grid and used solely for the production needs of the owner, produce a considerable and rising share of electricity in Indonesia (Figure 3.8). To date, IPPs have an installed capacity of about 5 000 MW against around 25 000 MW for PLN (PLN, 2009; Purra, 2010) and PLN maintains a monopoly in electricity sale, distribution and transmission. Estimates of installed capacity of captive power plants vary, but it appears to be substantial (World Bank, 2004; IEA, 2008).

Figure 3.8. **Private and captive power plant production**

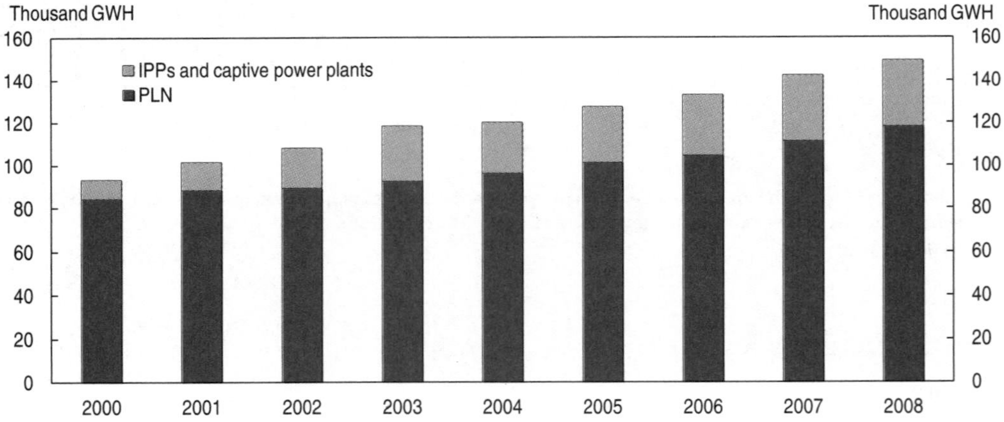

Source: Ministry of Energy and Mineral Resources.

StatLink http://dx.doi.org/10.1787/888932341708

The main obstacle to further private participation in electricity generation relates to the electricity price PLN charges to final consumers, which is set by the government at well below cost-recovery levels. This arrangement has made further private investment in electricity generation unprofitable and in some cases investment projects have been halted. From 2004 to 2009, PLN signed 45 new power purchase agreements with IPPs, but only 17 of them have reached the completion stage (PLN, 2009).

Electricity subsidies are at the core of reforming the sector, improving PLN finances and attracting private investment. The first objective should be to phase out electricity subsidies by increasing tariffs (see Chapter 2). The resulting savings could be used to provide targeted income support to low-income families or extend network coverage. Higher electricity coverage will generate benefits in terms of public health and educational outcomes. The recent government decisions to eliminate import duties on equipment needed to build power plants in the second phase of its fast-track electricity generating programme is a positive development but is unlikely to offer enough incentives to attract private investors, without reforming electricity subsidies.

In September 2009, the parliament approved a new electricity bill, which should come into force in 2010. The new law aims at increasing the role of private participation in electricity generation, transmission and distribution without violating the provisions of Article 33 of the Constitution.[6] IPPs are permitted not only to build and operate new generating stations, but also to establish their transmission network and sell electricity directly to final consumers. In addition, it is possible to charge different electricity tariffs across regions and customers. This goes in the direction of better aligning final prices with user costs and making electricity subsidies more selective. However, the law falls short of establishing a sectoral regulatory authority and states that the government must provide the guidelines for determining electricity tariffs for the retail market. More specifically, the new law specifies that retail electricity prices and tariffs to access others' electricity grid must be based on "sound business principles" (meaning transparency, accountability and fairness) and approved by central or local government. Further details on how to set retail power prices and grid rental tariffs will be specified in implementing regulations, which are yet to be issued. Overall, the guiding principle to set grid rental tariffs should be to minimise uncertainty and ensure cost recovery to spur investment in the sector so as to increase transmission and distribution capacity, reduce transmission losses and frequent blackouts.

Importantly, the new law recognises the role captive power plants might play in the electrification process. It states that that they can be owned and operated by both state-owned and private enterprises, but it does not make any provision concerning their connection to the electricity grid to integrate them into the market. The government needs to develop a clear strategy for integrating captive power plants into the grid. A first step could involve developing an inventory of all captive power plants to gauge their installed capacity and characteristics. When feasible, their integration into the electricity grid will help accelerate electrification in rural areas.

Although the new legal system allows for private participation in the generation, transmission, distribution and sale of electricity, it also makes provision for a preferential treatment of the state-owned enterprise, stating it must be given "priority" with respect to IPPs in the electricity-supply business. Overall, it is yet unclear how the new law will affect the electricity market's structure. PLN is likely to maintain its dominant position as the new law does not contain any provision to unbundle its operations.

To extend electrification in rural areas, a coherent plan should be developed involving the auction of subsidies, similar to what the government has already started in telecommunications. The entry of additional firms in electricity generation, transmission and distribution, as the new law allows, will increase competition in the electricity sector and may allow the government to start auctioning rural electrification subsidies competitively, instead of allocating them to a single company. The experience of Chile in this sense is encouraging (Box 3.5).

Box 3.5. Rural electrification programme in Chile

Chile is one interesting example of a successful rural electrification programme implemented through an innovative subsidy scheme. Traditionally, in Chile state-owned power companies had the responsibility for delivering centrally developed rural electrification plans relying on subsidies provided by the government or cross-subsidies. By early 1990s more than 50% of the rural population had still no access to electricity. According to data of the National Energy Commission (CNE), the rural electrification programme, launched in 1994 (*Programa Nacional de Electrificación Rural*) increased the rural electrification rate to 76% by 2000 and to 93% by 2007, not far from 2010 government target of 96%. The programme aims at attracting private participation into rural electrification through subsidies. It involves allocating a one-time direct subsidy to private electricity distribution companies, through an annual auction, to cover part of their investment costs. It is based on the following principles:

- **Decentralised decision-making.** The programme is essentially designed as demand-driven to ensure local participation and commitment. Local communities without electricity can propose to the municipality an electrification project supported by local distribution companies interested in investing in the project. A technical unit within the regional government then evaluates the projects. The final decision on which projects to finance is taken by the regional council according to pre-specified criteria. The central government provides economic and technical assistance through the CNE to coordinate the institutions involved in the programme. The programme allows only for projects with at least a 10% real rate of return on investment over 30 years.
- **Cost sharing.** The responsibility for financing the electrification projects is shared among users, distribution companies and the State. Users have to cover the costs of in-house wiring, the electricity meter and the connection to the grid. These expenditures can be substantial. To help poorer households to participate, these costs are initially financed by the electricity distribution company and repaid by users over time. The distribution company sponsoring the electrification project is required to invest a certain amount determined using a formula set by the government. The State provides subsidies to cover part of private distribution company investment costs.
- **Appropriate technologies.** Different electricity distribution schemes are considered. The preferred choice must abide by certain technical standards and ensure electricity supply for 24 hours per day. However, if this option proves to be too expensive for some areas, alternatives can be considered.
- **Competition.** To minimise costs and decrease the risk of politicisation competitive pressures were introduced at different levels: among communities, for financing projects; among distribution companies, for implementation; among regions, for subsidies provided by the central government; and among technologies.

At the completion of the project, distribution companies are responsible for managing and maintaining it and can recover operating costs by charging users the electricity tariffs set by CNE. Private participation has been key for implementing the programme. Given the absence of exclusive distribution rights, existing distribution companies have participated in the programme strategically to deter entry by competitors.

Source: Jadresic (2000a and 2000b) and CNE (2010).

Water and sanitation services

Water and sanitation is probably the infrastructure sector in Indonesia where reforms are the most needed. Like in other countries, policy responsibilities are fragmented between different ministries and local governments. The responsibility for planning, development and provision of water and sanitation services falls upon regency (*kabupaten*) and city (*kota*) governments, whereas the role of provincial governments is limited to co-ordinating functions spanning the boundaries of different districts along with mandates over inter-city activities and disputes (Water and Sanitation Programme, 2006; World Bank, 2004). Water tariffs are highly politicised. They must be approved by local parliaments, with the Ministry of Home Affairs providing guidelines on how to set them. As a result, water prices are generally well below cost-recovery levels.

Access to piped water remains low, particularly in rural areas. Private participation in the water sector is rare. The most notable example concerns Jakarta where two private foreign companies with local partners signed concession agreements in 1997 for a 25-year period (see Box 3.6). Whereas investment has not increased as expected, the concessions have at least raised the transparency and efficiency level of the water sector in Jakarta (Figure 3.9). After 1998, when the concession agreements started, water supply in Jakarta experienced significant efficiency gains when compared with other provinces, although not all expected gains in terms of service coverage and quality have materialised.

Box 3.6. **The experience of private-sector participation in the water sector in Jakarta**

In 1995 President Suharto instructed the Ministry of Public Works to consider the privatisation of the water-supply sector in Jakarta. At that time, only 41% of households in Jakarta had access to the system; non-revenue water was 57% of the total; water was of low quality; and supply was intermittent. Because of its dire financial condition, Jakarta Water Supply Company (PAM JAYA) could not obtain loans from banks to expand services and improve quality. Through an unsolicited review process two foreign private companies, Thames Water International from the United Kingdom and la Lyonnaise des Eaux from France, with two local partners Kati and GDS respectively, were selected to sign cooperation agreements, which became effective in early 1998. Jakarta was divided in two parts, east and west, following the natural boundary of the Ciliwung River. The two concessionaires had responsibility for investment, management and operation of one part of the network for a 25-year period. The Asian crisis put the co-operation agreements under severe strain and led to renegotiation in October 2001. The main reasons to renegotiate the contracts were: *i)* the devaluation of the *rupiah*; *ii)* the freeze of retail water tariffs until 2001 to protect the poor; and *iii)* the unclear status of 50% of PAM JAYA employees who were transferred to the payroll of the concessionaires.

One of the major changes of the restated cooperation agreements concerned the introduction of the Jakarta Water Supply Regulatory Body (JWSRB). At the beginning of its operation, JWSRB had a minimal set of responsibilities, focusing mainly on dispute resolution and technical issues. This was probably the best choice at that time, since JWSRB needed some time to build the necessary expertise and credibility and establish its authority. Although government regulations state that JWSRB is an independent body, on some important issues, such as tariffs, it has purely an advisory role since they have to be approved by the Governor of Jakarta province.

Box 3.6. **The experience of private-sector participation in the water sector in Jakarta** *(cont.)*

After ten years, the assessment of the water privatisation experience in Jakarta is mixed. Indicators suggest that water service has improved, but not all the expected gains in terms of service coverage and quality have materialised. Average tariffs are higher in Jakarta (USD 0.7 per m^3 in 2005) than in other Southeast Asian cities, such as Bangkok (0.29), Manila (0.35), Kuala Lumpur (0.22) and Singapore (0.55) and much higher than in the rest of Indonesia. Whereas this obviously presents a social challenge that needs to be addressed, it also signals a more sustainable water-pricing policy than in the rest of the country. Non-revenue water decreased from 61% in 1998 to around 50% in 2008, although it made virtually no progress from 2005 to 2008, against a 2008 target of 41.7%. Coverage increased from 46% at the beginning of the concession period to 64% in 2008, slightly below that year's target of 68%.

JWSRB has gained experience over time, and its relationship with the government has evolved. For its first three-year term (2001-04), its members were selected by the Governor of Jakarta province. However, in 2005 a new regulation made the selection process of board members more open and accountable. JWSRB still suffers from weak legitimacy because it was established through a Governor Regulation, which was supposed to be a temporary measure until local or national legislation was issued, which has yet to happen. Accountability towards all stakeholders has improved, by means of, for instance, a consumer communication forum through which complaints can be addressed. JWSRB has built expertise and credibility, but it still needs to resist tendencies to staff itself exclusively with ex-PDAM employees. A database containing detailed technical information on the operation of concessionaires has yet to be set up. This would greatly help the work of JWSRB to assess the performance of and obstacles facing concessionaires.

Source: Lanti (2006) and Lanti *et al.* (2009).

To date, the most common form of water supply involves self-provision (Chapter 4). This consists of household- and community-based water-supply systems, relying on wells, pumps and storage tanks. Community-based systems have traditionally been the mainstay form of water supply in rural areas. These have been established by communities themselves or built with support from national and international donors. However, national and international experience has shown that supply-driven projects that did not involve local communities in the planning and managing of the system often failed because of a lack of participation by local residents. As a consequence, a new generation of demand-driven community-based systems has been built with some encouraging results (Gatti, 2007).

Sanitation and wastewater treatment are marred by even more acute problems than the water-supply sector. The legal framework provides general statements about the importance of achieving good health and sanitation conditions and recognises the citizenry's right to a clean and healthy environment, but lacks specific provisions for the effective governance and supply of sanitation services. The current legal setting *de facto* treats sanitation as a private responsibility (World Bank, 2004; Robinson, 2008). Although local authorities are responsible for the provision of sanitation services, this does not imply they have the obligation to undertake the delivery of these services or have the capacity to do so. Therefore, public finance devoted to sanitation remains limited, and households and developers are expected to invest in on-site facilities. The vast majority of the population

Figure 3.9. **Distribution of productivity levels of water-supply establishments across provinces**[1]

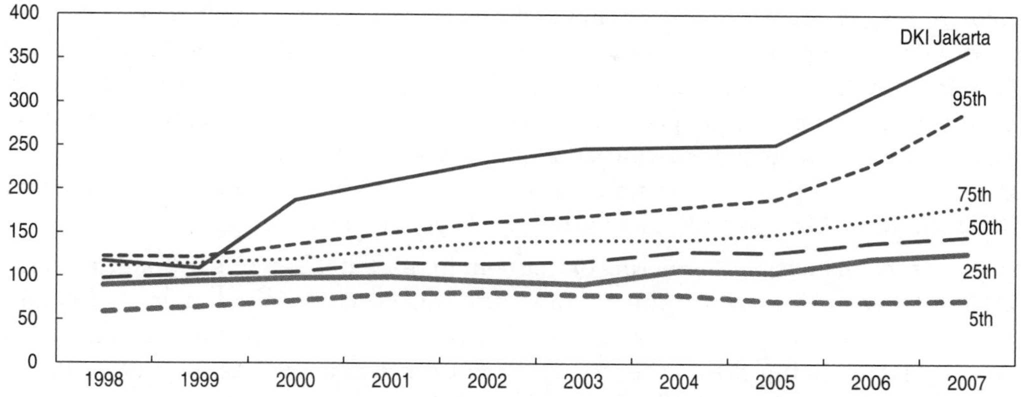

1. The lines correspond to different percentiles of the productivity distribution across provinces. Productivity is computed as the number of water-supply establishments' connections over their number of workers in each province. Figures are 2-year averages. The province of Bangka Belitung, Kep Riau, Banten, Sulawesi Barat, Gorontalo, Maluku Utara and Papua Barat are excluded because of missing data for some years.

Source: BPS and OECD calculations.

StatLink http://dx.doi.org/10.1787/888932341727

relies on such facilities as septic tanks and pit latrines, while many low-income households rely on polluted drains and urban waterways. Formal sewerage systems have been constructed in selected areas of a few large cities, but most are underutilised and underfunded.

The Water Resources Law 7/2004 introduced important changes to the water-supply legal framework. These include: *i)* ending public monopolies by clarifying the role of private-sector participation in the water sector; *ii)* eliminating the need for local parliament approval of water-tariff increases in case of cooperation contracts with the private sector; and *iii)* making provisions for the establishment of the National Water Regulatory Agency (NWRA) to implement regulations and monitor service delivery norms. The law also clarifies the roles and responsibilities of regional governments.

The law has been challenged before the Constitutional Court on the ground that the constitution requires the water sector to be totally under State control. The Court asserted the law to be only conditionally constitutional, meaning that its constitutionality depends on how it is interpreted and applied through implementing regulation (Al'Afghani, 2006). This has particular importance for the determination of water tariffs. The law is vague in this respect, simply stating that drinking water must be provided at an "affordable price" and achieving a balance between the consumer and service provider.

Water tariffs need to be raised in most jurisdictions to cost-recovery levels so as to encourage investment in the sector. Poor households would be protected from the attendant rise through existing cash transfers schemes. Moreover, a coherent national policy for network connection subsidies should be developed to extend access, especially among the poor as the connection fee might be prohibitively expensive for them. Higher tariffs, in addition to leading to a more efficient use of water resources, may make increasing the number of connections financially viable. Retail water tariffs should also reflect wastewater treatment costs.

Decentralisation has not translated into service improvements in the water-supply sector. Local government owned water utilities – *Perusahaan Daerah Air Minum* (PDAM) – which are responsible for the financing and provision of water supply, remain seriously underfunded. The precarious economic condition of most PDAMs has resulted in debt obligations to the central government amounting to around USD 600 million. The government has started a programme guaranteeing long-term bank loans to PDAMs at subsidised rates so as to increase investment in the sector. These loans are conditional on PDAMs restructuring their operations to be competently managed and raising average tariffs to, at least, average unit costs for the whole period of the guarantee.[7]

One of the main issues hindering investment in the water sector is the large arrears of PDAMs with the central government. To rectify this situation, the Ministry of Finance should accelerate the programme of debt restructuring and forgiveness it has already started, thus allowing PDAMs to access long-term financing. As at May 2010, only 15 PDAMs, out of the 175 in need, have restructured their debt obligations under the *aegis* of the Ministry of Finance (PERPAMSI, 2010). The recent government's initiative to offer partial loan guarantees and interest rate subsidies to PDAMs conditional on making their operations financial viable in the long term is commendable and needs to be continued. To increase efficiency in the water sector, merging the smallest PDAMs would allow them to increase the average number of connections and thus benefit from scale economies. In addition, this could help rationalise operations through defining service areas based on watersheds and not just jurisdictional boundaries.

Many PDAMs are small and cannot benefit from economies of scale. The average number of connections is about 20 230. Only around 8% of them serve more than 50 000 households whereas 79% count less than 20 000 (PERPAMSI, 2010). Their level of efficiency is in general low. They are overstaffed, and non-revenue water in many cases exceeds 50% (Godman, 2005). Service areas are determined by regency and city boundaries and not by watershed boundaries, resulting in additional operational inefficiencies. Merging the smallest PDAMs would allow them to increase their average number of connections and thus benefit from scale economies. In addition, this could help rationalise operations through defining service areas based on watersheds and not just jurisdictional boundaries. In 2004 the national association of water utilities (PERPAMSI) started a water-utility benchmarking programme with the intent to disseminate international and local best practices. The Indonesian authorities should focus on strengthening this programme so as to extend the benchmarking exercise and make its results widely available. An initial assessment of benchmarking in different countries suggests that it increases competition, helps disseminate best practices, improves efficiency and reduces non-revenue water (Cabrera, 2008). In addition, it could be used as a jumping board towards formally introducing yardstick competition in the water and sanitation sector.

To overcome long-term financing obstacles in the water and sanitation sector, the creation of revolving funds, managed by provinces, could be considered. These funds could help finance water and sanitation projects through pooling project risks within provinces and the provision of credit enhancement from the central government (Box 3.7). Entrusting provinces with the responsibility of managing these funds would also go some way towards granting them greater powers to co-ordinate water and sanitation projects among districts. The establishment of such funds should be preceded by an assessment of provincial governments' capacity to manage. Overall provincial governments should also strengthen their capacity in water and sanitation development, including planning

Box 3.7. State revolving funds: The US experience

The US federal government established the clean water and drinking water state revolving funds (CWSRF and DWSRF) in the mid-1980s, in connection with the federal Clean Water Act. These programmes aim at reducing wastewater and drinking water supply project costs by providing below-market rate loans for water-treatment and drinking-water projects. Today state revolving funds (SRFs) are recognised as a critical source of funding to enable communities to renew aging municipal infrastructure.

Assets used in SRFs are lent to communities at favourable rates and eventually returned to the fund through interest and principal repayments. States may also obtain additional funds for their programmes through issuing bonds or bank credits. Some states use the funds they receive through SRFs to back the issue of pooled bonds to meet the financing needs of local governments lacking the creditworthiness and expertise to access credit markets. In general, pooled SRF state bonds will have a credit rating far higher than what local governments could obtain. Yet, whereas the use of leverage provides an immediate increase in available funds and allows states to comply with matching-funding requirements, it may diminish the available funds over time as financial resources that could be disbursed for new projects are instead used to repay principal and interest.

One of the primary objectives of SRF programmes is to maintain, in perpetuity, the seed capital contributed to the programme and use it efficiently. Both the CWSRF and DWSRF are expected to revolve, thereby providing financial assistance far into the future. Interest rates on loans should not be set so low that inflation erodes the long-term SRF purchasing power. On the other hand, rates should not be so high as to offer too small a financial benefit to borrowers. As of 2008, CWSRF has disbursed USD 2.41 for every dollar provided by the federal government since its inception.

States have considerable flexibility to direct funds toward their most pressing needs and achieve the greatest environmental results. They must prepare an annual Intended Use Plan describing how they will use the funds in their SRF programmes. Communities that are interested in receiving assistance, through a SRF, must present their projects to their state, which will rank them in priority order. States also evaluate the financial condition of applicants to ascertain if they have established a dedicated revenue source for loan repayment.

capacity as well as coordination between inter-government offices (*Dinas*), governments and communities. The working group on water supply and sanitation (*Pokja AMPL*) that has been established throughout local governments in Indonesia, both at provincial and district/city levels, should be deployed as a means to connect stakeholders and achieve a better sector-development planning and coordination.

Road transport

Road infrastructure is currently regulated by Law 38/2004 (which covers regulation, maintenance, development and supervision of roads and regulatory authority) and implementing regulations. The Ministry of Public Works is responsible for building and maintenance of road infrastructure whereas the Ministry of Transport has responsibility over circulation of vehicles. The Indonesia Toll Road Authority (BPJT), an agency within the Ministry of Public Works, has an advisory role and its tasks and powers mainly involve: recommending toll-road tariff levels and their adjustment mechanism to the Minister of Public Works; taking over and managing toll roads at the end of their concession period;

soliciting private investment in toll roads through conducting feasibility studies and transparent and competitive bidding procedures; and implementing toll-road regulation and verifying compliance by private operators.

Indonesia currently has a toll road network of around 690 km, mostly concentrated on the Island of Java. Paved roads rose from around 45% of the total at the beginning of the 1990s to about 60% in 2008, but most of the gains took place prior to the Asian crisis (Figure 3.10).

Figure 3.10. **Total length of road networks and share of paved roads**[1]

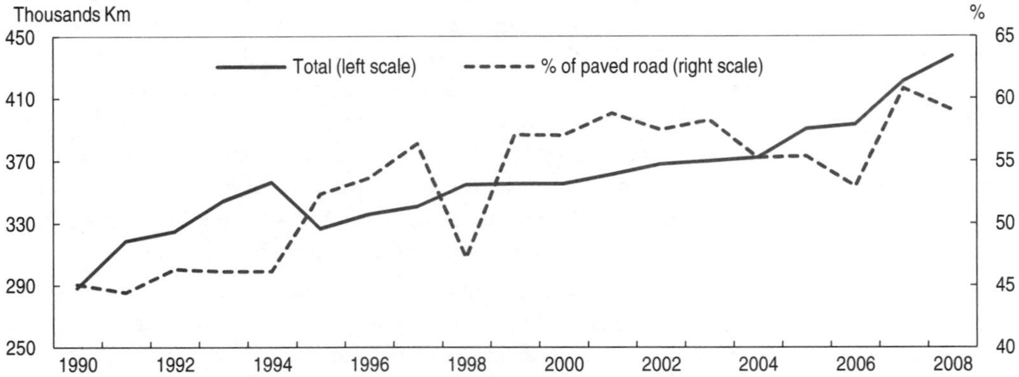

1. East Timor excluded from 1999 onwards.

Source: BPS.

StatLink http://dx.doi.org/10.1787/888932341746

Land acquisition is one of the main obstacles hindering toll-road development and infrastructure more generally. As a result, Indonesia has built, on average, only 23 kilometres of toll roads per year since it started in 1978, and the total length of its toll road network compares poorly with that of Malaysia, for instance, whose toll road network is fully 6 000 kilometres long. Current legislation on eminent domain (*i.e.* the power of the state to seize private property for public or civic use paying due monetary compensation to the owner) mandates that compensation has to be based on fair market value of land and buildings located on it. Because of a lack of an independent agency to decide fair prices, legal disputes over land values end up in courts and are very slow to be resolved. In addition, the practice of selling land, which has been selected for infrastructure projects, to third parties puts upward pressure on the final price investors will be asked to pay.

To overcome land-acquisition problems, the government has set up a land revolving fund of USD 160 million (IDR 1.49 trillion) managed by BPJT to provide bridging finance for toll roads' land acquisition. The authorities are also considering amending the eminent-domain legislation. One option being considered involves lowering, from 75 to 51, the percentage of the needed land for a project the government must have already acquired to trigger court-led consignment, whereby work can start even if there are still pending legal disputes over the remaining land. According to the draft law currently under discussion, owners will have three months to agree on the compensation proposed by an expert assessor certified by BPN (The National Land Agency). If the parties do not reach an agreement within this deadline formal court proceedings will follow. Moreover, to protect private investors over spiralling costs of land acquisition once negotiation starts, the government will be responsible for any increase in land price above 110% of the level stipulated in the contract with private investors. For this purpose the government has allocated about USD 543 million (IDR 4.89 trillion) to the Land Capping Fund for the next 5 years. The law would also make it illegal for the owner of land selected for infrastructure projects to sell it to third parties. These measures are likely to assuage investors' fear over escalating costs for land procurement and further private investment.

The planned amendment to the eminent-domain legislation is a step in the right direction toward reforming the process for securing land for infrastructure projects. Authorities should focus on passing and implementing the new law on eminent-domain legislation expeditiously. To determine more swiftly the market price of land to be expropriated, the government could also consider allocating this responsibility to BPN, which is likely to already have the expertise to reach fair solutions. This may shorten markedly the time required to reach a final decision on compensation, when compared to relying on civil courts, thereby lowering uncertainty about final land acquisition costs.

In general, building and maintenance of national and provincial roads is financed through the DAK (Feaver, 2008). A Road Preservation Fund was created in 2009 to tackle deteriorating road quality. Its resources will be used for road maintenance and rehabilitation only. Road users can be charged, although details about funding, organisation and management of the Fund still have to be determined in implementing regulations. The government should concentrate on rapid implementation of necessary regulations to define the source of funding, organisation and management of the Road Preservation Fund and make it operational. It also needs to provide more incentives to sub-national governments to allocate higher local budget resources to road maintenance, since most of the road network (around 90%) is under their responsibility. Incentives for upkeep could take the form of making central-government transfers for additional investment in the road sector conditional on appropriate road maintenance.

Telecommunications

Indonesia started to modernise its telecommunications sector in the mid-1990s through the partial privatisation of Telkom and Indosat. Following the Asian crisis the government issued a "Sector Blueprint" setting forth the basic principles it intended to use to reform the sector and achieve full competition by 2010. In 1999, momentous changes were introduced in the sector including: the possibility for privately owned enterprises to provide telecommunications services without entering in joint ventures or concession agreements with SOEs; sanctioning the abuse of dominant positions and prohibiting *de facto* monopoly practices; determining tariffs by operators based on a formula set by the government, instead of being decided by the government; assigning network operators the obligation to provide interconnection services; and allowing the government to retain its regulatory power with the option of delegating it to a regulatory agency. This change in the sector's legal framework was accompanied by a further reduction in the government's participation in Telkom and Indosat and termination of their exclusivity rights for specific services before schedule.[8]

In 2003 the government created the regulatory agency for the telecommunications sector (*Badan Regulasi TelekomunikasiIndonesia*, BRTI). BRTI is supposed to be independent from government and private operators and its role is to guarantee a transparent, independent and fair telecommunications industry. Its specific duties involve organising and establishing network and service operations (such as evaluating and awarding licenses), and supervision and control over the telecommunication network and service operations. In fulfilling its duties, BRTI must seek opinions and inputs from the parties affected by its decisions.

BRTI it is not actually a fully independent body. It is comprised of the Directorate General of Post and Telecommunications and the Telecommunications Regulatory Committee. The Director General of Post and Telecommunications, who is a public servant, is BRTI chairman, *ex-officio*. Besides, BRTI's budget is 100% funded through government appropriation. Still, it is at least functionally separate from the government since the members of the Telecommunications Regulatory Committee are not civil servants but are chosen, by the government, from the private, public and academic sectors on the basis of their expertise (Latifulhayat, 2008).

Overall the BRTI appears to have served the industry and consumers well. BRTI's members possess technical expertise and have been appointed openly and transparently. In turn, BRTI has sought the input and opinion of different parties to inform its decisions. However, the government still plays a conflicting role as simultaneously being the major shareholder in Telkom and the regulator. Granting BRTI more independence from the executive power would go towards clearly separating these conflicting roles. This could involve removing the need for ministerial approval in BRTI's decisions and eliminating the rule that the Director General of Post and Telecommunications, or any other civil servant, has to chair BRTI. One way to make the regulator more independent could also involve funding its budget with licence fees and levies from operator turnover.

Competition in the telecommunications sector has increased substantially since reforms were launched in 1999, but the market, although counting 15 operating companies, is still dominated by a few large operators. The share of the population with telecommunications devices has increased notably in recent years (Table 3.1), although a large divide still remains between urban and rural areas. Wireless and fixed-wireless services have experienced robust growth, whereas fixed-line services have grown more slowly, partly because of fixed-wireless substitution. Regarding internet services, competition among service providers has strengthened, but access to the internet still lags well behind regional peers and OECD levels, with dial-up being the dominant mode of access. Limited internet access is attributable to a lack of fixed lines and the low spread of personal computers, especially in rural areas. Access to telecommunication services is rarer among poor than well-off households (Table 3.8). The gap between them for owning a computer and a mobile phone increased from 2005 to 2008 and narrowed for fixed lines.

Table 3.8. **Access to telecommunications services by income levels, 2008**

	Lowest quintile	2nd quintile	3rd quintile	4th quintile	Highest quintile	Difference: Highest – Lowest	
						2008	2005
Fixed line phone	0.9	2.3	4.4	9.3	30.1	29.2	37.0
Mobile phone	12.2	32.3	49.6	67.5	88.4	76.2	54.5
Own a computer	0.5	1.7	3.6	8.2	33.2	32.7	12.1
Internet connection	0.6	1.7	2.5	3.8	8.2	7.6	..

Source: Susenas and OECD calculations.

In 2007 the government started to auction subsidies to companies willing to provide basic telecommunication services in designated areas currently lacking them, as a way to meet its universal service obligation. The government applied the same approach for internet services in 2009. Tenders have been completed for telecommunication services in 2009 and internet services in 2010. Subsidies are limited to five years. The initiative to auction subsidies for extending services in underserved areas is laudable, as it is likely to narrow substantially and eventually eliminate the digital divide among different areas, and the government needs to press it forward to meet the universal service obligation.

Current legislation is ill suited to prepare service convergence (*i.e.* the confluence of previously distinct media services on single devices) as it is based on a concept of the industry as comprising vertically separated services. To overcome this problem, the government has recently reorganised the Ministry of Communications and Information Technology, whose functions and tasks have been structured to manage and regulate the process towards convergence. In addition, the government is considering introducing the unified access service license for telecommunications services, which would allow the same operator to offer a variety of services. New regulations need to be issued to manage and accelerate the convergence process. The introduction of a unified access service license would be a big step in this direction and would strengthen competition, contributing to lower prices.

Ports and shipping

Indonesia is an archipelago country spread over around 18 000 islands. It counts around 1 700 ports, which are organised in a hierarchical system consisting of 111 *commercial* ports, about 1 000 *special-purpose* ports (*i.e.* private terminals serving the needs of individual companies) and around 600 *non-commercial* ports, which tend to be unprofitable and of little strategic value. In all commercial ports one of four SOEs, also known as *Pelindos*, has a legislated monopoly with the result of playing the dual role of port authority and sole port operator. As port authorities, they set the tariffs shipping companies have to pay to access these services and have regulatory authority over private-sector terminals.

The legislative framework is currently in a state of flux. A new shipping law, approved in 2008, provides a comprehensive reform of the port system, but it will not be fully implemented until 2011. This law replaces the previous 1992 legislation, which seems to have constrained the growth of Indonesia's shipping industry and made it less efficient by undercutting competitive pressures (Dick, 2008). Ray (2008) reports that the Jakarta International Container Terminal, although one of the most efficient Indonesian ports, is one of the poorest performing in all of Southeast Asia with respect to productivity and unit costs.

The new legislation introduces a simpler regulatory structure, specifically in business licensing and port management. Local governments are now in charge of issuing licences for inland waterways and ferries and coastal passenger transport. In addition, the law sets easier requirements than the previous system to obtain a shipping licence, which could boost competition in the industry.[9] The new legal framework also makes provision for the creation of port authorities, thus recognising the distinction between port management and regulation. Powers and responsibilities of port authorities are shaped around the management concept of *landlord port*. In this model, the port authority owns the land and basic infrastructure such as wharves, which are rented or leased to private operators. Operators invest in cargo-handling equipment, hire personnel and negotiate contracts with shipping companies to unload and load cargo.

The main benefit of the new system is that it holds the promise of breaking the monopoly of the four SOEs, which are supposed to turn into port operators. The port authorities will regulate one or more commercial ports and, in consultation with local government, will issue concessions to port operators and regulate their activities. Similar changes in Mexico have resulted in significant improvements in the productivity of ports and reductions in cargo handling charges (Estache *et al.*, 2004). In the case of Indonesia, however, the law stipulates that port authorities will be staffed by civil servants and will be under ministerial authority, thus granting them little independence from the executive.

The new regulatory framework also specifies that *special-purpose* terminals may be converted into public ports. This may lead to increased inter-port competition, but it is unclear whether private owners will forsake their ownership rights when details about the new regulatory framework have yet to be set in implementing regulations. Under the new law, private ports will not be able to handle third-party cargo, thus limiting the inter-port competition private ports will be able to provide.

The separation of port operations from their regulation with the creation of port authorities around the concept of landlord port management is a welcome development and promises to improve ports' efficiency significantly. The authorities should focus on issuing implementing regulations necessary to make the new port authorities operational soon. Their ability to perform their duties effectively could be jeopardised by the requirement that they must be staffed solely by civil servants. The authorities should consider the alternative of recruitment based on experience and qualifications instead. In addition, the authorities will need to develop a plan to manage the transition of those currently employed by port management companies to new port authorities or other companies.[10]

The new system also legislates that the right to cabotage (*i.e.* the transport of goods or passengers between two points in the same country) is reserved to national shipping companies, using Indonesia-flag vessels and crewed by Indonesian nationals. Restrictions on cabotage, requiring domestic sea cargo to be shipped by national vessels, were re-introduced in 2005, if only partially, and appear to have been inspired by protectionist considerations, which are unlikely to be consistent with the objective of developing a competitive and modern sea transport sector. There is some evidence that this policy has decreased the share of foreign charter ships operated by foreign companies, probably exerting a negative effect on competitive pressures (Figure 3.11).

Figure 3.11. **Share of ships by type of ownership**

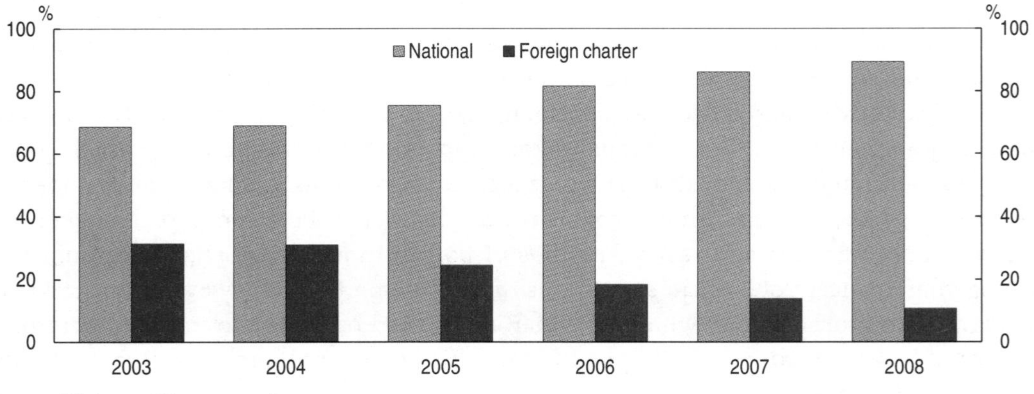

Source: Ministry of Transportation.

StatLink http://dx.doi.org/10.1787/888932341765

Reducing restrictions on foreign cabotage will prove to be beneficial to the Indonesian shipping industry in the long term because of the enhanced competitive pressures it will generate. Although restrictions on cabotage by foreign vessels are applied in many countries, they are likely to have more pernicious effects in Indonesia because of its geography and the importance sea-transport has. Also, foreign competition in the shipping and port management sectors is already limited since port services and domestic sea transport are still on the "Negative Investment List" which limits foreign ownership to 49%.

In addition, according to the new shipping law the State will control routes through a highly complex system-wide network to manage inter-island shipping.[11] The new shipping law also confers powers on the government to set passenger fares. Inter-island freight rates can in principle be freely determined by shipping companies and their clients, but the law mandates that these will have to be consistent with the tariff types, structure and categories defined by the government. The same requirement will apply to port service tariffs charged by port operators. How freight tariff types, structure and categories are determined will impinge on the ability of shipping companies and port operators to set tariffs and freight rates on a commercially viable basis. If rates are set too low, they will discourage entry or the opening of new routes. A better option would involve letting shipping companies freely determine their tariff rates, thus stimulating competition. In order to satisfy any regional policy objective or ensure national unity, the government could then auction subsidies to ensure the provision of services over unprofitable routes.

Box 3.8. **Summary of policy recommendations: Infrastructure**

Improving infrastructure spending

- Consider increasing the planned public spending on infrastructure from 2011 to 2014 by 0.2% of GDP beyond what is currently planned.
- Use the Medium-Term Expenditure Framework more effectively to improve multi-year budget appropriations for infrastructure projects and improve coordination among ministries responsible for infrastructure development.
- Commission sector studies to gauge yearly maintenance expenditure in different sectors and allocate budget resources accordingly.
- Undertake rigorous value-for-money tests to assess the relative and absolute cost-effectiveness of PPPs. Carefully monitor whether the private sector bears the appropriate share of risk.
- Thoroughly assess demand-side risks the government may be assuming in PPP projects by appointing independent advisors to provide conservative and independent demand forecasts.
- Provide incentives to local governments to allocate budget resources for roads, water and sanitation by making transfers conditional on appropriate upkeep.

Strengthening the regulatory framework

- Establish independent regulatory bodies in the sectors currently lacking them; initially they could be created as having a purely advisory role.
- Lower regulatory uncertainty by legally entrenching the power and responsibilities of regulatory bodies.
- Grant independence to existing regulatory entities by eliminating the need for ministerial approval of their decisions and by funding their budgets through licence fees and levies on firms.

Box 3.8. **Summary of policy recommendations: Infrastructure** *(cont.)*

- Eliminate any requirement that regulatory bodies be staffed by civil servants and base recruitment on qualification and experience only.
- Consider conferring on regulatory bodies the power to resolve contractual disputes between concessionaires and public authorities before going to arbitration or the courts.
- Further strengthen the public accountability of regulatory bodies by formally evaluating their operations at regular intervals and increasing their transparency.
- Lower FDI restrictions on equity and on foreign key personnel in telecommunications, transport and electricity.

Electricity

- Phase out electricity subsidies and compensate low-income households through existing cash-transfer programmes or subsidies to new connection to the grid.
- Develop a coherent plan to extend electrification in rural areas by auctioning subsidies competitively.
- Develop a plan to integrate captive power plants into the grid.

Water and sanitation

- Accelerate the restructuring programme of the debt of local government utilities (PDAMs).
- Consider the creation of revolving funds managed by provinces.
- Strengthen the role of the National Association of Water Utilities (PERPAMSI) and extend its benchmarking exercise to disseminate best practices.
- Realign average water tariffs to cost-recovery levels and use existing cash-transfer programmes to compensate low-income households.

Road transport

- Reform eminent-domain legislation to expedite the process of land acquisition. Consider allocating to BPN (the National Land Agency) the responsibility to resolve disputes over land value.
- Swiftly issue implementing regulations to establish the Road Preservation Fund.

Ports and shipping

- Expedite release of implementing regulations to establish port authorities.
- Reduce restrictions on cabotage by foreign vessels so as to raise competition in the shipping industry.
- Develop a plan to manage the transition of employees currently employed by port management companies (*Pelindos*) to new port authorities or other companies.
- Allow shipping companies to determine freely their freight and passenger tariffs, and, if necessary, auction subsidies to ensure the provision of services over unprofitable routes.

Telecommunications

- Make the sectoral regulator (BRTI) more independent.
- Press forward the plan of auctioning subsidies as a cost-effective way to extend telecommunication services in underserved areas to meet universal service obligations.
- Issue regulations consistent with the ongoing service convergence process and introduce the unified access service license.

Notes

1. The other constraints considered in the survey are: land access; business licensing; local government and business interaction; business development programmes; capacity and integrity of the mayor; local taxes and use charges; security and conflict resolution; and local regulations.
2. DAK accounts for a non-negligible share of the total infrastructure budget, around 7.4% in 2009. DAK is a fund used to make *specific* fiscal transfers to regional and district governments needing additional financial resources to raise the provision of public services in different sectors, among which infrastructure, and finances mainly physical capital investment.
3. Hellowell and Pollock (2009) report on the experience of the United Kingdom on value-for-money exercises concerning capital investment in the health sector. They stress how PPPs have come out, in virtually all instances, as the most cost-efficient saving option, as value-for-money exercises have allocated risks to private providers, which they were not contractually obliged to bear.
4. Price regulation is common in network industries because of the existence of natural monopoly, the presence of positive externalities generated through widespread access to the network, and the high political and social sensitivity of some sectors. Regulating prices is also a necessity when the core monopoly network provider must ensure access to it for different service operators under payment of an access fee – as in the electricity transmission network – or when only competition for the market is feasible – as in concessions for toll roads or water supply.
5. The FDI index is computed considering restrictions in four areas: *i)* foreign equity restrictions; *ii)* screening and prior-approval requirements; *iii)* rules for key personnel, such as executives; and *iv)* other restrictions on the operation of foreign enterprises. The highest score in any area is one, when it fully restricts foreign investment in the sector, whereas the lowest is zero, in case there are no regulatory impediments to FDI. The overall score for each sector is computed by summing the scores for the different types of restrictions (OECD, 2010). No attempt is made to appraise the overall restrictiveness of the regulatory regime as it is actually implemented.
6. Article 33 requires the State to control: *i)* all branches of production that are important for the State; and *ii)* all natural resources. In 2004, the Constitutional Court declared unconstitutional a 2002 law attempting to reform the electricity sector by increasing private participation and creating a regulatory body. A labour union of PLN has challenged the validity of the new law before the Constitutional Court.
7. According to Presidential Decree 29/2009, the guarantee covers 70% of the subsidised loan (40% by the central government and 30% by the local government).
8. Despite its divestiture of Telkom, at the end of 2008 the government's participation still stood at 52.5% (Telkom, 2009). In addition, the Ministry of Finance holds a "golden" share with special voting rights, giving it veto power on some strategic issues. At the end of 2009 the government held around 14% of Indosat's capital in common stock (Indosat, 2010).
9. These involve being a legal entity and owning an Indonesia-flag vessel of at least 175 gross tonnes, whereas the previous regulations required holding already two licences, namely business and operating licences, before obtaining shipping permission.
10. Similar transitional issues were experienced by the two concessionaires of Jakarta's water supply, which "inherited" more than 50% of the former public-owned water supplier's employees (Lanti *et al.*, 2009).
11. All companies are required to be part of this network, which is to be specified by the central and regional governments, the Indonesia Ship-owners Association and the Association of Sea Transport Users, considering the distribution of economic activity, regional development and national unity.

Bibliography

ADB (2009), *Indonesia: Rural Infrastructure Support Project*, Asian Development Bank, Manila.

Agénor, P.R. and B. Moreno-Dodson (2006), "Public Infrastructure and Growth: New Channels and Policy Implications", *Policy Research Working Paper* No. 4064, World Bank, Washington, DC.

Al'Afghani, M.M. (2006), "Constitutional Court Review and the Future of the Water Law in Indonesia", *Law, Environment and Development Journal*, 2(1), 3-18.

Albala-Bertrand, J.M. and E.C. Mamatzakis (2004), "The Impact of Public Infrastructure on the Productivity of the Chilean Economy", *Review of Development Economics*, 8(2), 266–278.

Andres, L., J. Guasch and S. Straub (2007), "Does Regulation and Institutional Design Matter for Infrastructure Sector Performance?", *Policy Research Working Paper* No. 4378, World Bank, Washington, DC.

APEC (2009), *Meeting APEC's Post-Crisis Infrastructure Challenge: Towards Commonality in PPP Infrastructure Markets*, Commonwealth of Australia.

Bougheas, S., P.O. Demetriades and E.L. Morgenroth (1999), "Infrastructure, Transport Costs and Trade", *Journal of International Economics*, 47(1), 169–189.

Brown, A.C., J. Stern and B.W. Tenenbaum (2006), *Handbook for Evaluating Infrastructure Regulatory Systems*, World Bank Publications, Washington, DC.

Cabrera, E.J. (2008), "Benchmarking in the Water Industry: a Mature Practice?", *Water Utility Management International*, 3(2), 5-7.

CNE (2010), Comisión Nacional de Energía website, *www.cne.cl*, accessed April 2010.

Cubbin, J. and J. Stern (2006), "The Impact of Regulatory Governance and Privatization on Electricity Industry Generation Capacity in Developing Economies", *World Bank Economic Review*, 20(1), 115-141.

Dick, H. (2008), "The 2008 Shipping Law: Deregulation or Re-regulation?", *Bulletin of Indonesian Economic Studies*, 44(3), 383–406.

Djankov, S., C.L. Freund and C.P. Pham (2006), "Trading on Time", *Policy Research Working Paper* No. 3909, World Bank, Washington, DC.

Donaldson, D. (2008), "Railroads of the Raj: Estimating the Impact of Transportation Infrastructure", unpublished manuscript.

Égert, B. (2009), "Infrastructure Investment in Network Industries: The Role of Incentive Regulation and Regulatory Independence", *Working Paper Series* No. 2642, CESifo, Munich.

Égert, B., T. Kozluk and D. Sutherland (2009), "Infrastructure Investment: Links to Growth and the Role of Public Policies", *Economics Department Working Papers* No. 686, OECD, Paris.

Esfahani, H. S. and M.T. Ramirez (2003), "Institutions, Infrastructure, and Economic Growth", *Journal of Development Economics*, 70(2), 443–477.

Estache, A. and A. Goicoechea (2005), "How Widespread Were Private Investment and Regulatory Reform in Infrastructure Utilities During the 1990s?", *Policy Research Working Paper Series* No. 3595, World Bank, Washington, DC.

Estache, A. and M. Fay (2007), "Current Debates on Infrastructure Policy", *Policy Research Working Paper* No. 4410, World Bank, Washington, DC.

Estache, A., B.T. de la Fe and L. Trujillo (2004), "Sources of Efficiency Gains in Port Reform: a DEA decomposition of a Malmquist TFP index for Mexico", *Utilities Policy*, 12(4), 221–30.

Feaver, D. (2008), "A Regulatory Analysis of the Special Allocation Fund (DAK) and Horizontal Equalization in Indonesia", *Research Institute Working Paper Series*, SMERU, Jakarta.

Gatti, M. (2007), *Best Practices in Water Supply and Sanitation: Learning from Successful Projects*, Asian Development Bank, Manila.

Godman, A (2005), "The WBI-PERPAMSI Twinning Program: Capacity Building Components for NRW Reduction", Presented at the *World Bank Water Week 2005 Conference*, Washington, DC.

Guasch, J.L, J. Laffont and S. Straub (2003), "Renegotiation of Concession Contracts in Latin America", *Policy Research Working Paper* No. 3011, World Bank, Washington, DC.

Guasch, J.L., J. Laffont and S. Straub (2007), "Concessions of Infrastructure in Latin America: Government-led Renegotiation", *Journal of Applied Econometrics*, 22(7), 1267-94.

Guasch, J.L., J. Laffont and S. Straub (2008), "Renegotiation of Concession Contracts in Latin America: Evidence from the Water and Transport Sectors", *International Journal of Industrial Organization*, 26(2), 421-42.

Gutiérrez, L.H. (2003), "The Effect of Endogenous Regulation on Telecommunications Expansion and Efficiency in Latin America", *Journal of Regulatory Economics*, 23(3), 257-286.

Hellowell, M. and A.M. Pollock (2009), "The Private Financing of NHS Hospitals: Politics, Policy and Practice", *Economic Affairs*, 29(1), 13–19.

Henisz, W.J. (2002), "The Institutional Environment for Infrastructure Investment", *Industrial and Corporate Change*, 11(2), 355-89.

Henisz, W.J. and B.A. Zelner (2001), "The Institutional Environment for Telecommunications Investment", *Journal of Economics and Management Strategy*, 10(1), 123–147.

Hodge, G. and C. Greve (2009), "PPPs: The Passage of Time Permits Some Sober Reflection", *Economic Affairs*, 29(1), 33-39.

IEA (2008), *Energy Policy Review of Indonesia*, OECD/IEA, Paris.

Indosat (2010), *2009 Annual Report*, *www.indosat.com/Investor_Relations/Investor_Relations/Annual_Report*, accessed June 2010.

Jadresic, A. (2000a), "A Case Study on Subsidizing Rural Electrification in Chile", in P. Brooks and S. Smith (eds.), *Energy Services for the World's Poor*, World Bank, Washington, DC.

Jadresic, A. (2000b), "Promoting Private Investment in Rural Electrification: The Case of Chile", *World Bank Viewpoint Note 214*, World Bank, Washington, DC.

JETRO (2009), *Survey of Japanese-affiliated Firms in Asia and Oceania*, Japanese External Trade Organisation, Tokyo, *www.jetro.go.jp/en/reports/survey/biz/*, accessed November 2009.

Keefer, P. (1996), "Protection against a Capricious State: French Investment and Spanish Railroads 1845-1875", *Journal of Economic History*, 56(1), 170–192.

KPPOD (2008), *Local Economic Governance in Indonesia*, *http://kppod.org/ind/datapdf/rating/2007/LEGI2007.pdf*.

Lanti, A. (2006), "A Regulatory Approach to the Jakarta Water Supply Concession Contracts", *International Journal of Water Resources Development*, 22(2), 255–76.

Lanti, A., F. Ali, A. Kretarto, R. Nugroho and A. Zulfikar (2009), "The First Ten Years of Implementation of the Jakarta Water Supply 25-year Concession Agreement (1998-2008)", *Jakarta Water Supply Regulatory Body*, *www.jakartawater.org/images/stories/unduh/10tahunbrEng.pdf*, accessed 10 January 2010.

Latifulhayat, A. (2008), "The Independent Regulatory Body: A New Regulatory Institution in the Privatised Telecommunications Industry (The Case of Indonesia)", *International Journal of Technology Transfer and Commercialisation*, 7(1), 15–33.

Levine, P., J. Stern and F. Trillas (2003), "Independent Utility Regulators: Lessons from Monetary Policy", *Department of Economics Discussion Papers* 0403, Department of Economics, University of Surrey.

Limao, N. and A.J. Venables (2001), "Infrastructure, Geographical Disadvantage, Transport Costs, and Trade", *The World Bank Economic Review*, 15(3), 451-479.

Majone (2005), *Agency Independence and Accountability*, Proceedings of an Expert Meeting in London, United Kingdom, 10-11 January 2005.

Melody, W.H. (1997), "On the Meaning and Importance of 'Independence' in Telecom Reform", *Telecommunications Policy*, 21(3), 195–199.

OECD (2005), *OECD Guidelines on Corporate Governance of State-owned Enterprises*, OECD Publishing, Paris.

OECD (2007), *OECD Principles for Private Sector Participation in Infrastructure*, OECD Publishing, Paris.

OECD (2008), *Indonesia Economic Assessment*, OECD Publishing, Paris.

OECD (2009), *OECD Reviews of Regulatory Reform Regulatory Impact Analysis: A Tool for Policy Coherence*, OECD Publishing, Paris.

OECD (2010), *Indonesia Investment Review*, forthcoming.

Kalinova, B., A. Palerm and S. Thomsen (2010), "OECD's Foreign Direct Investment Restrictiveness Index: 2010 Update", *OECD Working Papers on International Investment*, No. 2010/3.

PERPAMSI (2010), *Peta Masalah PDAM*, *www.perpamsi.org/online_document_detail.php?id=30*.

PLN (2009), *Annual Report 2008*, *www.pln.co.id/pro-e/images/stories/annual_report/*, accessed March 2009.

Posner, P., S.K. Ryu and A. Tkachenko (2009), "Public-Private Partnerships: The Relevance of Budgeting", *OECD Journal on Budgeting*, 9(1), 41-66.

Purra, M. (2010), "The Indonesian Electricity Sector: Institutional Transition, Regulatory Capacity and Outcomes", *Lee Kuan Yew School of Public Policy Research Paper* No. LKYSPP10-006-CAG, National University of Singapore.

Ray, D. (2008), "Indonesian Port Sector Reform and the 2008 Shipping Law", *SENADA (Indonesia Competitiveness Development) Project*, USAID, Jakarta, *http://pdf.usaid.gov/pdf_docs/PNADN188.pdf*.

Robinson, A. (2008), *Enabling Environment Assessment for Scaling up Sanitation Programs: East Java, Indonesia*, Water and Sanitation Program, World Bank, Washington, DC.

Saghir, J. (2005), "Energy and Poverty: Myths, Links, and Policy Issues", *Energy Working Notes No. 4*, World Bank, Washington, DC.

Serven, L. (1997), "Irreversibility, Uncertainty and Private Investment: Analytical Issues and Some Lessons for Africa", *Journal of African Economies*, 6(3), 229–68.

Stern, J. (2007), "Evaluating Regulatory Decisions and Sector Outcomes in Infrastructure Industries: Results from Africa and other Developing Countries", *PPIAF Working Paper* No. 3, World Bank.

Straub, S. (2008), "Infrastructure and Growth in Developing Countries: Recent Advances and Research Challenges", *Policy Research Working Paper* No. 4460, World Bank, Washington, DC.

Telkom (2009), *Annual Report 2008*, *www.telkom.co.id/investor-relation/reports/annual-reports*, accessed December 2009.

Wallsten, S. (2002), "Does Sequencing Matter? Regulation and Privatization in Telecommunications Reforms", *World Bank Policy Research Working Paper* No. 2817, World Bank, Washington, DC.

Warwick, H. and A. Doig (2004), *Smoke – The Killer in the Kitchen*, ITDG Publishing, London.

Water and Sanitation Programme (2006), *Review of Public Financing for Water Supply and Sanitation in Indonesia*, World Bank, Washington, DC.

World Bank (2004), *Averting an Infrastructure Crisis*, World Bank Office, Jakarta.

World Bank (2007), *Spending for Development*, World Bank, Washington, DC.

Chapter 4

Enhancing the effectiveness of social policies

Indonesia has made considerable progress over the years in improving the social conditions of its population, especially among disadvantaged groups, not least by raising government spending and strengthening social protection programmes. Nevertheless, in some respects social outcomes remain sub-par in relation to regional peers. In particular:

– A rapid increase over the years in government expenditure on education has yet to deliver marked improvements in student performance, which is somewhat weaker than in comparator countries. Enrolment is particularly low in secondary education, suggesting the need to improve the transition from primary to higher levels of education. Efforts are also needed to enhance the quality of teaching. Indonesia will need to at least sustain current levels of education spending in relation to GDP over the longer term to ensure durable improvements in outcomes.

– Government spending on health care and utilisation rates are lower than in comparator countries. Outcomes are also comparatively poor. As in the case of education, regional discrepancies in the health status of the population are narrowing, possibly due in part to the decentralisation of service delivery since the early 2000s. A publicly funded health insurance plan was launched in 2005 to protect vulnerable individuals against the risk of falling into poverty as a result of illness. The programme is being expanded to cover the entire targeted population of very poor, poor and near-poor individuals.

– Indonesia has a number of social-assistance programmes for protecting vulnerable groups against adverse income shocks in periods of crisis. These programmes are reasonably well targeted, but there is considerable room for improvement. Social protection has been strengthened since 2005 with the implementation of government-funded conditional cash transfers and community-based development programmes. Emphasis is now shifting from crisis mitigation towards an extension of the coverage of unconditional and conditional income support. The main challenge in this area is to extend social protection, especially through social security, to informal-sector workers, while strengthening co-ordination and seeking synergies among the existing programmes.

Indonesia's social programmes – especially in the areas of education, health care and social protection – are being strengthened. Government social spending has risen concomitantly. Educational outcomes are somewhat weaker than in regional peers and compare particularly unfavourably against OECD benchmarks. As for health, Indonesia often fares poorly in comparison with regional benchmarks, suggesting ample room for policy action. Emphasis is now being placed on a much needed strengthening of insurance mechanisms for poor and near-poor households. Indonesia's experience with targeted support for vulnerable social groups in periods of economic duress provides invaluable lessons for countries with a comparable level of development. The focus of policy in this area is now rightly shifting towards increasing support to population groups that have so far been left behind, as well as a strengthening of conditional cash transfers to the poor.

This chapter reviews Indonesia's main programmes in the areas of education, health care and social protection. The main challenges policymakers will have to face in the coming years will be to make room in the budget for the increase in coverage of formal social protection and health insurance and to ensure that cost-effective initiatives are put in place to improve educational attainment and the population's health status. Discussions on the design of social policies will need to include the tradeoffs associated with different financing instruments. Moreover, given the long periods of time required for social policies to come to fruition, Indonesia will need to formulate appropriate policies and to be able to maintain them over many years to gradually close the performance gap that currently exists in some areas with respect to regional peers and, especially, with the wealthier countries in the OECD area.

Education

Main issues

Successive Indonesian governments have placed increasing emphasis on human capital accumulation since the return to democracy in the late 1990s. Government spending on education has risen considerably over the last ten years, and Indonesia's education expenditure-to-GDP ratio now exceeds the average of regional peers, although it is still significantly lower than that of OECD countries (Table 4.1). As in other Southeast Asian countries, education accounts for a comparatively high share of total government outlays in Indonesia, in part as a result of the introduction in 2002 of a targeted spending floor for education, at 20% of government spending, which was reached in 2008. Recurrent spending has also risen over time, due predominantly to increases in teachers' compensation, which has reduced to some extent the room in the budget for financing capital outlays. Spending levels nevertheless vary a great deal across the provinces (Table 4.2). Although empirical evidence suggests that Indonesia's spending ratio is in line with the country's income level and socio-demographic indicators (Arze del Granado *et al.*, 2007), the composition of government spending is tilted towards primary

Table 4.1. **Basic education indicators: International comparisons**

	Indonesia			Southeast Asia, 2007	OECD, 2007
	1990	2000	2007		
Inputs					
Public spending on education					
in per cent of GDP	..	2.5[3]	3.5	2.7[4]	5.5[5]
in per cent of government expenditure	..	11.5[3]	17.5	16.1[3]	12.0[5]
Pupil-teacher ratio					
Primary	23.3	22.4	18.8	19.3	15.3
Secondary	12.9	15.8	13.0	17.8	13.3
Outputs and outcomes					
Net enrolment rates (per cent)[1]					
Primary	98.1[2]	94.3	94.8	93.1	95.6
Secondary	..	49.7	69.7	..	91.3
Tertiary (gross)	9.5[2]	14.8[3]	18.0	22.5	71.6
Completion rate, primary (per cent of age group)	93.6	98.2[3]	108.1	99.8	98.5
Persistence to grade 5 (per cent of cohort)	..	95.3	92.8[5]	..	..
Repetition rate (per cent of primary school enrollment)	9.8	6.2[3]	3.3	1.6	0.4[5]
Literacy rate (per cent of 15+ population)	81.5	..	92.0[5]	93.1[6]	99.4
Males	88.0	..	95.2[5]	96.0[6]	99.6
Females	75.3	..	88.8[5]	90.1[6]	99.3

Note: OECD excludes Chile, Israel, Mexico, Poland, Slovenia and Turkey.
1. Net enrolment rates adjust gross enrolment by age-grade mismatches.
2. 1991.
3. 2001.
4. 2004.
5. 2006.
6. 2008.

Source: World Bank (*World Development Indicators*).

schooling to the detriment of higher levels of education, where private financing is predominant (Box 4.1).

Enrolment has risen over the years but remains comparatively low for secondary and higher levels. This suggests that there may be obstacles to the transition from primary education, where attainment is already relatively high, to higher levels of education. Empirical evidence shows that children from low-income households, girls and those living in areas with abundant employment opportunities are most likely to drop out of school after primary education (Suryadarma *et al.*, 2006) and therefore to have comparatively low educational attainment (Table 4.3). Repetition rates are also higher in Indonesia than in comparator countries, even if they have come down sharply. In addition, there are important discrepancies in educational attainment across the different regions, with a number of poor provinces lagging far behind the more prosperous parts of the country (Table 4.4).

An increase in school enrolment has not been accompanied by commensurate improvements in student performance. Indonesia fares poorly in international standardised tests, even after taking socio-economic conditions into account. In 2003, Indonesia ranked 33rd out of 45 countries in the Third International Mathematics Science Study (TIMSS) and 50th out of 57 countries in the 2006 PISA in science, reading and mathematics. The relatively poor performance of Indonesian students is due to a large extent to poor health conditions (discussed below), given that the incidence of child malnutrition and the prevalence of water-borne diseases are considerably higher than in

Table 4.2. Education and health care: Total spending by province, 2008

In per cent of household non-food expenditure

	Education	Health care
Aceh	4.63	7.29
Sumatera Utara	7.25	7.38
Sumatera Barat	7.14	6.46
Riau	5.85	5.78
Jambi	5.13	6.47
Sumatera Selatan	6.25	6.47
Bengkulu	7.30	6.88
Lampung	6.06	7.35
Bangka-Belitung	4.55	5.35
Kepulauan Riau	5.35	5.01
Jakarta Raya	6.95	5.84
Jawa Barat	7.93	7.12
Jawa Tengah	8.68	6.76
Yogyakarta	10.55	6.58
Jawa Timur	9.10	7.62
Banten	7.63	6.48
Bali	4.81	7.68
Nusa Tenggara Barat	7.35	6.78
Nusa Tenggara Timur	4.64	6.26
Kalimantan Barat	7.42	7.18
Kalimantan Tengah	3.60	4.49
Kalimantan Selatan	4.50	5.89
Kalimantan Timur	6.04	4.91
Sulawesi Utara	4.73	7.14
Sulawesi Tengah	4.65	6.30
Sulawesi Selatan	5.68	5.33
Sulawesi Tenggara	6.21	5.30
Gorontalo	7.69	8.24
Sulawesi Barat	4.90	5.44
Maluku	5.77	4.47
Maluku Utara	5.88	5.22
Papua Barat	3.29	3.93
Papua	4.30	4.17
Memorandum item:		
Indonesia	**6.62**	**6.48**

Source: BPS (*Susenas*).

Box 4.1. Indonesia's education system: An overview

The education system

The Indonesian education system comprises pre-school education (kindergarten, two years), primary education (six years), lower-secondary education (three years), upper-secondary education (three years) and higher education. Compulsory education includes the primary and lower-secondary levels (children aged 7-15 years). Secondary education can be formal or vocational.

Education services are provided in a decentralised manner. As a result of comprehensive fiscal decentralisation in 2001, the provinces and local governments (*kota* and *kapubaten*) are responsible for service delivery and the maintenance of schools. Policymaking and standard setting are prerogatives of the central government. The provinces are responsible for planning and quality oversight. School management is carried out by the schools themselves.

Box 4.1. **Indonesia's education system: An overview** *(cont.)*

Public institutions are under the authority of the Ministry of National Education, whereas the private or non-governmental sector is dominated by religious institutions under the oversight of the Ministry of Religious Affairs. Private *madrasahs* account for 12% to 15% of enrolment in primary and lower-secondary education. These institutions follow the general curriculum of regular schools in addition to providing religious teaching.

Private schools play an important role at the secondary level of education: only 7% of primary schools are private, as against 56% at the lower-secondary and 67% at the upper-secondary levels.

Performance assessment and eligibility for enrolment at higher levels of education are carried out on the basis of a national exam (UAN, *Ujain Akhir Nasional*) at the end of lower-secondary and upper-secondary education. Students also sit exams designed by individual schools at the end of primary education.

Recent legislation

Legislation was enacted in 2003 (Law on National Education and the Constitution Amendment No. 3) to introduce the right to publicly funded basic education for all Indonesians aged 7-15 years. A spending floor was introduced for education at 20% of total government expenditure at all levels of administration (OECD, 2008).

The 2005 Teacher Law changed employment conditions, compensation and certification requirements for teachers. The Law introduced new benefits for teachers depending on their functional area, place of work and qualifications on the basis of national certification exams. Teacher certification applies to all schools (public and private) and levels of schooling, for teachers with at least undergraduate education or four-year diplomas (Ministry of National Education, 2007; SMERU, 2009). Certification is carried out on the basis of an assessment of the teacher's competencies. Implementation started in 2007.

A three-pillar strategic plan for 2005-09 was set up by the Ministry of Education focusing on efforts to increase access to education, improve the quality of education and enhance the governance of the education sector. In addition, the government launched the School Operations Fund (BOS, *Bantuan Operasional Sekolah*) in 2005, allowing public funds to be channelled directly to schools and greater managerial autonomy at the school level.

Selected targeted programmes

Indonesia's experience with targeted education-related programmes dates back to the 1998 crisis. The social safety net that was put in place at the time of the crisis (JPS, *Jaring Pengaman Sosial*) also included a targeted scholarship system for poor students enrolled in primary and secondary education. The programme was introduced at the beginning of the 1998-99 school year and was maintained for five years. The main aim of the programme was to safeguard access to education for vulnerable groups, which are most adversely affected by transitory income losses related to economic crises. Targeting was carried out in a decentralised manner at the community and district levels.

Empirical evidence suggests that the programme was fairly pro-poor and that as a result enrolment rose to its pre-crisis level, especially for poor primary-school children living in rural areas (Sparrow, 2007).

During 2001-05, a targeted scholarship programme (BKM) was introduced using part of the budgetary savings arising from lower fuel subsidies. BKM was downsized in 2005 and in part replaced by BOS, intended to protect the poor from further reductions in fuel subsidies in March and October 2005. BOS consists of per-pupil block transfers to primary

Box 4.1. **Indonesia's education system: An overview** *(cont.)*

and lower-secondary schools to cover part of non-payroll operational expenditures. Funds are disbursed directly to schools, reducing the scope for leakages and misuse. By covering part of the schools' recurrent outlays, the programme aims to reduce the need for user charges. Virtually all schools now benefit from the measure. A new sub-programme now focuses on assistance for the purchase of school books. Schools enjoy considerable discretion over the use of funds.

Empirical evidence suggests that BOS has been successful at improving motivation among students from disadvantaged backgrounds, although the programme's impact on drop-out rates at the lower-secondary level has been small (SMERU, 2006).

Table 4.3. **Educational attainment by income level, 1996 and 2008**

Highest qualification, in per cent of population aged at least 5 years

	1996		2008	
	Lowest quintile	Highest quintile	Lowest quintile	Highest quintile
No primary education	52.66	27.09	45.87	23.82
Primary education	35.85	26.01	34.73	19.80
Lower-secondary education				
General	6.52	15.73	11.85	16.08
Vocational	0.88	2.08	0.40	0.82
Upper-secondary education				
General	2.12	14.20	4.97	20.33
Vocational	1.68	8.79	1.71	7.01
Higher education				
Diploma I/II (One/two years of higher education)	0.10	0.93	0.18	1.90
Diploma III (Three years of higher education)	0.08	1.84	0.11	2.53
Diploma IV (Four years of higher education)	0.11	3.33	0.20	7.71

Source: BPS (*Susenas*).

comparator countries. Low educational attainment and hence literacy among women is also known to affect student performance adversely.

Despite a sustained expansion of the school network over the years, supply constraints continue to pose important obstacles to raising educational attainment. The empirical evidence reported in Annex 4.A1, based on Indonesia's experience with large-scale school infrastructure development in the 1970s, shows that each new school built per 1 000 children results in an additional 0.2 average years of educational attainment.[1] A case could also be made for tackling supply constraints by improving the quality of school infrastructure and improving teacher qualifications (Table 4.5). Only a minority of teachers have the minimum qualification required by the Ministry of Education, a feature of the Indonesian education system that indicates the need for increasing emphasis in policy design and evaluation on teacher training and certification. Despite a predominance of private institutions at higher levels of education, there do not appear to be significant differences in the quality of schools, teacher qualifications and pupil-teacher ratios between public and private institutions.[2]

Despite progress in recent years, teacher absenteeism remains a problem in many parts of the country. Although reliable information is scarce, according to a survey conducted in ten local governments in 2002-03, about 19% of teachers had not shown up to

Table 4.4. **Educational attainment by province, 2008**

Highest qualification, in per cent of population aged at least 5 years

	No primary education	Primary education	Lower-secondary education		Upper-secondary education		Higher education		
			General	Vocational	General	Vocational	Diploma I/II	Diploma III	Diploma IV
Aceh	29.3	26.0	18.4	1.2	17.0	2.7	1.4	1.1	3.0
Sumatera Utara	31.6	23.9	18.2	0.7	15.6	5.7	0.8	1.1	2.5
Sumatera Barat	34.8	22.1	16.1	1.0	14.0	5.7	1.5	1.4	3.4
Riau	31.6	26.6	16.8	0.8	15.1	4.6	1.1	1.0	2.4
Jambi	34.3	28.3	16.9	0.5	12.1	3.8	1.2	0.8	2.2
Sumatera Selatan	34.4	30.0	15.3	0.6	12.7	3.4	0.7	0.9	2.1
Bengkulu	33.7	27.3	17.4	0.6	13.2	3.5	1.0	0.7	2.7
Lampung	34.7	28.4	17.4	0.6	10.7	4.7	0.9	0.8	1.9
Bangka-Belitung	35.3	28.5	13.9	0.8	12.4	5.2	0.8	1.1	1.9
Kepulauan Riau	30.1	25.0	14.6	0.8	17.3	7.7	1.1	1.3	2.2
Jakarta Raya	19.2	19.5	17.3	1.0	20.9	10.8	0.7	3.3	7.4
Jawa Barat	30.0	33.2	14.9	0.7	11.2	5.3	0.8	1.3	2.9
Jawa Tengah	31.4	32.2	16.3	0.6	9.8	5.2	0.9	1.2	2.5
Yogyakarta	22.4	23.5	16.5	0.6	17.4	9.2	1.2	2.5	6.7
Jawa Timur	30.6	30.4	16.1	0.8	11.5	5.7	0.7	0.8	3.5
Banten	32.6	27.6	15.8	0.5	12.4	5.9	0.6	1.3	3.3
Bali	27.6	27.3	15.2	0.5	17.5	5.3	1.8	0.9	4.0
Nusa Tenggara Barat	35.4	25.4	15.1	0.5	15.5	2.8	1.2	0.8	3.4
Nusa Tenggara Timur	43.4	29.8	11.2	0.4	8.6	3.2	0.7	0.8	1.9
Kalimantan Barat	40.9	26.4	15.1	0.6	10.5	3.2	0.8	0.9	1.6
Kalimantan Tengah	30.9	33.6	17.3	0.5	11.4	2.4	1.3	0.6	2.0
Kalimantan Selatan	35.8	28.7	15.7	0.5	11.2	3.6	1.2	0.7	2.6
Kalimantan Timur	29.3	24.8	17.2	0.8	16.7	5.8	1.0	1.2	3.2
Sulawesi Utara	31.6	24.0	17.3	1.3	15.9	5.3	0.8	0.9	2.9
Sulawesi Tengah	31.8	31.4	16.1	0.5	12.3	3.2	1.5	0.6	2.6
Sulawesi Selatan	36.1	27.1	14.5	0.6	12.9	3.5	1.1	0.9	3.4
Sulawesi Tenggara	34.1	25.6	16.4	0.4	15.2	2.8	1.6	0.7	3.0
Gorontalo	44.2	28.0	11.8	0.5	9.3	2.8	0.7	0.8	1.8
Sulawesi Barat	39.4	29.9	13.7	0.4	9.9	2.8	1.1	0.6	2.3
Maluku	33.8	26.7	15.8	0.7	15.4	3.5	1.4	0.6	2.1
Maluku Utara	36.4	25.7	15.9	0.5	14.5	2.6	1.5	0.6	2.4
Papua Barat	34.6	24.1	17.4	0.5	13.6	4.9	0.7	1.1	3.0
Papua	36.9	23.8	14.9	1.1	14.6	4.7	0.6	0.9	2.7

Source: BPS (*Susenas*).

work on the days the survey was conducted. Absent teachers are predominantly male, better educated and on temporary contracts (Usman *et al.*, 2004). According to the survey, the main reasons for absenteeism are a lack of adequate transportation to schools and poor quality of school facilities. To some extent, absenteeism can also be related to the structure of compensation for teachers, given that salaries are typically low and grade schedules are flat, leaving limited room for career progression and compensation for incremental qualifications (Ministry of National Education, 2007). Better educated teachers may therefore seek opportunities in more rewarding activities while maintaining a formal attachment to the school system. In any case, empirical analysis shows that absenteeism impinges on student performance, at least for primary school pupils (Suryadarma *et al.*, 2004), which calls for remedial policy action.

Reliance on private institutions at the pre-school and secondary levels creates problems of access for students from disadvantaged backgrounds. Only about 57% of

Table 4.5. **Teacher qualifications and school conditions, 2001-02 and 2007-08**

	Public					Private			
	Share of public institutions (per cent)	Teacher qualification (at least minimum requirement) (per cent)	Classroom conditions (at least good) (per cent)	Pupil/ teacher ratio	Pupil/ class ratio	Teacher qualification (at least minimum requirement) (per cent)	Classroom conditions (at least good) (per cent)	Pupil/ teacher ratio	Pupil/ class ratio
2001-02									
Kindergarten	0.6	81.9	91.2	11	20	52.6	81.3	13	20
Primary	93.2	45.1	35.6	22	26	44.5	70.3	20	26
Lower secondary	52.0	65.1	86.5	17	40	61.7	85.6	13	37
Upper secondary	30.2	67.3	89.5	15	40	59.5	88.9	13	36
General	37.6	69.1	89.7	15	41	59.7	89.7	12	35
Vocational	17.6	57.5	88.9	13	37	56.1	88.0	15	38
2007-08									
Kindergarten	1.1	26.0	78.0	11	21	25.9	53.8	12	20
Primary	91.7	2.0	49.7	19	27	21.1	63.3	17	26
Lower secondary	57.2	87.9	77.6	15	38	82.8	81.1	11	33
Upper secondary	36.7	86.8	88.0	13	37	81.6	86.9	11	37
General	43.9	83.3	88.2	14	36	70.0	88.1	11	34
Vocational	25.9	79.2	87.2	12	39	75.8	85.8	12	40

Source: Ministry of Education.

schools at the lower-secondary level are public, against over 91% at the primary level. Co-payments also put a burden on household budgets, which are often prohibitive for low-income families, and have helped to motivate the introduction of the BOS programme in 2005 (described in Box 4.1 above), which consists of direct block transfers to schools on a per-student basis to finance non-payroll recurrent expenditures. Expenditure on tuition fees, transport, uniforms, books and supplies rises with household non-food expenditure, which implies that children in lower-income households do not in general enrol beyond the primary level (Table 4.6).

Table 4.6. **Household expenditure on education and health care, 1996 and 2008**

In per cent of household non-food expenditure

	Education		Health care	
	1996	2008	1996	2008
Lowest quintile	2.85	4.10	6.50	7.27
Quintile 2	5.13	6.37	6.78	6.81
Quintile 3	6.43	7.08	6.92	6.50
Quintile 4	7.60	7.41	7.11	6.07
Highest quintile	8.83	8.14	6.71	5.76

Source: BPS (*Susenas*).

Education services are provided in a decentralised manner by the provinces and local governments. Although they account for the bulk of spending on education, local authorities have had limited autonomy in personnel management and in the allocation of funds transferred to them by the central government. Recurrent expenditure is based essentially on historical budgeting, and most investment programmes are designed and financed by the central government through grants. The governance of the education system is nevertheless beginning to change with the implementation of the BOS programme since 2005. Although it is now fully implemented, decentralisation may well be contributing to the reduction in disparities in school enrolment across the country (Figure 4.1).

Figure 4.1. **The effect of decentralisation on educational enrolment at the provincial level**

The dots represent the provinces

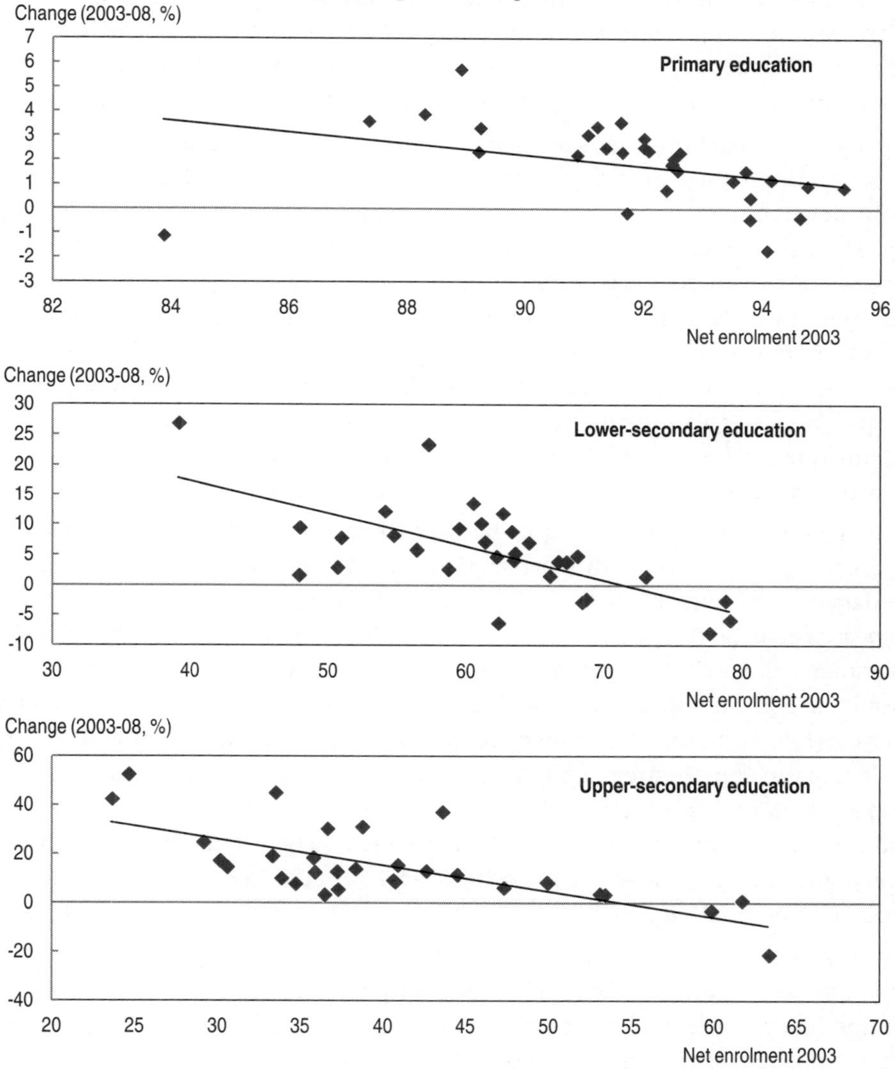

Source: BPS.

StatLink http://dx.doi.org/10.1787/888932341784

Policy considerations

School enrolment needs to be raised at the secondary and tertiary levels. Emphasis on secondary education is justified on the basis of estimated social rates of return, which seem to be higher in Indonesia at the secondary level than for primary education (Arze del Granado *et al.*, 2007). A case can be made for raising government spending – notwithstanding the 20% spending floor introduced in 2002 and met for the first time in 2008 – in support of initiatives to improve school enrolment. Incremental spending could be financed by eliminating fuel and electricity subsidies (as recommended in Chapter 2), which are inequitable and inefficient. There is also likely to be room for reallocating budgetary resources within the education sectors towards cost-effective programmes. Higher spending would allow supply constraints to be tackled, including by improving the quality of schools, which is much needed. Efforts to boost school enrolment beyond primary education would be supported by extension of the PKH income-support programme (discussed below) to the whole country, because PKH conditions assistance on enrolment of school-age children in primary and lower-secondary education. This measure would go in the direction of increasing the opportunity cost of dropping out of school, which is currently low for low-income individuals living in areas with plentiful employment opportunities.

The quality of teaching needs to improve. Indonesia does not suffer from a shortage of teachers, although they are in general poorly qualified. The 2005 Teacher Law is an important development in the direction of creating incentives for teachers to engage in training. The Law recognises that the current career streams and compensation packages do not create the necessary incentives for teachers to invest in human capital accumulation throughout their working lives. To remedy this situation, the Law introduces compensation for staff on the basis of certified qualifications. However, for these initiatives to deliver better educational outcomes, they will need to be complemented by efforts to monitor progress in teaching quality through regular assessments of teachers' pedagogical skills. Continued effort to tackle absenteeism would also be needed. At a minimum, teacher attendance will need to be monitored more effectively.

Financial assistance to schools could be strengthened through various means. There has been increasing emphasis on direct transfers to schools, rather than to students from disadvantaged backgrounds. This is the case of a shift from BKM scholarships to BOS funding in 2005 (described in Box 4.1), which is welcome. While existing support mechanisms could be used to enhance the ability of schools to improve teaching conditions in general, it should be recognised that it is often costlier to provide adequate services to students from disadvantaged backgrounds than for their more affluent counterparts. BOS assistance could therefore target schools located in remote areas and catering predominantly for poor students through a higher per-student transfer. International experience with differentiated transfer mechanisms, such as that of Chile's education vouchers, suggests that they go in the direction of equalising expenditure needs at the school level by recognising the existence of service delivery cost differentials arising from students' socio-economic backgrounds (OECD, 2007).

There is scope for improving the targeting of financial support to students from disadvantaged backgrounds. Indonesia has a long experience of using geographical and community-based mechanisms for identifying the intended beneficiaries of government-funded income-support programmes, especially in periods of economic strain. Assessments of these mechanisms are in general very positive, although they are not perfect, and leakages often occur. Indonesia is in a privileged position in relation to most countries with comparable income levels in that it has large household, labour market and village-level surveys, such as *Susenas*, *Sakernas* and PODES, that are conducted regularly and provide a wealth of information on the socio-economic characteristics of individuals and households, which can be – and have been – used extensively for proxy means-testing. These proxy devices are appropriate, because means-testing is very difficult in countries with a large informal labour market. A focus on primary education in targeted support is justified on the grounds that Indonesian households tend to protect education for older children at the expense of younger siblings when faced with transitory adverse income shocks (Thomas *et al.*, 2004).

Decentralisation could be deepened by giving local governments greater policymaking autonomy. The main advantage of decentralised service delivery is its scope for boosting cost-effectiveness and accountability by allowing the local authorities, who are closer to the people, to match provision to local preferences and needs. Decentralisation is obviously not without pitfalls, including those related to governance and the risk of capture of the benefits of provision by local interest groups. Notwithstanding these caveats, Indonesia could gain from greater autonomy at the local level, especially as far as human resources management is concerned. Efforts in this area would complement the ongoing strengthening of the BOS programme, which relies on decentralised (school-level) management of central government support for non-payroll recurrent expenditure.

Health care

Main issues

Total spending – public and private – on health care is fairly low in Indonesia, even by the standards of neighbouring countries (Table 4.7). This is despite a rapid increase in government outlays following fiscal decentralisation in 2000-01 (Box 4.2). Legislation introduced in 2009 requires the central government to spend 5% of its budget and the local

Table 4.7. **Basic health indicators: International comparisons**

	Indonesia			Southeast Asia, 2007	OECD, 2007
	1990	2000	2007		
Inputs					
Expenditure					
Total (per cent of GDP)	..	..	2.2	4.1	11.4
Private (per cent of GDP)	..	..	1.0	2.2	4.4
Public (per cent of GDP)	..	..	1.2	1.9	7.0
Public (per cent of government expenditure)	..	..	6.2	9.9[6]	17.1
Per capita (current USD)	..	..	41.8	96.2	4 618.4
Hospital beds (per 1 000 people)	0.7	..	..	2.1[6]	6.2[6]
Physicians (per 1 000 people)	0.1	0.2	..	1.5[5]	2.6[4]
Sanitation facilities (per cent of population with access)	51.0	52.0	52.0[6]	65.6[6]	99.9[6]
Water source (per cent of population with access)	72.0	77.0	80.0[6]	87.4[6]	99.6[6]
Outputs and outcomes					
Malnutrition, weight for age (per cent of children under 5)	31.0[1]	24.8	19.6	11.9[7]	..
Incidence of tuberculosis (per 100 000 people)	342.8	269.7	228.0	137.9[7]	13.1[7]
Mortality rate, under 5 (per 1 000)	91.0	48.0	40.5[7]	28.5[7]	5.8[7]
Births attended by skilled health staff (per cent of total)	31.7[2]	64.2[3]	79.4	89.2[7]	99.5[7]
Pregnant women receiving prenatal care (per cent)	76.2[2]	..	93.30	90.9[7]	..
Immunisation rates (in per cent of children aged 12-23 months)					
DPT	60.0	75.0	77.0[7]	92.3[7]	95.4[7]
Measles	58.0	72.0	83.0[7]	91.4[7]	92.5[7]
Life expectancy at birth, total (years)	61.7	67.5	70.8[7]	72.2[7]	80.1[7]
Males	60.0	65.7	68.8[7]	70.4[7]	77.4[7]
Females	63.5	69.4	72.8[7]	74.0[7]	82.9[7]

Note: OECD excludes Chile, Israel, Mexico, Poland, Slovenia and Turkey.
1. 1989.
2. 1991.
3. 2001.
4. 2002.
5. 2005.
6. 2006.
7. 2008.

Source: World Bank (*World Development Indicators*).

Box 4.2. **The Indonesia health-care system: An overview**

Indonesia's health care system was originally set up as a publicly funded primary care system with national coverage. Because of chronic underfunding, a health insurance pillar was created, including mixed private and public insurers to cover private provision. A Health Insurance Law (promulgated in 2004-05) provides a blueprint for the system in the years to come. It leans towards a mixed-economy approach with multiple health care schemes, including a government financed scheme for low-income individuals (described in Box 4.3).

As in the case of education, health care is provided in a decentralised manner. Following fiscal decentralisation in 2001, responsibility for managing government-financed health-care facilities and medical personnel (doctors, nurses and midwives) was delegated to the provinces and local governments. The local authorities have the power to set fees and user charges for public health services and to allocate the transfers received from the central government to finance provision. The central government sets employment and pay conditions for medical personnel and manages the health-insurance scheme for the poor.

Each sub-district has at least one health centre headed by a doctor, usually supported by two or three sub-centres, usually headed by nurses. At the village level, the integrated Family Health Post provides preventive-care services. These health posts are established and managed by the community with the assistance of health centre staff. To improve maternal and child health, midwives are being deployed to the villages.

There has been increased use of health care-related conditionality in the design of targeted income support (discussed below) with the launching of the *PNPM* and PKH programmes in 2007 (see Box 4.4 below).

governments to spend 10% of their budgets on health care (excluding personnel outlays). Local governments already account for about one-half of government outlays, a proportion that is likely to rise when the health insurance scheme for the very poor, poor and near-poor (*Jamkesmas*, see below) is fully operational. Low spending also reflects administrative and managerial weaknesses, given that budgetary appropriations are often not fully executed. Private sources account for the bulk of expenditure, and most private spending is out of pocket, due to low health-insurance coverage. There is no pricing regulation or quality-control mechanism for private health-care providers. Spending levels vary considerably among the provinces (see Table 4.2 above). Curative and out-patient (as opposed to preventive) care accounts for the bulk of spending (Ministry of Health, 2008).

Non-monetary indicators, such as the density of medical staff, suggest that there are important deficiencies in service delivery. The share of doctors in the population is considerably lower in Indonesia than in neighbouring countries, although that of nurses and midwives is higher than the average in comparator countries. To some extent, the supply of doctors is limited by regulations in professional services, which impose stringent barriers to entry in the medical profession, including for foreigners. In addition, as in the case of education, absenteeism is high: survey-based evidence suggests that up to 40% of doctors have been found to be absent from their posts without valid reasons during official working hours (World Bank, 2008a).

Despite low spending, provision is considered adequate at the primary health care level. There is one public health centre (*Puskesmas*) for every 30 000 inhabitants on average (10 000 if sub-centres are considered). Nevertheless, with only about 0.7 beds per

1 000 inhabitants, at close to one-tenth of OECD levels, the supply of in-patient hospital care is deficient. In addition, the quality of services is in general poor, because public health-care facilities often suffer from a lack of equipment and supplies. Possibly as a result of poor service quality, coupled with limited access to health insurance, utilisation rates are low, with bed occupancy rates in the vicinity of 56% in both public and private facilities.

Consistent with important shortcomings in service delivery, Indonesia continues to fare poorly on the basis of several health-status indicators. Immunisation rates are comparatively low, and child malnutrition are well above the average of neighbouring countries. Progress has been significant in reducing the incidence of tuberculosis. Indonesia is also well off-track in meeting the Millennium Development Goal (MDG) of reducing maternal mortality by 2015, the MDG that is most closely related to health system performance, despite impressive progress in this area over the years. Life expectancy at birth and child mortality indicators are nevertheless on a par with those of regional comparators. To some extent, these mostly poor outcomes are due to deficiencies in other areas, such as access to clean water and sanitation, which affects the health status of the population. Low educational attainment, particularly among women, also contributes to poor health outcomes, especially for children. Health-status indicators also differ among income groups and, as expected, are often worse for low-income households (Table 4.8).

Table 4.8. **Health indicators by social group**

	Morbidity rate (per cent)		Last birth attended by skilled staff (per cent)	
	1995	2006	1999	2006
Consumption quintile				
1 (bottom)	23.0	27.4	38.2	53.3
2	24.2	27.9	51.7	66.2
3	25.7	28.5	62.1	74.3
4	26.7	29.0	73.5	83.8
5 (top)	27.3	28.1	88.7	93.1
Indonesia	**25.4**	**28.1**	**60.1**	**72.4**

Source: Ministry of Health.

Access to health care is fairly uneven among the different social groups. Out-of-pocket (OOP) spending, which is a conventional metric for utilisation, is particularly low among less affluent households in part due to the fact that poor individuals tend to seek treatment in public health institutions, where care is provided free of charge. But low OOP spending may also indicate that user charges, especially for in-patient care, make treatment prohibitively expensive in the absence of affordable health insurance. Low-income individuals may therefore be unable to pay for health care and therefore forego it. Self-treatment and recourse to traditional medicine are often the first source of care in the event of illness for the majority of people, even in urban areas (Table 4.9). In the case of out-patient care, the gap in utilisation among the different income groups is lower, especially for public health facilities.

Purchases of pharmaceuticals account for the bulk of OOP spending on health care. Together with ambulatory care, household spending on medicines exceeds that on in-patient care, which is typically provided free of charge in public institutions. The share of OOP spending on medicines is higher for poorer households and those living in rural areas,

Table 4.9. **Utilisation rates in rural and urban areas, 1997 and 2006**

Per cent

	Urban		Rural	
	1997	2006	1997	2006
Public hospital	23.7	22.1	29.4	25.4
Private hospital	31.0	15.7	25.3	7.0
Traditional care	1.2	0.7	3.4	0.9
Self-treatment	35.7	70.4	38.0	72.2
Other treatment	n.a.	1.1	n.a.	1.3

Source: Ministry of Health.

possibly due to self-medication. Recourse to unlicensed vendors of drugs and traditional medicines is not uncommon among low-income groups. But, in the absence of appropriate health insurance, expenditure is now higher as a proportion of non-food consumption among the poor, because there is no public refund mechanism for the cost of medicines prescribed during treatment and purchased directly by patients (Table 4.6).

The incidence of catastrophic health payments is particularly high among the poor, who are most exposed to unforeseeable health events, although it appears to be declining. Such payments affect living conditions in the short run, when the costs of treatment are financed by cutting back current consumption, and/or in the long run, when treatment is financed through indebtedness, which needs to be repaid at the sacrifice of future consumption or the depletion of accumulated savings or assets. These households tend to rely on government support, especially through *Jamkesmas*, a health insurance programme for poor and near-poor households that has been set up to mitigate at least in part the adverse impact of catastrophic health risk on poor and near-poor individuals (Box 4.3). By

Box 4.3. **Indonesia's experience with health insurance**

Government-financed programmes

A health-insurance programme (*Jamkesmas*) was introduced in 2008 to mitigate at least in part the adverse impact of catastrophic health risk on vulnerable (poor and near-poor) individuals. The programme covers comprehensive out-patient care in public health clinics and third-class hospital comprehensive in-patient care, and aims to protect vulnerable individuals who might otherwise fall into poverty as a result of unanticipated health events that would prevent them from working. *Jamkesmas* currently covers about 35% of the population and builds upon existing schemes (*Askeskin*, JPS health card and JPK-Gakin) that have been put in place since the 1998 crisis (see below). *Jamkesmas* is being extended to cover the entire targeted population of 93 million very poor, poor and near-poor individuals. Beneficiaries are identified by the local authorities. The authorities intended *Jamkesmas* beneficiaries to be accepted by both private and public health care providers, but only about one-third of private hospitals currently do.

Early attempts to shield vulnerable social groups from the risk of falling into poverty as a result of poor health focused on price subsidies for public health care targeted on the poor. These programmes have been in operation since the economic crisis of 1998 and include the JPS health-card programme, which was part of the social safety net that was put in place during the crisis, and a pilot health-insurance programme (JPK-Gakin), which was implemented after the crisis.

Box 4.3. Indonesia's experience with health insurance *(cont.)*

The JPS health-card programme introduced a user-fee waiver for public health care. Indirect-care costs, as well those related to access to care in remote areas, are important deterrents to health-care utilisation among the poor. A more comprehensive health-insurance programme (*Askeskin*) was introduced in 2005 as part of the compensating measures to protect vulnerable social groups from the loss in purchasing power associated with a reduction in fuel subsidies. *Askeskin* had national coverage and open membership, and was publicly funded. Beneficiaries were entitled to free-of-charge comprehensive out-patient and in-patient care at public health centres and in-patient services at public third-class hospitals. Special health services were also provided under *Askeskin* in remote areas and isolated islands, as well as obstetric and mobile health services, immunisation and pharmaceuticals.

Askeskin differed from the JPS health-card programme by focusing on individuals, rather than households, and by conditioning refunds to health-care providers for the services actually delivered to programme beneficiaries. The JPS health-card programme was based on a price subsidy associated with the use of the health card. As with the JPS health-card programme, targeting was carried out in a decentralised manner, whereby beneficiaries were identified at the community level. While the authorities intended *Askeskin* cards to be accepted by both private and public health providers, more than 30% of private providers did so.

Privately financed programmes

In addition to publicly provided programmes, there are occupational health-insurance schemes for civil servants (*Askes*), the police and armed forces (*Asabri*) and private-sector employees (*Jamsostek*), in addition to community health insurance and privately funded health insurance. It is estimated that at most 20% of the total population had health insurance in 2004 (Sparrow *et al.*, 2009), though by 2008 that figure seems to have risen to nearly 30%.

Under *Askes*, civil servants contribute 2% of their basic salary (matched by the government) to the publicly managed insurance fund. The scheme covered about 6% of the population in 2007 (13.8 million beneficiaries, comprising 4.5 million civil servants and their 9.3 million their dependents). Old-age and survivor pensions for civil servants are also provided under *Taspen*.

Jamsostek, which is also publicly managed, covers individuals working in private enterprises employing at least 10 workers and turnover of over 1 million *rupiah* (and their families). *Jamsostek* offers old-age pensions, life and health insurance, and job-related disability and illness compensation. Employers pay 3 or 6% of salary depending on the employee's marital status. Companies can opt out of the scheme, if they offer comparable or better health insurance. Because of the opt-out clause, out of a total 19.8 million employees enrolled at *Jamsostek* in 2005, only 2.7 million were covered by health insurance. As discussed in the 2008 *Economic Assessment* (OECD, 2008), informal-sector workers, who account for the vast majority of employment in Indonesia, are not covered.

contrast, contributive programmes, such as schemes sponsored by employers, are more prevalent among the more affluent social groups (Table 4.10).

Indonesia's experience with the targeting of health insurance is by and large positive but could be improved considerably. Empirical analysis shows that the JPS health-card programme – one of the earlier initiatives in this area and a precursor to *Jamkesmas* – was

Table 4.10. **Coverage of health insurance by income level, 2008**

In per cent of households

	Lowest income quintile	Quintile 2	Quintile 3	Quintile 4	Highest income quintile
Government pension	0.72	1.31	2.79	6.71	16.27
Employer-financed health-care reimbursement	0.2	0.67	1.45	2.6	4.62
Health security for civil servants	0.1	0.16	0.36	0.69	1.95
Employer-financed health insurance (*Jamsostek*, etc.)	0.14	0.3	0.6	1.15	2.98
Social security health insurance (JPS health card, etc.)	26.82	20.96	16.73	12.63	6.68
Community-based health care	0.6	0.54	0.57	0.51	0.37
Other	3.5	3.21	3.06	3.15	2.75

Source: BPS (*Susenas*).

reasonably well targeted, despite leakages to the non-poor population for both in-patient and out-patient care (Pradhan *et al.*, 2007; Sparrow, 2008). In the case of *Askeskin*, most beneficiaries were low-income individuals, suggesting that targeting was adequate (Sparrow *et al.*, 2009).[3] Utilisation of both out-patient and in-patient care was found to have risen among programme beneficiaries after introduction of *Askeskin*. Experience with these programmes also suggests the presence of barriers to utilisation among the poor, reflecting a lack of knowledge about entitlements and the cost of transport to health-care facilities, which may be high in remote areas.

Access to government-sponsored health insurance improves utilisation by the underserved population. The empirical evidence reported in Annex 4.A2 shows that several social groups, including individuals living in rural areas, women and informal-sector workers, have a lower probability of visiting a health-care facility in the event of illness. By contrast, utilisation rates are high for individuals in possession of health insurance, especially government- and enterprise-sponsored schemes. This suggests that a carefully designed programme could increase the affordability of health care and therefore help to remove the constraints that currently prevent certain individuals from seeking treatment when confronted with a health problem.

Poor infrastructure is also affecting the health status of the population. Access to basic sanitation is very unequal among the different income groups (Table 4.11). Despite some progress in recent years, a lack of access to clean water among the poor has been a major cause of child mortality. According to WHO data, in 2008 the percentage of deaths among children under five years of age due to diarrhoeal diseases was around 15 in Indonesia against an average of 3 for Southeast Asia (Malaysia, Philippines, Thailand and Vietnam) and 0.6 in the OECD area.

As in the case of education, comprehensive fiscal decentralisation since 2001 has possibly contributed to a reduction in regional disparities in health indicators (Figure 4.2). The level of government spending and the distribution of doctors and midwives nevertheless vary a great deal across provinces. To a large extent, this is due to the fact that sub-national spending on health care is calculated on the basis of historical budgeting, rather than expenditure needs that would take regional specificities into account. Differentials in spending levels among the provinces have therefore not narrowed since decentralisation. Another characteristic of intergovernmental fiscal arrangements in Indonesia that has a direct bearing on the efficiency of government spending is that service delivery costs are financed by the central government through the transfer and grant

Table 4.11. Access to water and sanitation infrastructure by income levels, 2008

	Lowest quintile	2nd quintile	3rd quintile	4th quintile	Highest quintile	Difference between highest and lowest quintiles	
						2008	2005[1]
Sources of drinking water							
Piped water	5.3	7.9	11.3	15.2	23.8	18.6	28.1
Pump	9.9	11.4	12.9	13.3	13.7	3.8	6.2
Well	46.6	44.6	41.2	37.9	26.3	–20.3	–19.7
Spring	24.2	18.8	14.6	10.6	5.6	–18.7	–18.2
Other	14.0	17.4	20.1	23.0	30.6	16.6	3.7
Waste water disposal							
Septic tank	27.1	36.8	45.1	55.7	73.5	46.3	52.0
Untreated disposal	29.7	26.2	23.3	18.1	9.9	–19.8	–12.2
Hole	39.7	34.1	29.2	24.3	15.4	–24.3	–16.3
Other	3.5	2.9	2.5	2.0	1.3	–2.3	–23.5
Toilet facilities							
Private	36.9	47.3	56.9	68.3	85.0	48.1	42.1
Shared	15.8	14.5	13.1	10.7	6.3	–9.5	–5.7
Other	47.3	38.3	30.0	20.9	8.7	–38.6	–36.4

1. Refers to 1996 for waste water disposal.

Source: *Susenas* and OECD calculations.

Figure 4.2. Decentralisation and health-care indicators

The dots represent the provinces

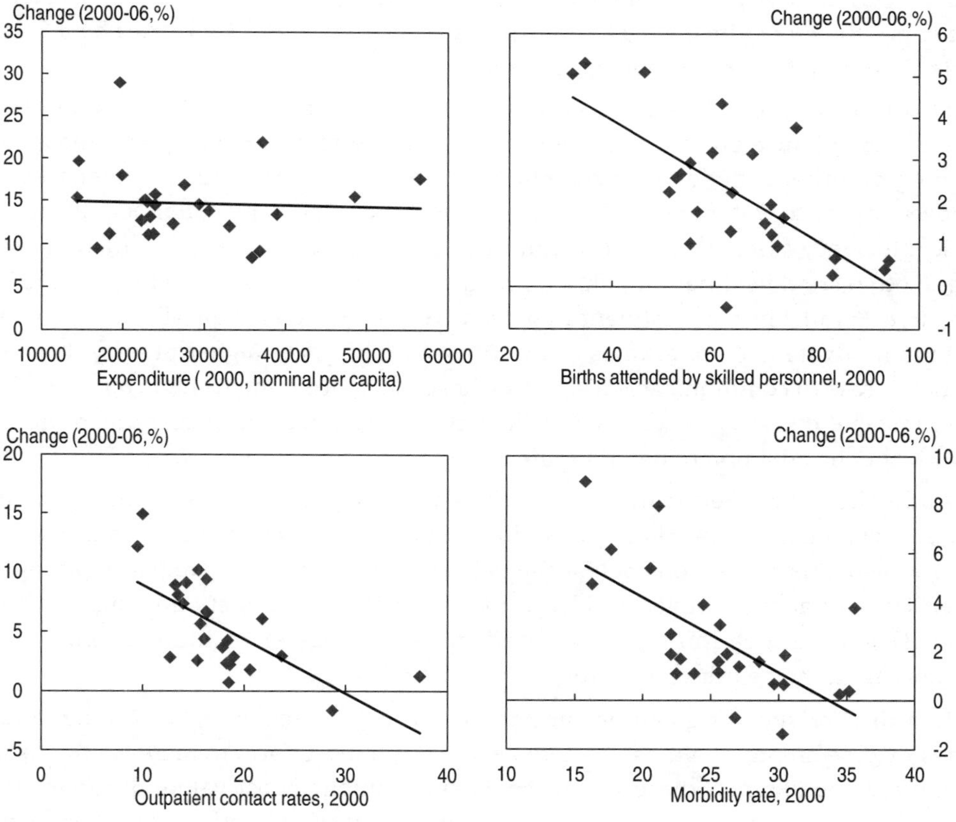

Source: BPS.

StatLink http://dx.doi.org/10.1787/888932341803

system. This creates incentives for the recipient jurisdictions to increase their payroll with limited concern for cost-effectiveness. In addition, the sub-national jurisdictions have limited autonomy to punish absenteeism.

Empirical evidence suggests that local governments hike spending on health care in tandem with increases in their revenue base. This is especially the case of infrastructure development spending, for which the elasticity of outlays to revenue is estimated to be greater than one (Kruse *et al.*, 2009). Recurrent spending on health care is particularly sensitive to changes in the general allocation grants (DAU), which underscores the importance of intergovernmental transfers for financing the decentralised provision of health care.

Policy considerations

Indonesia's current level of health-care spending is insufficient to ensure the provision of adequate health services to the population. Growth in household income, as well as changes in the population's demographic structure and epidemiological risks will change the demand for services towards increasingly sophisticated care, a trend that is likely to put additional pressure on the budget in the years to come, even though part of health insurance is privately funded.[4] The authorities estimate the additional cost to the budget of extending *Jamkesmas* to the entire targeted population to be small. But policy initiatives will be needed to create room in the budget for accommodating current and emerging demands for government services over the longer term. The authorities intend to contain health costs by increasingly relying on DRG (diagnosis-related group) methods for payments, which are already used in hospitals providing care to *Jamkesmas* beneficiaries. Efforts should therefore continue in this area.

Efforts to improve the population's health status should be complemented by measures to enhance efficiency in service delivery and to secure adequate financing for spending on other functional areas that have an impact on health outcomes, such as improved access to water and sanitation, female literacy and early childhood nutrition. Of course, efficiency gains depend on a multitude of initiatives, which are difficult to single out and often straddle different policy domains. But there are areas where gains are likely to be large. For instance, investment in preventive care, which is typically associated with substantial private and social rates of return, should be given higher priority. This is the case not only with communicable diseases, whose incidence remains high, but also of non-communicable diseases, where health literacy is particularly important as a means of encouraging the adoption of healthier life styles.

As in the case of education, initiatives to tackle absenteeism among medical personnel would also have a large payoff in terms of improving health outcomes. Because local governments are responsible for the delivery of services, they are better placed than higher levels of administration to identify and punish misconduct and abuse. The local authorities should therefore be granted increased power to monitor and punish absenteeism in the health-care sector.

Health-care spending can become more pro-poor. Because health indicators are typically worse among the most vulnerable social groups, efforts to increase the focus of government spending on these groups could substantially boost value for money in the health-care sector. Experience with *Askeskin* shows that the targeting of *Jamkesmas* could be improved – budget conditions permitting – by including coverage for indirect costs, such as for transport, which are likely to increase utilisation rates among the poor, especially in remote areas. Informal user fees are additional important deterrents to utilisation of health-care facilities by low-income individuals, but it is difficult to ascertain whether or not informal side-payments are often requested. Efforts to monitor and punish this practice would therefore also be welcome.

It is important to strengthen health insurance by reforming *Jamsostek*, the privately financed health insurance scheme for private-sector employees. Participation is currently low in part because of an opt-out clause for employers who prefer to make alternative arrangements for their employees and the exclusion of own-account workers and employees in small enterprises from membership. The opt-out clause should be revoked, so that participation would be mandatory for all eligible private-sector enterprises. Employers willing to offer broader coverage than *Jamsostek*'s would continue to be able to do so through complementary schemes. At the same time, the size of enterprises allowed to participate could be reduced from the current threshold of ten employees. As recommended in the 2008 *Economic Assessment* (OECD, 2008), participation in *Jamsostek* could also be extended to the self-employed on an optional basis. The main advantage of a single-provider arrangement for privately financed health insurance is that risk-pooling can be improved by preventing cream-skimming, whereby firms would hire younger, less risky individuals to minimise insurance costs. At the same time, wasteful competition for low-risk enrolees can be reduced, and service delivery can become more homogenous. Of course, a number of conditions would have to be met. *Jamsostek*'s technical capacity would need to be enhanced, including for conducting actuarial analysis, and regulation would need to be improved to protect the interests of enrolees. Effort should also be put into enhancing enforcement and credibility in the programme so as to increase compliance and to encourage individuals who can afford to participate, but currently prefer not to do so.

A strengthening of *Jamsostek* would complement efforts to extend the coverage of health insurance to the entire population, which the authorities hope to achieve by 2014. To this end, consideration could be given to merging the existing insurance schemes for civil servants (*Asabri*, *Taspen* and *Askes*) into a single programme. This architecture would provide a third pillar to Indonesia's health insurance system, together with *Jamsostek* and *Jamkesmas*,

Intergovernmental fiscal relations could be improved in support of cost-efficiency in the provision of health care. This is because the local governments are at the forefront of service delivery in the social area and financing is provided through intergovernmental transfer arrangements. Nevertheless, current intergovernmental transfer mechanisms do not create the necessary incentives for the recipient jurisdictions to seek efficiency gains, because transfers are based essentially on historical budgeting. At a minimum, transfers to local governments should be based on expenditure needs, rather than historical budgeting, with the aim of assuring provision according to standards and norms set by the central government.

Social protection

Main issues

Indonesia's experience with government-financed social protection has focused on initiatives to shield vulnerable groups from income losses in periods of economic duress. A first generation of poverty alleviation programmes was put in place at the time of the 1997-98 crisis (Box 4.4).[5] More recent initiatives have aimed to compensate vulnerable

Box 4.4. Indonesia's social-assistance programmes

Crisis-related programmes

Rice for Poor Families (RASKIN) was implemented during the 1997-98 crisis to alleviate poverty through the distribution of a regular ration of subsidised rice to vulnerable households. About one-third of the population benefitted from the programme at the time of the crisis. The programme is relatively well targeted: nearly 85% of the subsidy accrues to households deemed needy by village leaders. RASKIN was also used as an additional compensatory mechanism for protecting the poor against fuel price hikes in 2002-03 and 2005.

The *Fuel Subsidy Reduction Compensation Fund* (PKPS-BBM) was launched in 2005 to compensate poor households for a reduction in fuel subsidies. The budgetary savings arising from a reduction in outlays on fuel subsidies were used to finance the disbursement of targeted transfers to poor households to finance basic health care and insurance against income losses, the School Operations Fund (BOS) described above, financing for the development of infrastructure at the local level and unconditional cash transfers.

Assessments of these transfer programmes are by and large positive. Of particular interest are innovative targeting mechanisms, given the need to implement programmes rapidly in times of crisis and the difficulties associated with formal means-testing. Village leaders, who command respect among the recipient population, were used to identify the targeted population and self-targeting methods. Moreover, there is little evidence to suggest that these programmes are contributing to the creation of poverty traps, which would discourage work effort.

In addition to these programmes, a number of sectoral initiatives have been put in place, often with the aim of linking poverty alleviation and crisis-related measures to the fulfilment of broader social objectives. This is the case of the targeted scholarship programme for poor students enrolled in primary and secondary education and the JPS health-card programme that were implemented as part of JPS, as well as the targeted scholarships (BKM) and school support fund (BOS) introduced in 2005 at the time of the reductions in fuel subsidies.

Conditional cash transfers

In 2007, the authorities launched two pilot conditional cash transfer programmes: Community Cash Transfer (*PNPM*) and Conditional Cash Transfer (PKH, *Program Keluarga Harapan*). While PNPM is a block grant to communities, allowing them autonomy in designing and managing their own activities in pursuit of programme objectives, PKH is a conditional cash transfer targeting poor households (Rahayu *et al.*, 2008; World Bank, 2008c). The programmes' objectives include five of the eight MDGs: poverty and hunger reduction, universal coverage of basic education, gender equality and maternal and child mortality reduction. These programmes were motivated by the fact that Indonesia lags behind regional comparator countries in key education and health-care indicators. Their impact on poverty and vulnerability has yet to be fully assessed.

Coverage of the conditional cash transfer programmes was extended to 720 000 households in 2009 and is planned to be extended gradually by 2013 to all 2.9 million households estimated to be in poverty. Implementation is expected to be strengthened through the payment of benefits by means of bank cards, rather than the postal service, although the limited availability of ATMs in rural areas and outside Java remains an important constraint. Targeting is carried out in part through the use of proxy instruments, given the difficulties of relying fully on means-testing in a country with a sizeable informal labour market.

households for rising fuel prices due to reductions in fuel subsidies in 2002-03 and 2005. The right to government-funded social protection is a constitutional entitlement, and the current administration is committed to meeting the Millennium Development Goal of halving the incidence of poverty by 2015. Efforts to boost coordination among the authorities overseeing the various social protection programmes include the creation of a Poverty Commission under the Vice-President's purview in 2009.

Indonesia is now shifting attention in the design of social protection programmes from crisis mitigation to strengthening conditional support for vulnerable households (predominantly through the PKH programme since 2007) in a manner that helps them to pull themselves out of poverty, by raising awareness about their situation of deprivation, links social protection to sustained improvements in social outcomes and equips poor individuals with the means to prevent a durable fall into poverty in the presence of adverse income shocks. Complementary initiatives to empower vulnerable individuals have also been launched, including government-sponsored micro-credit programmes. At the same time, there has been increasing emphasis on universal programmes, such as social and health insurance and community-based development initiatives since 2007, so as to extend formal social safety nets to needy groups that have so far been neglected, such as the elderly, the disabled, individuals living in isolated communities, single-parent households and indigenous groups. Options for introducing unemployment insurance are discussed in Chapter 1.

Poverty continues to decline. Based on Indonesia's national poverty line, which is set at the provincial level for urban and rural households separately, the incidence of poverty has fallen steadily since the 1997-98 crisis to nearly 15.5% in 2008, or about 36 million people. An alternative measure of poverty, defined as one-half of median household consumption per capita, points to a somewhat lower incidence of poverty relative to that calculated on the basis of the national poverty line (Table 4.12). As noted in the 2008 *Economic Assessment* (OECD, 2008), there continues to be a concentration of individuals around the national poverty threshold, given that the income and poverty gap ratios remain fairly low, suggesting that the consumption level of the average poor individual is close to median consumption threshold. On the basis of this alternative measure of poverty, inequality as gauged by the Gini coefficient has been fairly stable from 1996 to 2008, although the income share of individuals/households in the wealthiest income decile has increased relative to that of those in the lowest decile.

Educational attainment and labour-market status are powerful determinants of poverty in Indonesia. The empirical analysis reported in Annex 4.A3 shows that the probability of being poor rises with the size of households and the share of children and elderly members in the household. Households headed by women and unmarried individuals are also more likely to be poor. By contrast, the probability of being poor falls with educational attainment and in households with a higher share of individuals engaged in salaried occupations. As discussed in the 2008 *Economic Assessment* (OECD, 2008), low-skilled individuals tend to work in non-salaried jobs, which account for the bulk of the informal labour market. The decomposition analysis reported in the Annex shows that rising educational attainment has contributed strongly to reducing poverty between 2002 and 2008. These characteristics of poor households point to areas where formal social protection networks could be strengthened.

Table 4.12. **Poverty and income-inequality indicators, 1996 and 2008**

	1996	2008
Poverty incidence[1]		
Poverty headcount (per cent)	7.7	11.0
Income gap[2] (per cent)	15.9	21.8
Poverty gap[2] (per cent)	1.2	2.4
Income distribution		
Gini coefficient	0.36	0.35
Ratio of income shares of highest to lowest income deciles	4.4	4.7
Ratio of income shares of highest to lowest income quintiles	2.6	2.6
Memorandum item:		
Poverty headcount based on national poverty lines (per cent)	17.6	15.4

1. Based on a poverty line of one-half of median household consumption per capita (28 493 *rupiah* per capita per month in 1996 and 186 857 *rupiah* per capita per month in 2008).
2. The income gap ratio is the average per capita consumption shortfall of the population below the poverty line. It is defined as $IG = \frac{z-\bar{c}}{z}$, where z is the poverty line and $\bar{c}$ is average per capita consumption of the population below the poverty line. The poverty gap ratio is the sum of the income gap ratio for the population below the poverty line divided by total population. It is defined as $PG = \frac{1}{n}\sum_{i=1}^{q}\frac{(z-c_i)}{z}$, where *n* is total population, c_i is per capita consumption of household *i* and *q* is the population below the poverty line. Therefore, the poverty gap ratio can be calculated as the product of the income gap ratio and the headcount ratio.

Source: BPS (*Susenas*, *Indonesia Social Indicators*) and OECD calculations.

The incidence of poverty is also closely related to adverse income shocks, with a large number of individuals falling below the poverty line in periods of economic difficulty.[6] Empirical evidence suggests that the transition in and out of poverty is relatively smooth during an economic crisis, with many households experiencing relatively short periods of poverty when faced with an economic shock (Suryahadi *et al.*, 2003). Notwithstanding this flexibility, regional effects are often important, and the incidence of poverty varies a great deal among the provinces (Table 4.13), in part because the transmission of economic shocks is constrained by Indonesia's geography and infrastructure bottlenecks that pose obstacles to labour mobility and the adjustment of internal labour markets in periods of crisis.[7]

Considerable effort has been placed on improving the targeting of income-support programmes. It is difficult to implement formal means-testing in developing countries with large informal sectors because of a lack of information of the income of potential beneficiaries. Indonesia has a large experience with proxy instruments (which are based on individual and household characteristics that are correlated with poverty, as well as hard-to-hide assets that are used to predict consumption) and community-based targeting (where village residents select programme beneficiaries, often using scoring mechanisms based on proxy means-testing). Different methodologies may be appropriate under different circumstances, and determining which one works best in essentially an important empirical question from the viewpoint of policy design and evaluation. Evidence based on field experiments shows that proxy means-testing performs better than community-based targeting in identifying the poor, particularly near the poverty threshold (Alatas *et al.*, 2010).[8]

Despite much progress in recent years, Indonesia has yet to introduce an affordable contributory system of social insurance. As discussed in the 2008 *Economic Assessment* (OECD, 2008), a National Social Security Law (*Jamsosnas*, enacted in 2004 but so far not yet regulated) extends contributory social security arrangements to informal-sector workers and the self-employed. The scheme would be publicly run and cover old-age and survivors'

Table 4.13. **Poverty headcount by province, 2008**

In per cent of households

	Poverty line[1]	
	Province-specific	National
Aceh	9.9	5.7
Sumatera Utara	8.9	8.4
Sumatera Barat	8.9	6.2
Riau	9.2	2.4
Jambi	6.5	4.9
Sumatera Selatan	9.4	7.6
Bengkulu	13.6	11.9
Lampung	11.2	15.3
Bangka-Belitung	6.4	0.7
Kepulauan Riau	8.0	1.1
Jakarta Raya	6.1	0.1
Jawa Barat	9.7	9.6
Jawa Tengah	8.6	15.5
Yogyakarta	12.7	10.9
Jawa Timur	8.6	15.0
Banten	9.9	6.4
Bali	5.5	4.4
Nusa Tenggara Barat	10.5	18.1
Nusa Tenggara Timur	15.2	25.8
Kalimantan Barat	9.8	9.6
Kalimantan Tengah	8.6	4.6
Kalimantan Selatan	7.5	5.2
Kalimantan Timur	11.7	4.1
Sulawesi Utara	8.4	8.7
Sulawesi Tengah	11.4	16.4
Sulawesi Selatan	11.1	14.5
Sulawesi Tenggara	10.0	18.1
Gorontalo	11.5	18.6
Sulawesi Barat	9.1	16.5
Maluku	15.0	20.4
Maluku Utara	13.3	8.7
Papua Barat	16.8	11.2
Papua	24.4	18.1

1. Poverty lines defined as of one-half of median household consumption per capita.

Source: BPS (*Susenas*) and OECD calculations.

pensions, as well as death and disability insurance. A minimum pension would be set at 70% of the statutory minimum wage. The retirement age would be only 55 years, and workers would be eligible for a pension after as little as 15 years of contribution. Although contribution rates are not yet known, the retirement age and the shortness of the length of contribution required for eligibility for an old-age pension are too generous and would therefore put considerable strain on the budget, in addition to the cost of an announced contribution subsidy for poor individuals.

Policy considerations

Because poverty is a multi-dimensional phenomenon, corrective policies need to be multi-faceted. Indonesia has considerable experience with linking poverty alleviation efforts to broader policies related to crisis mitigation and has put in place innovative programmes building on existing social networks at the community level. Although a case can be made for placing increasing emphasis on strengthening universal, unconditional social and health insurance, as is currently intended, the benefits of creating synergies across policy domains through conditionality should not be underestimated. Conditionality could be introduced in income-transfer programmes so as to require beneficiaries to keep their children at school and to pay regular visits to health clinics. As recommended above, conditionality could be used to complement policy action to raise secondary school enrolment. Experience with conditional income support has been very positive in other regions, notably in Latin America, where a number of programmes are currently in place.[9]

Indonesia's flagship conditional income-support programmes – community-based PNPM and household-based PKH – are well thought-out and are working reasonably well, although there is room for improvement. They are both underpinned by the need to tackle the root causes of material deprivation in conjunction with providing vulnerable groups with the means to pull themselves out of poverty in a sustained manner. To this end, Indonesia is also taking steps to strengthen measures focused on empowering the needy, including micro-credit schemes sponsored by the government. But these two streams of social protection mechanisms need to be better integrated, and programme implementation needs to be strengthened, so that entry into these empowerment initiatives is a natural step following exit from conditional income support. It is also important to tackle design problems that may lead to inclusion and exclusion errors in the identification of the programme's intended beneficiaries.

Efforts to improve the targeting of social assistance have been constrained by the difficulty of reaching informal-sector workers. This is a common challenge for countries, such as Indonesia, where widespread informality in the labour market is an obstacle to greater reliance on formal means-testing. As a result, proxy-targeting could be used more extensively to target informal-sector workers. The fairly large body of empirical research that is currently available on the main determinants of poverty in Indonesia and on the characteristics of the social groups who are most likely to fall into poverty as a result of adverse economic shocks could therefore be used for identifying targeting instruments. Since large households and/or those headed by women and less-educated individuals are particularly at risk of being poor, they could therefore be targeted by existing income-support programmes.

The Indonesian authorities are taking steps to strengthen contributive social insurance while increasing the coverage of formal social safety nets. Progress has so far been considerably more timid in setting up social insurance than in expanding publicly funded social-assistance programmes. In any case, as discussed in the 2008 *Economic Assessment* (OECD, 2008), a more fundamental policy consideration is how to finance the broadening and strengthening of formal safety nets over the longer term. Appropriate actuarial costing of the existing schemes, especially *Jamkesmas*, is imperative, as noted above. Such efforts should be extended to all social-protection programmes, so that appropriate sources of finance and their associated tradeoffs can be identified. Most countries rely on a combination of general taxation and social contributions to finance social protection, and the tradeoffs associated with different funding instruments will become increasingly prominent in the policy debate. OECD experience suggests that the negative employment effects of the tax wedge are especially strong for low-paid employment, notably in the presence of a binding minimum wage.

Box 4.5. **Summary of policy recommendations: Social policies**

Education

- Raise government spending on education, especially at the secondary level, to finance the extension of conditionality of existing income-transfer programmes to secondary school enrolment.
- Carry out regular assessments of teachers' pedagogical skills and regular monitoring of teacher attendance to tackle the problem of their absenteeism.
- Target BOS (School Operations Fund) assistance on schools located in remote areas and catering predominantly for poor students through a higher per-student transfer.
- Grant greater autonomy to local governments in human resources management.

Health care

- Raise government spending on health care, and carry out a comprehensive costing of *Jamkesmas.*
- Maintain adequate financing for programmes in functional areas that are also associated with improvements in health outcomes, such as improved water and sanitation, female literacy and early childhood nutrition.
- Public finances permitting, include coverage for transport and related costs under *Jamkesmas.*
- Revoke the opt-out clause for participation in *Jamsostek*, reduce the eligibility condition for membership to fewer than ten employees, and allow the self-employed to participate on an optional basis.
- Gradually shift emphasis in the design of transfers to the local governments away from historical budgeting and towards a formula-based system founded on expenditure needs.

Social assistance

- Make further use of conditionality in the design of income-transfer programmes so as to require beneficiaries to keep their children at school and to pay regular visits to health clinics.
- Better integrate conditional income-support and empowerment programmes.
- Use proxy instruments more extensively to target informal-sector workers.
- Carry out a comprehensive actuarial costing of existing social protection programmes to allow for appropriately identifying the associated financing instruments.

Notes

1. Indonesia engaged in a massive programme to build schools (*Sekolah Dasar INPRES*) between the school years of 1973-74 and 1978-79 using the revenue accruing from the development of oil and gas reserves. As a result more than 61 000 primary schools were built during 1973-79. Empirical evidence shows that the cohort of individuals born in the districts that benefited from the programme was more likely to stay longer at school and to earn more once joining the labour force. In addition, the increase in the proportion of educated workers as a result of the programme encouraged the participation of both educated and uneducated workers in the formal labour market (Duflo, 2001 and 2004).
2. Nevertheless, there appears to be a considerable gap in earnings between graduates from public and private schools. Based on survey data, Fahmi (2009) shows that graduates from public schools earn 25% and 35% more than their counterparts from private non-religious and private religious schools, respectively.

3. This finding is in line with empirical evidence for government spending on subsidised health care, which suggests that public outlays contribute to reducing income inequality, although they are not necessarily pro-poor (O'Donnell *et al.*, 2007). In-patient care tends to be more pro-rich than out-patient care.
4. The incidence of communicable diseases is in decline, although it remains comparatively high for tuberculosis and measles, while that of non-communicable diseases, such as diabetes, cardio-vascular conditions and cancer, is on the rise.
5. See Perdana and Maxwell (2004) for a detailed discussion of the micro-level effects of a number of poverty-alleviation programmes in Indonesia.
6. The bulk of the existing literature on household poverty in Indonesia focuses on the financial crisis of the late 1990s. See Frankenberg, Thomas and Beegle (1999), Skoufias and Suryahadi (2000), Suryahadi, Sumarto and Pritchett (2003), Strauss et al. (2004) and Suryahadi and Sumarto (2005) for more information and empirical evidence.
7. See Bidani and Ravallion (1993) and Pradhan *et al.* (2000) for more information and empirical evidence.
8. This is because community-based methods tend to reflect how individual community members rank each other, rather than actual poverty as measured on the basis of per capita expenditure or income.
9. See Rawlings and Rubio (2005) for more information.

Bibliography

Alatas, V., A. Banerjee, R. Hanna, B.A. Olken and J. Tobias (2010), "Targeting the Poor: Evidence from a Field Experiment in Indonesia", *NBER Working Paper*, No. 15980, National Bureau of Economic Research, Cambridge, MA.

Arze del Granado, F.J., W. Fengler, A. Ragatz and E. Yavuz (2007), "Investing in Indonesia's Education: Allocation, Equity and Efficiency of Public Expenditure", *Policy Research Working Paper*, No. 4329, World Bank, Washington, DC.

Bidani, A. and M. Ravallion (1993), "A Regional Poverty Profile for Indonesia", *Bulletin of Indonesian Economic Studies*, 29, 37-68.

Comola, M. and L. de Mello (2009) "The Determinants of Employment and Earnings in Indonesia", *OECD Economics Department Working Paper*, No. 690, OECD, Paris.

Duflo, E. (2001), "Schooling and Labour Market Consequences of School Construction in Indonesia: Evidence from an Unusual Policy Experiment", *American Economic Review*, 91, 795-813.

Duflo, E. (2004), "The Medium Run Effects of Educational Expansion: Evidence from a Large School Construction Programme in Indonesia", *Journal of Development Economics*, 74, 163-97.

Fahmi, M. (2009), "School Choice and Earnings: A Case of Indonesia", *Working Paper in Economics and Development Studies*, No. 20014, Padjadjaran University, Bandung.

Frankenberg, E., D. Thomas and K. Beegle (1999), "The Real Costs of Indonesian Economic Crisis: Preliminary Findings from the Indonesia Family Life Surveys", *Working Paper, No.* 99-04, RAND Corporation Publications Department, Santa Monica, CA.

Kruse, I., M. Pradhan and R. Sparrow (2009), "Health Spending and Decentralisation in Indonesia", unpublished manuscript.

Ministry of Health (2008), *The Indonesian National Health Accounts, 2002-04*, Ministry of Health, Jakarta.

Ministry of National Education (2007), *Reforming Teachers: Towards Educational Equality and Quality*, Ministry of National Education, Jakarta.

O'Donnell, O., E. van Doorslaer and R.P. Rannan-Eliya (2007), "The Incidence of Public Spending on Healthcare: Comparative Evidence from Asia", *World Bank Economic Review*, 21, 93-123.

OECD (2007), *Economic Survey of Chile*, OECD, Paris.

OECD (2008), *Economic Assessment of Indonesia*, OECD, Paris.

Perdana, A. and J.Maxwell (2004), "Poverty Targeting in Indonesia: Programs, Problems and Lessons Learned", *CSIS Economics Working Paper Series*, No. WPE083, CSIS, Jakarta.

Pradhan, M., F. Saadah and R. Sparrow (2007), "Did the Health Card Program Ensure Access to Medical Care for the Poor during Indonesia's Economic Crisis?", *World Bank Economic Review*, 21, 125-50.

Pradhan, M., A. Suryahadi, S. Sumarto and L. Pritchett (2000), "Measurements of Poverty in Indonesia: 1996, 1999, and Beyond", *SMERU Working Paper*, SMERU, Jakarta.

Rahayu, S.K., N. Toyamah, S. Hutagalung, M. Rosfadhila and M. Syukri (2008), "Qualitative Baseline Study for *PNPM Generasi* and PKH: The Availability and Use of the Maternal and Child Health Services and Basic Education Services in the Provinces of West Java and East Nusa Tenggara", *Research Report*, SMERU, Jakarta.

Rawlings, L.B. and G.M. Rubio (2005), "Evaluating the Impact of Conditional Cash Transfer Programmes", *World Bank Research Observer*, No. 20, 29-55.

Skoufias, E. and A. Suryahadi (2000), "Changes in Household Welfare, Poverty and Inequality during the Crisis", *Bulletin of Indonesian Economic Studies*, 36, 98-114.

SMERU (2006), "A Rapid Appraisal of the PKPS-BBM Education Sector: School Operational Assistance (BOS)", *Research Report*, SMERU, Jakarta.

SMERU (2009), "Implementation of the 2007 Teacher Certification Programme", *Policy Brief*, SMERU, Jakarta.

Sparrow, R. (2007), "Protecting Education for the Poor in Times of Crisis: An Evaluation of a Scholarship Programme in Indonesia", *Oxford Bulletin of Economics and Statistics*, 69, 99-122.

Sparrow, R. (2008), "Targeting the Poor in Times of Crisis: The Indonesian Health Card", *Health Policy and Planning*, 23, 188-99.

Sparrow, R., A. Suryahadi and W. Widyanti (2009), "Public Health Insurance for the Poor: Targeting and Impact of Indonesia's *Askeskin* Programme", Presented at the 2009 Harmonising Health and Economics Conference, 12-15 July, Beijing.

Strauss, J., K. Beegle, A. Dwiyanto, Y. Herawati, D. Pattinasarany, E. Satriawan, B. Sikoki, Sukamdi and F. Witoelar (2004), *Indonesian Living Standards: Before and After the Financial Crisis*, Rand Corporation, USA and Institute of Southeast Asian Studies, Santa Monica, CA.

Suryadarma, D., A. Suryahadi and S. Sumarto (2004), "The Determinants of Student Performance in Indonesian Public Private Schools: The Role of Teachers and Schools", *Working Paper*, SMERU, Jakarta.

Suryadarma, D., A. Suryahadi and S. Sumarto (2006), "Causes of Low Secondary School Enrolment in Indonesia", *Working Paper*, SMERU, Jakarta.

Suryahadi, A., S. Sumarto and L. Pritchett (2003), "The Evolution of Poverty during the Crisis in Indonesia, 1996 99", *World Bank Policy Research Working Paper*, No. 2435, World Bank, Washington, DC.

Suryahadi, A. and S. Sumarto (2005), "Update on the Impact of the Indonesian Crisis on Consumption Expenditure and Poverty Incidence – Results from the December 1998 Round of 100 Village Survey", East Asian Bureau of Economic Research, *Development Economics Working Papers*, No. 116, Jakarta.

Suryahadi, A., W. Widyanti and S. Sumarto (2003), "Short Term Poverty Dynamics in Rural Indonesia during the Economic Crisis", *Journal of International Development*, 15, 133 144.

Thomas, D., K. Beegle, E. Frankenberg, B. Sikoki, J. Strauss and G. Teruel (2004), "Education in a Crisis", *Journal of Development Economics*, 74, 53-85.

Usman, S., Akhmadi and D. Suryadarma (2004), "When Teachers Are Absent: Where Do They Go and What Is the Impact on Students?", *Field Report*, SMERU, Jakarta.

World Bank (2008a), *Investing in Indonesia's Health: Challenges and Opportunities for Future Public Spending*, Public Health Expenditure Review, World Bank, Washington, DC.

World Bank (2008b), "Giving More Weight to Health: Assessing Fiscal Space for Health in Indonesia", *Report*, No. 46847, World Bank, Washington, DC.

World Bank (2008c), "Cash Transfers in Indonesia: Baseline Survey Report Program Keluarga Harapan and PNPM-Generasi", *Report*, No. 46548, World Bank, Washington, DC.

Yun, M. (2004), "Decomposing Differences in the First Moment", *Economics Letters*, 82, 275-80.

ANNEX 4.A1

The effect of school infrastructure development on education attainment

This Annex uses individual-level data to estimate the effect of government spending on school infrastructure development on educational attainment in Indonesia.

The data

The data set is available from the 2004 wave of the National Labour Force Survey (*Sakernas*). *Sakernas* is an annual cross-section survey that focuses on the socio-economic and labour-market characteristics of individuals and households. Data started to be collected in 1976. The 2004 wave includes 75 371 households (comprising 237 290 individuals).

For the purpose of the empirical analysis reported below, *Sakernas* data are combined with information on the number of schools built in each district under *Sekolar Dasah IMPRES* in 1973-74 and 1978-79. Over 61 000 primary schools were built nation-wide under that programme. Exposure of school-age children to the programme has been used extensively in the empirical literature to identify the effect of educational attainment on earnings and labour-market outcomes. Empirical evidence shows that the cohorts of individuals who have been exposed to this programme are more likely to stay longer at school and to earn more once in the labour force.[1]

The impact of government investment in education on attainment

Information on the number of new schools built in the district of birth of individuals of different age cohorts is used as a determinant of educational attainment. Following Duflo (2001), exposure of an individual to the school-construction programme is determined both by the intensity of school-construction activity in his/her district of birth and his/her age when the programme was launched. The district-level programme intensity variable is defined as the number of schools built between 1973-74 and 1978-79 divided by the number of children aged 5-14 years living in the district in 1971 (in thousands). Since most Indonesian children attend primary school between the ages of 6 and 12, children are assumed to benefit from the construction of schools only if they were aged 11 or less in 1974, when the programme was launched. A proxy for programme exposure is defined as the programme intensity in district of birth of individuals aged 11 or less in 1974, and zero otherwise.[2]

The results

The results of a standard OLS regression of educational attainment, measured in terms of years of schooling, on exposure to the school-construction programme for a sample of adult individuals (aged 15-65 in 2004) are reported in Table 4.A1.1.[3]

The main covariate of interest is programme exposure, which captures the intensity of school construction in the district of birth of those individuals who were young enough to benefit from the programme. The regression also includes control variables: place of residency (district dummies), age and age squared, gender, marital status and its interaction with gender, the age dependency ratio (computed as the number of household members who are younger than 15 or older than 65 divided by the number of household members aged 15-65) and its interaction with gender, and household's educational attainment (computed as the average years of schooling of the other adult household members).

Table 4.A1.1. **Impact of school construction on educational attainment**

Dependent variable: years of schooling

	Estimated parameter
Programme exposure	0.2348 ***
	(0.010)
Place of residency (rural areas)	–0.9864 ***
	(0.019)
Age	0.1302 ***
	(0.004)
Age squared	–0.0025 ***
	(0.000)
Gender (female)	–0.6043 ***
	(0.025)
Marital status (married)	–0.0945 ***
	(0.024)
Female* married	–0.7859 ***
	(0.028)
Age dependency ratio	–0.2275 ***
	(0.035)
Female* dependency ratio	0.3531 ***
	(0.047)
Household level of education	0.4430 ***
	(0.003)
Intercept	3.1433 ***
	(0.209)
No. of observations	192 119
R-squared	0.464

Note: The regression is estimated by OLS and includes district dummies (not reported).

Source: Data available from BPS (*Sakernas*), and OECD estimations.

The regression results show an increase of 0.23 years of education for each new school built per 1 000 children. This effect is larger, yet comparable with the one estimated by Duflo (2001) (0.15 additional years of education for each new school) using another dataset, which covers only men born between 1950 and 1972.

The control variables are signed as expected: rural individuals have lower educational attainment, years of schooling rises with age (albeit in a non-linear manner), and being a woman, married and living in a household with a high dependency ratio all correlated negatively with years of schooling. With regard to the interaction effects, being a woman further decreases the (already negative) effect of being married, but more than compensates for the negative coefficient associated with the dependency ratio. Family background, proxied by the average years of schooling of all other adult household members, is positively signed, as expected.

Notes

1. See Duflo (2001) and Comola and de Mello (2009) for more information.
2. Duflo (2001) shows how the variable *program intensity* has a good explanatory power in both the educational attainment and earnings equations. Although it is not obvious to assume that the district of residency is also the district where pupils attend primary school, Duflo reports that 91.5% children surveyed in the Indonesian Family Life Survey were still living in the district of birth at age 12.
3. *Sakernas* reports only the highest educational qualification attained by respondents. The reported levels were used to compute the number of years of schooling required in Indonesia to obain the corresponding qualification. For instance, primary school is coded as 6 years of schooling, while Diploma III (which corresponds to a Bachelor's degree) corresponds to 15 years of schooling.

ANNEX 4.A2

Health insurance and utilisation in Indonesia

This Annex uses household-survey data to estimate the impact of health insurance on utilisation of health care facilities in Indonesia.

Data and variables

Individual-level information is available from the 2008 wave of Indonesia's household survey (*Susenas*). Attention is focused on individuals who reported having had a health problem (defined as fever, cough, cold, asthma, diarrhoea, headache, toothache or other) during the month prior to the survey.

Based on the sample of individuals who reported having had a health problem, a binary dependent variable, *consultation*, is constructed as taking the value of 1 if the respondent declared to have visited a governmental/private hospital, medical practice, community health center (*Puskesmas*), polyclinic or nurse practice at least once during the month prior to the survey, and 0 otherwise. The different types of health insurance are defined on the basis of a set of dummy variables that equal 1 if the respondent declared to have a government pension (*JPK PNS, veteran, pensiun*), employer-financed health insurance (*Jamsostek*), health insurance for civil servants (*Askes*), employer-financed health-care reimbursement (*Tunjangan/penggantian biaya oleh perusahaan*), social security health insurance (*JPS health card, JPK-Gakin, Askeskin*) or community-based health care (*Dana Sehat*), and 0 otherwise.

The set of control variables includes individual characteristics, such as age, years of schooling and a number of dummy variables to identify residents of rural areas, females and unmarried individuals.* Labour-market status is controlled for through the inclusion of two dummy variables equalling 1 if the individual is a wage-earner or has a non-salaried occupation, and 0 otherwise (the omitted category is inactive). Household characteristics include size (the logarithm of the number of household members), the share of household members aged less than 15 (children) and more than 65 (elderly) years of age, and household per capita consumption. Provincial dummies are also included. Descriptive statistics are reported in Table 4.A2.1.

* As noted in Annex 3.A1, *Sakernas* only reports the highest educational qualification attained by respondents. The reported levels were used to compute the number of years of schooling required in Indonesia to obtain the corresponding qualification.

Table 4.A2.1. **Descriptive statistics**[1]

Variable	Mean	Minimum	Maximum	Standard deviation
Individual characteristics				
Consultation	0.40	0	1	0.49
Age	29.28	0	98	21.71
Place of residency (rural)	0.66	0	1	0.47
Years of schooling	5.01	0	19	4.33
Gender (female)	0.50	0	1	0.50
Marital status (unmarried)	0.53	0	1	0.50
Labour-market status (salaried)	0.12	0	1	0.32
Labour-market status (non-salaried)	0.33	0	1	0.47
Type of health insurance/benefit				
Government pension	0.06	0	1	0.23
Employer-financed health insurance	0.02	0	1	0.14
Health insurance for civil servants	0.01	0	1	0.09
Employer-financed health care reimbursement	0.01	0	1	0.11
Social security health insurance	0.19	0	1	0.39
Community-based health care	0.01	0	1	0.08
Household characteristics				
Household size (in log)	0.92	0	3.33	0.63
Share of children	0.34	0	1	0.32
Share of elderly	0.06	0	1	0.20
Per capita consumption (in thousands of rupiah per month)	8.62	0.15	929.92	10.32

1. The number of individuals is 318 547.
Source: BPS (*Susenas*) and OECD computations.

Estimation results

The results of the probit regressions reported in Table 4.A2.2 suggest that all types of health insurance have a significantly positive impact on the probability of visiting a health-care facility, especially the government health insurance and pension. Government pension, employer-financed health insurance and reimbursement have the strongest effect on utilisation rates. The effects of social security health insurance (JPS health card, JPK-Gakin, *Askeskin*, etc.) and community-based health care are somewhat weaker, partly reflecting additional constraints to utilisation among the beneficiary population. Such constraints include the cost of transport to health-care facilities, awareness of entitlements, etc.

As expected, individuals living in rural areas, women and unmarried individuals have a lower probability of visiting a health care facility when they are confronted with a health problem. The interaction *female*unmarried* is positively signed and the size of the estimated coefficient suggests that being married more than compensates for the negative effect of being female. Educational attainment is also negatively signed. Moreover, the estimation results suggest that wage-earners and workers engaged in non-salaried jobs are less likely to visit a health-care facility than inactive individuals. Household size has a negative impact on the utilisation probability. Finally, high per capita consumption and share of dependent members are associated with a high utilisation probability.

Table 4.A2.2. **Health insurance and utilisation: Probit regressions**[1]

Dependent variable: Consultations

	Estimated parameter
Individual characteristics	
Age	0.0003 ***
	(0.000)
Place of residence (rural)	–0.0187 ***
	(0.002)
Years of schooling	–0.0087 ***
	(0.000)
Gender (female)	–0.0148 ***
	(0.003)
Marital status (unmarried)	–0.0345 ***
	(0.003)
Female* unmarried	0.0191 ***
	(0.004)
Labour-market status (salaried)	–0.0452 ***
	(0.003)
Labour-market status (non-salaried)	–0.0626 ***
	(0.002)
Type of health insurance/benefit	
Government pension	0.0956 ***
	(0.004)
Employer-financed health insurance	0.0847 ***
	(0.006)
Health insurance for civil servants	0.0481 ***
	(0.010)
Employer-financed health-care reimbursement	0.1005 ***
	(0.008)
Social security health insurance	0.0454 ***
	(0.002)
Community-based health care	0.0414 ***
	(0.010)
Household characteristics	
Number of household members	–0.0150 ***
	(0.002)
Share of children	0.0605 ***
	(0.003)
Share of elderly	0.0395 ***
	(0.005)
Per capita consumption	0.0019 ***
	(0.000)
Number of observations	318 547

1. Probit marginal effects are reported. Statistical significance at the 1, 5 and 10% levels is denoted by, respectively, ***, ** and *. Robust standard errors are reported in parentheses. The regression includes a set of place of residency dummies.

Source: BPS (*Susenas*) and OECD estimations.

ANNEX 4.A3

The determinants of poverty in Indonesia

This Annex uses household-level data and probit modelling to estimate the determinants of poverty in Indonesia.

Data and variables

Data are available from Indonesia's household survey (*Susenas*) for 2002 and 2008. The 2002 and 2008 waves contain information on around 208 000 and 274 000 households, respectively. The empirical analysis reported below is restricted to households with at least one adult member (*i.e.* aged 15-65). A household is classified as poor if its per capita consumption (defined as the sum of food and non-food consumption expenditure divided by the number of household members) is below one-half of the province-level sample median. The dependent variable, *poor*, equals 1 if the household is considered poor, and 0 otherwise.

The set of poverty determinants includes household composition indicators, educational attainment and geographical dummies. The household composition indicators include household size (the logarithm of the number of household members), the share of household members aged less than 15 years (children) and more than 65 years (elderly), the average age and years of schooling of the adult members of the household,[1] an illiteracy dummy (equaling 1 if at least one adult member is illiterate, and 0 otherwise), a gender dummy (equaling 1 if the household head is female, and 0 otherwise), and a marital status dummy (equaling 1 if the household head is unmarried, and 0 otherwise). Labour-market status is controlled for through the inclusion of the shares of salaried and non-salaried adult workers in the household, while the omitted category refers to those who are inactive.[2] Provincial dummies are included in all regressions and not reported to economise on space). Descriptive statistics are reported in Table 4.A3.1.

Estimation results

The marginal effects reported in Table 4.A3.2 suggest that household size and age dependency are important determinants of the incidence of poverty in Indonesia. Large households and those with a high share of children and elderly members are more likely to be poor. By contrast, age and educational attainment have the effect of reducing the probability of being poor, although the average age of adult household members is significant for 2008 only. The finding that the presence of an illiterate member in the household reduces the probability of being poor (for 2002 only) once household years of schooling is controlled for is probably due to the fact that the accumulation of human

Table 4.A3.1. Descriptive statistics[1]

Variable	Mean	Minimum	Maximum	Standard deviation
2002 wave				
Poor	0.089	0	1	0.285
Household size (number of members, in log)	1.472	0	4.248	0.600
Share of children	0.271	0	0.857	0.210
Share of elderly members	0.033	0	0.857	0.103
Average age of adult household members	35.112	15	65	8.580
Average years of schooling (adult members)	7.212	0	19	3.322
Illiteracy dummy	0.162	0	1	0.369
Female head of household dummy	0.124	0	1	0.330
Unmarried head of household dummy	0.160	0	1	0.367
Share of salaried workers	0.192	0	1	0.271
Share of non-salaried workers	0.428	0	1	0.357
2008 wave				
Poor	0.135	0	1	0.341
Household size (number of members, in log)	1.481	0	3.871	0.579
Share of children	0.275	0	0.857	0.206
Share of elderly members	0.040	0	0.8	0.110
Average age of adult household members	36.018	15	65	8.514
Average years of schooling (adult members)	7.550	0	19	3.335
Illiteracy dummy	0.134	0	1	0.341
Female head of household dummy	0.129	0	1	0.335
Unmarried head of household dummy	0.154	0	1	0.361
Share of salaried workers	0.203	0	1	0.278
Share of non-salaried workers	0.485	0	1	0.367

1. The number of individuals is 207 712 in 2002 and 274 224 in 2008.
Source: BPS (*Susenas*) and authors' computations.

Table 4.A3.2. The determinants of poverty: Probit regressions, 2002 and 2008[1]

Dependent variable: Poor

	2002	2008
Household size	0.1842 ***	0.2325 ***
	(0.001)	(0.001)
Share of children	0.0305 ***	0.0968 ***
	(0.003)	(0.003)
Share of elderly members	0.0858 ***	0.1794 ***
	(0.007)	(0.006)
Average age of adult household members	0.0001	–0.0004 ***
	(0.000)	(0.000)
Average years of schooling of adult household members	–0.0105 ***	–0.0207 ***
	(0.000)	(0.000)
Illiteracy dummy	–0.0058 ***	–0.0023
	(0.002)	(0.002)
Female head of household dummy	0.0131 ***	0.0216 ***
	(0.002)	(0.003)
Unmarried head of household dummy	0.0392 ***	0.0470 ***
	(0.002)	(0.003)
Share of salaried workers	–0.0143 ***	–0.0506 ***
	(0.003)	(0.003)
Share of non-salaried workers	–0.0041 *	0.0034
	(0.002)	(0.002)
Provincial dummies	YES	YES
Number of observations	207 712	274 224

1. Probit marginal effects are reported. Statistical significance at the 1, 5 and 10% levels is denoted by, respectively, ***, ** and *. Robust standard errors are reported in parentheses.
Source: BPS (*Susenas*) and authors' estimations.

capital among the other household members compensates for the illiteracy of a single member. Finally, gender and marital status also matter. The impacts of a female head of household and an unmarried head of household on poverty are both positive, but the coefficient of the former is smaller in magnitude than that of the latter.

The labour-market status of adult household members is an important determinant of poverty. A higher share of wage-earners (and non-salaried workers in 2002) in the household decreases the probability of being poor. This is in line with the fact that the Indonesian labour market is segmented, as discussed in the 2008 *Economic Assessment* (OECD, 2008) and that less qualified individuals tend to be more numerous in non-salaried occupations.

Decomposition analysis

The results of the probit analysis can be used to decompose changes in the incidence of poverty during 2002-08 between changes in individual and household characteristics (captured by changes in the variables included in the regressions) and structural changes in the economy (captured by changes in the estimated coefficients). Several methodologies are available to carry out such a decomposition, including that of Yun (2004). The basic idea is that the incidence of poverty, denoted by Y, is a function of several structural and individual/household characteristics, such that it can be written as $Y = F(X'\beta)$, where F is a normally distributed cumulative density function, as in the probit model; X is a set of regressors, which includes the main determinants of poverty, and β is a vector of estimated coefficients. The decomposition exercise consists of re-writing Y as follows:

$$\overline{Y}_t - \overline{Y}_{t+1} = \overline{F(X_t'\beta_t)} - \overline{F(X_{t+1}'\beta_{t+1})} = \overline{F(X_t'\beta_t)} - \overline{F(X_{t+1}'\beta_t)} + \overline{F(X_{t+1}'\beta_t)} - \overline{F(X_{t+1}'\beta_{t+1})}$$

Changes in Y $(\overline{Y}_t - \overline{Y}_{t+1})$ can therefore be written as a sum of two components. The first term $(\overline{F(X_t'\beta_t)} - \overline{F(X_{t+1}\beta_t)})$ accounts for changes over time in the variables included in the regressions (the determinants of poverty included in X), whereas the second term $(\overline{F(X_{t+1}'\beta_t)} - \overline{F(X_{t+1}'\beta_{t+1})})$ accounts for changes in the estimated coefficients (β).

The results of the decomposition analysis – based on the Oaxaca-Blinder decomposition of outcome differentials in its nonlinear version for binary outcomes proposed by Yun (2004) – are reported in Table 4.A3.3. The decomposition is restricted to those provinces that did not change between the two waves of *Susenas*.[3] The results suggest that the raw difference in the poverty headcount ratios between 2002 and 2008 (0.044) is almost entirely attributable to changes in the estimated coefficients, rather than in sample characteristics.

Table 4.A3.3. **Poverty incidence decomposition, 2002 and 2008**[1]

	Coefficient	Percentage change
Raw	0.044388	100%
Sample characteristics	–0.00875	–19.71%
Estimated coefficients	0.057542	129.63%
Interaction	–0.0044	-9.92%

1. The decomposition is carried out for the 2002 sample.
Source: BPS (*Susenas*) and OECD estimations.

The coefficients reported in Table 4.A3.4 confirm that most of the change in poverty outcomes is explained by changes in coefficients. The larger effects of household size and educational attainment on the incidence of poverty in 2008 than in 2002 are particularly noteworthy.

Table 4.A3.4. **Poverty incidence decomposition coefficients, 2002 and 2008**[1]

	Changes in variables	Changes in coefficients
Household size	0.0001	–0.0517 ***
	(0.000)	(0.002)
Share of children	1.4E-05 **	0.0090 ***
	(0.000)	(0.001)
Share of elderly members	0.0002 ***	0.0011 ***
	(0.000)	(0.000)
Average age of adult household members	4.3E-05	–0.0124 ***
	(0.000)	(0.004)
Average years of schooling of adult household members	–0.0012 ***	–0.0235 ***
	(0.000)	(0.003)
Female head of household dummy	1.7E-05 ***	0.0001
	(0.000)	(0.000)
Unmarried head of household dummy	–0.0001 ***	–0.0014 ***
	(0.000)	(0.000)
Illiteracy dummy	0.0001 ***	0.0003
	(0.000)	(0.000)
Share of salaried workers	–0.0001 ***	–0.0037 ***
	(0.000)	(0.001)
Share of non-salaried workers	–0.0001 *	0.0021 *
	(0.000)	(0.001)
Provincial dummies	YES	YES
Number of observations	207 712	274 224

1. Statistical significance at the 1, 5 and 10% levels is denoted by, respectively, ***, ** and *. Standard errors (reported in parentheses) are computed using the delta method.

Source: BPS (*Susenas*) and OECD estimations.

Notes

1. As noted above, *Sakernas* only reports the highest educational qualification attained by respondents. The reported levels were used to compute the number of years of schooling required in Indonesia to obain the corresponding qualification.
2. An adult household member is considered inactive if he/she declared not to have worked during the week prior to the survey. Respondents who declare themselves to have worked (not necessarily as primary activity) can be employed as wage-earners or in non-salaried jobs (self-employed with or without assistance, or unpaid/family/casual workers).
3. As discussed in the 2008 *Economic Assessment* (OECD, 2008), Indonesia went through a period of administrative refom during 2001-05 that resulted in the creation of a number of provinces by splitting existing jurisdictions. Since the decomposition technique requires that the set of regressors included in the probit analysis remains unchanged over time, the provinces that do not appear in both waves of *Susenas* (1 province for 2002 and 4 provinces for 2008) were omitted. Omission of these provinces implies a loss of less than 1% of observations for 2002 and 5% for 2008. Of course, omission of these provinces does not solve the problem of shifts of population among the provinces that were split as a result of administrative reform.

ORGANISATION FOR ECONOMIC CO-OPERATION AND DEVELOPMENT

The OECD is a unique forum where governments work together to address the economic, social and environmental challenges of globalisation. The OECD is also at the forefront of efforts to understand and to help governments respond to new developments and concerns, such as corporate governance, the information economy and the challenges of an ageing population. The Organisation provides a setting where governments can compare policy experiences, seek answers to common problems, identify good practice and work to co-ordinate domestic and international policies.

The OECD member countries are: Australia, Austria, Belgium, Canada, Chile, the Czech Republic, Denmark, Finland, France, Germany, Greece, Hungary, Iceland, Ireland, Israel, Italy, Japan, Korea, Luxembourg, Mexico, the Netherlands, New Zealand, Norway, Poland, Portugal, the Slovak Republic, Slovenia, Spain, Sweden, Switzerland, Turkey, the United Kingdom and the United States. The European Commission takes part in the work of the OECD.

OECD Publishing disseminates widely the results of the Organisation's statistics gathering and research on economic, social and environmental issues, as well as the conventions, guidelines and standards agreed by its members.

OECD PUBLISHING, 2, rue André-Pascal, 75775 PARIS CEDEX 16
(10 2010 18 1 P) ISBN 978-92-64-08340-0 – No. 57661 2010